Sport as a Business

Also edited by Harald Dolles and Sten Söderman

HANDBOOK OF RESEARCH ON SPORT AND BUSINESS

DEVELOPING INTERNATIONAL SPORT

MEGA-SPORTING EVENTS IN ASIA
Impacts on Business, Society and Management

Also edited by Sten Söderman

EMERGING MULTIPLICITY
Integration and Responsiveness in Asian Business Development

Also edited by Harald Dolles

SINO-GERMAN BUSINESS RELATIONSHIPS DURING THE AGE OF ECONOMIC REFORM (*with Torsten M. Kühlmann*)

Sport as a Business

International, Professional and Commercial Aspects

Edited by

Harald Dolles

and

Sten Söderman

Selection, introduction and editorial content © Harald Dolles and Sten Söderman 2011
Individual chapters © the contributors 2011

All rights reserved. No reproduction, copy or transmission of this publication may be made without written permission.

No portion of this publication may be reproduced, copied or transmitted save with written permission or in accordance with the provisions of the Copyright, Designs and Patents Act 1988, or under the terms of any licence permitting limited copying issued by the Copyright Licensing Agency, Saffron House, 6-10 Kirby Street, London EC1N 8TS.

Any person who does any unauthorized act in relation to this publication may be liable to criminal prosecution and civil claims for damages.

The authors have asserted their rights to be identified as the authors of this work in accordance with the Copyright, Designs and Patents Act 1988.

First published 2011 by
PALGRAVE MACMILLAN

Palgrave Macmillan in the UK is an imprint of Macmillan Publishers Limited, registered in England, company number 785998, of Houndmills, Basingstoke, Hampshire RG21 6XS.

Palgrave Macmillan in the US is a division of St Martin's Press LLC, 175 Fifth Avenue, New York, NY 10010.

Palgrave Macmillan is the global academic imprint of the above companies and has companies and representatives throughout the world.

Palgrave® and Macmillan® are registered trademarks in the United States, the United Kingdom, Europe and other countries.

ISBN 978–0–230–24925–7 hardback

This book is printed on paper suitable for recycling and made from fully managed and sustained forest sources. Logging, pulping and manufacturing processes are expected to conform to the environmental regulations of the country of origin.

A catalogue record for this book is available from the British Library.

Library of Congress Cataloging-in-Publication Data
Sport as a business : international, professional and commercial aspects /
  [edited by] Harald Dolles, Sten Söderman.
    p. cm.
  Includes index.
  ISBN 978–0–230–24925–7 (hardback)
  1. Sports administration. 2. Sports—Management. 3. Sports—Economic aspects. 4. Sports—International cooperation. I. Dolles, Harald, 1961– II. Söderman, Sten.
  GV713.S67215 2011
  796.06′9—dc22   2011004893

10 9 8 7 6 5 4 3 2 1
20 19 18 17 16 15 14 13 12 11

Printed and bound in the United States of America

Contents

List of Figures and Tables vii

Notes on the Contributors ix

Sport as a Business: Introduction 1
Harald Dolles and Sten Söderman

Part I Sport Consumers' Perspective

1 'As American as Mom, Apple Pie and Dutch Soccer?': The Team Identification of Foreign Ajax FC Supporters 15
   Anthony K. Kerr, Narelle F. Smith and Alastair Anderson

2 Decision-making Styles in Purchasing Sport Products: An International Comparison Between American and Korean College Students 35
   Sungwon Bae

3 Travel Time Elasticities in Recreational Sports: Empirical Findings for the Professionalization in Sports Facility Management 53
   Tim Pawlowski, Christoph Breuer and Pamela Wicker

Part II Sport Events and Sport Facilities

4 Perceptions of the Impacts of Major Commercial Sport Events 75
   Christopher J. Auld, Kathleen M. Lloyd and Jennifer Rieck

5 Gender, Race and Nationality: An Examination of Print Media Coverage of the 2006 Winter Olympics 99
   Andrea N. Eagleman and Erin L. McNary

6 Enhancing Public Sports Facilities: A Representation of the Global Value 115
   Bernard Augé, Arnaud Pedenon and Alexandre Vernhet

Part III Sports Organizations and Governance

7 Sports Organizations, Professionalization and
   Organizational Conflict: A Review of the Literature   137
   John Schulz

8 International and Professional Dimensions of National
   Governing Bodies: Insights from the Gaelic Athletic
   Association   153
   Anne Bourke

9 The Role of Central Brokers and Their Influence on
   Effectiveness in an Intentionally Created Sports
   Professionalization Network   170
   Simon G. Martin, Maureen Benson-Rea and Nitha Palakshappa

10 Business Ecosystem Co-evolution: The Ultimate Fighting
   Championships   194
   Simon Ford and Clive Kerr

11 Learning from Failure: Is Major League Soccer Repeating
   the Mistakes of the North American Soccer League?   213
   John D. Francis

12 Learning from Success: Implementing a Professional
   Football League in Japan   228
   Harald Dolles and Sten Söderman

Index   251

List of Figures and Tables

Figures

6.1	The functional model of the value – an application of the value of a public sports facility	124
6.2	Representation of the convergences, Town A	129
6.3	Representation of the association matrix of the director of the town sports service in Town B	131
6.4	Representation of the association matrix of the elected town councillor in charge of sports in Town B	131
9.1	NZAS-North network stages of development	176
9.2	NZAS-Central network stages of development	177
9.3	NZAS-South Island network stages of development	179
10.1	Gate receipts for Las Vegas-based UFC events	201
10.2	Growth in the number of UFC events	203
12.1	Network of Value Captures in professional football	235
12.2	J-League – sample team emblems and mascots	244

Tables

1.1	Importance of reasons in original Ajax FC support	22
1.2	Mean scores of the important reasons in original Ajax FC support (satellite supporters versus expatriate fans)	24
1.3	Behaviour to support Ajax FC (during season)	26
1.4	Behaviour to support Ajax FC (out of season)	27
2.1	Factor loadings and Cronbach's alpha coefficients	40
2.2	Frequency of distribution and percentage	42
2.3	Nationality comparison of the United States and South Korea	44
2.4	The results of mean comparison for nationality	45
3.1	Descriptive statistics data set Stuttgart and Cologne	58
3.2	Descriptive statistics time variables Stuttgart and Cologne	61
3.3	Simulated time elasticities in Stuttgart and Cologne	62
3.4	Descriptive statistics involvement variables Stuttgart and Cologne	63

3.5	Multiple regression between MTIME and factors in Cologne	66
3.6	Multiple regression between MTIME and factors in Stuttgart	67
4.1	Sporting involvement	83
4.2	Perceived economic benefits agreement scores	84
4.3	Perceived social benefits agreement scores	85
4.4	Perceived economic and social costs agreement scores	86
4.5	Infrastructure investment agreement scores	87
4.6	Differences in costs and benefits scales mean scores	88
4.7	Correlations between sport participation, sport watching, attendance at events and agreement mean scores	90
5.1	2006 Olympic games coverage by gender	106
5.2	2006 Olympic games coverage by race	106
5.3	2006 Olympic games coverage by nationality	107
5.4	Readership demographics of news outlets examined	111
6.1	Global typology of the components of the value	120
6.2	Distribution of the variables between the components of the global value of a sports facility	126
8.1	Sport governing bodies – forms and activities	156
9.1	Summary of interviews	175
10.1	Significant rules change introduced to the UFC	199
10.2	Salaries of three selected UFC fighters	205
10.3	Number of bouts competed in by UFC fighters in 2007	206
10.4	UFC record of fighters leaving the organization in 2007	207
11.1	Key similarities and differences between NASL and MLS	220

Notes on the Contributors

Alastair Anderson is Research Fellow in the School of Management at La Trobe University in Melbourne, Australia. His research interests are in the socialization of children into sport, fan identification and the psychological and sociological aspects of fan violence. Other research interests include sport sponsorship, ageing and physical activity and drug use among professional athletes.

Bernard Augé has a PhD in management science and is currently Assistant Professor at the Institute of the Sciences of the Enterprise and Management and a member of the Research Team on Firm and Industry – Finance, Accounting, Control and Strategy Group, at the University of Montpellier 1, Montpellier, France. He is the author of conference papers, articles and books on sports management and governance. His research deals with control and assessment of performances of public sector and sports organizations. As a former treasurer of Montpellier Rugby Club, Bernard is a member of the Board of the French National Association of the Elected Representatives in Charge of Sport (ANDES).

Christopher J. Auld is Professor and Dean of the Griffith Business School, Griffith University, Nathan, Queensland, Australia. Chris teaches in the area of sport economics and his current research interests include the recruitment, management and retention of sport volunteers, the impacts of major sport events and the board performance and governance in third sector organizations. In 2010, Chris was elected as a senior fellow and founding member of the World Leisure Academy.

Sungwon Bae received a BA in education at Yeungnam University and earned a Masters in sport administration from Ohio University, USA. After a two-year internship with Disney's Wide World of Sports, he obtained his PhD in sport management at Florida State University. Sungwon was an adjunct faculty member in the Department of Health, Physical Education and Recreation at Florida A&M University and Tallahassee Community College. He was also a visiting assistant professor in the Department of Health, Physical Education, Recreation and Dance at Cleveland State University. Sungwon is now teaching as an Assistant Professor in the Health, Exercise, & Sport Sciences Department at Texas Tech University, Lubbock, USA.

Maureen Benson-Rea is Senior Lecturer in the Department of Management and International Business at the University of Auckland, New Zealand. She holds a PhD in marketing and international business, a Henley MBA and a BA (Hons) in European studies. Maureen has held academic positions in the UK and New Zealand, and several European roles with a major UK business organization. She specializes in international business strategy, with a particular focus on Europe, and has research interests in networks, internationalization strategies and cooperative business strategies in general and the global wine industry.

Anne Bourke is Vice Principal for Teaching and Learning at University College Dublin, College of Business and Law, Dublin, Ireland. In that role, she organizes and coordinates seminars and workshops designed to enhance student and staff learning within the university and the School of Business. Her teaching expertise is in international business, services management and research methods. Anne's research interests include governance in national sports bodies, elite athlete development, managing university sport, curriculum design and continuing professional education. Anne has presented at many international seminars and conferences and is currently a Board member of the European Association of Sport Management (EASM).

Christoph Breuer is Professor of Sport Management at the German Sport University Cologne, Cologne, Germany and specializes in research on sport demand, sport organizations and sport sponsoring. His research mostly relates to forecasting sport demand, identifying key drivers of viability of sport organizations and measuring the economic value of sport sponsoring. Christoph has published several articles in journals such as *Research Quarterly for Exercise and Sport, Journal of Sport Economics, European Sport Management Quarterly, Sport Management Review* and *The German Journal of Sports Science*.

Harald Dolles is Visiting Professor (full-time) in International Business at the School of Business, Economics and Law at the University of Gothenburg, Gothenburg, Sweden. He received his Doctorate in International Business/Strategic Management from the University Erlangen-Nuremberg in Germany, with a focus on East Asia. He has been Assistant Professor at Bayreuth University (Germany) and taught on the university's sports business programme. During his professional career from 2001 to 2006, he was assigned by the German Ministry of Education and Science to serve in an official mission as expert on China and Japan at the economic section of the German Institute for Japanese Studies in Tokyo. He also taught in Japan before joining the German Graduate School of Management and Law as Professor of Management and International Business in 2006. Harald frequently contributes to scientific development in the fields of international business and international human resource management, entrepreneurship and innovations management, sports management and Asian studies. In this regard, he has a publication stream of articles and books, most recently 'Mega-sporting Events in Asia: Impacts on Society, Business & Management' (*Asian Business & Management*, June 2008, with Söderman); 'Developing International sport' (*International Journal of Sport Marketing and Sponsorship*, October 2008, with Söderman); 'Sponsoring the Beijing Olympic Games – Patterns of Sponsor Advertising' (*Asia-Pacific Journal of Marketing & Logistics*, January 2010, with Söderman), 'Addressing Ecology and Sustainability in Megasporting Events: The 2006 Football World Cup in Germany' (*Journal of Management and Organization*, September 2010, with Söderman) and 'Innovation, Creativity, Competitiveness and Globalization – European and International Perspectives' (*International Journal Business Environment*, April 2010, with Fernandes). Together with Sten Söderman he is currently editing the *Handbook of Research on Sport and Business* (Edward Elgar Publishing, 2012). Harald chairs the European Academy of Management (EURAM) Special Interest Group on 'Sport as a Business', a network of academics, practitioners, athletes and sport officials whose interests revolve around aspects of internationalization, professionalization and commercialization of sports in theory and in practice.

Andrea N. Eagleman is Assistant Professor in the Department of Physical Education at Indiana University-Purdue University Indianapolis in Indianapolis, USA. She earned her BA in journalism in 2001, a Master's in sport management and athletic administration in 2002 and her PhD in sport management with a minor in mass communication in 2008, all from Indiana University, Bloomington. Andrea's research interests focus on the portrayal of athletes in the mass media and the differences in media portrayals of race, nationality and gender.

Simon Ford is Research Associate at the Centre for Technology Management at the University of Cambridge, UK. He was an Advanced Institute of Management (AIM) Research Fellow on the Innovation and Productivity Grand Challenge from 2007 to 2009, during which he focused on how established firms generate breakthrough innovations. His current research activities include understanding how firms acquire external technologies and the protection strategies they can adopt, and the complex co-evolutionary dynamics underpinning industrial emergence.

John D. Francis is Assistant Professor of Management at San Diego State University (SDSU), San Diego, USA specializing in international strategic management. He teaches the globalization of sport business for SDSU's Sports MBA programme and has taught internationally in Taiwan and the Dominican Republic. His research focuses on the interface between institutions and internationalizing firms. His work has been published in *Journal of International Business Studies, Journal of World Business, Management International Review, International Business Review*, and the *Journal of Business Research*. John served on the faculty of Iona College and received his PhD from the University of Memphis before coming to SDSU.

Anthony K. Kerr is Lecturer in the School of Management (and member of the Centre for Sport and Social Impact) at La Trobe University, Melbourne, Australia. He earned his PhD from the University of Technology, Sydney, a MBA from the University of Oregon and a MS in Sport Management from the University of Massachusetts. He has worked in marketing, public relations and media relations for sport organizations worldwide and on consulting projects for some of the world's most famous brands. His research interests focus on the brand equity of professional sport teams in a global marketplace and team fandom in foreign markets.

Clive Kerr is Research Associate at the Centre for Technology Management at the University of Cambridge, UK. His current research interests are visual strategy, roadmapping, technology intelligence, technology insertion and through-life capability management. Prior to joining Cambridge, he was a research officer in Engineering Design at the Enterprise Integration Department of Cranfield University. Clive has a First Class Honours degree in electrical and mechanical engineering, a Diploma degree in economics, a Postgraduate Certificate in the social sciences and a Doctorate in engineering.

Kathleen M. Lloyd is Lecturer in the Department of Tourism, Leisure, Hotel and Sport Management at Griffith University, Nathan, Queensland, Australia. She currently teaches in the areas of venue and event management, sport facility planning and work integrated learning. Her research interests include the relationship between leisure and quality of life, planning liveable communities through the development of leisure initiatives, event impacts and the impacts of women's physical activity experiences on their psychological well-being.

Simon G. Martin has held a number of academic positions in New Zealand and the UK over the past 15 years, mainly teaching on sport marketing and management courses. His PhD examined high performance networks in an elite sports context, his research interests are in the sports industry and in particular in networks and business clusters. He also has ten years marketing and public relations experience in the sports and health sectors. Simon has a background in sport coaching and has a number of coaching awards. Currently Simon is Senior Lecturer at the Auckland University of Technology in the Centre for Interdisciplinary Studies, Auckland, New Zealand.

Erin L. McNary studied sport management at the University of Illinois Urbana-Champaign and received her graduate degrees from Indiana University, Bloomington. Currently, McNary serves as the Director of the Sports Management Program and is Sports Management Assistant Professor in the College of Global Business and Professional Studies at Fontbonne University, St Louis, MO, USA. Erin's research interests include the promotion of and ethics in youth sport, history, marketing and promotion of women and minority in sport, current media portrayals and historic media coverage of youth, women and minority in sport and pedagogy in sports management.

Nitha Palakshappa is Senior Lecturer in the Department of Communication, Journalism and Marketing at Massey University, Albany, New Zealand. Before coming to Massey she was at the University of Waikato. She has a PhD in Management from the University of Canterbury. Nitha specializes in teaching marketing strategy at both the undergraduate and post-graduate level. Her current research interests are in the area of alliances and networks in general. More recently she has been involved in research focusing on non-profits, social partnerships and social enterprises.

Tim Pawlowski is Junior Professor of Sport Economics at the German Sport University Cologne, Cologne, Germany and specializes in research on sports demand as well as league economics. His research mostly relates to factors influencing physical activity and stadium attendance, measurement of competitive balance in sports leagues and measurement of the fiscal political importance of sports. Tim has published in journals such as *Journal of Sport Economics, European Sport Management Quarterly* and *Sport Management Review*.

Arnaud Pedenon is a graduate in sports management from the Sports Science Department of the University Victor Ségalen–Bordeaux 2, France. Arnaud is currently manager of webstrategies, a communication consultant firm. He is the author of articles on sports management and is the co-founder of Sport Strategies.

Jennifer Rieck completed a BA in leisure management at Griffith University. Her research focused on South East Queensland University students' perceptions of the benefits and costs of hosting major sports events in the region. She is currently a research assistant in the Key Centre for Ethics, Law, Justice and Governance at Griffith University, Nathan, Queensland, Australia and is working on the Pathways to Prevention Project, a joint initiative with Mission Australia and Education Queensland that seeks to identify pathways to crime prevention for socially disadvantaged communities in Brisbane.

John Schulz worked for the Queensland Government Education Department for 13 years, providing technical support for the production of professional development resources. John also worked as a volunteer running wilderness camps for teenagers and sat on the Board of Directors of several large charities and volunteer-based organizations. John studied sport and outdoor recreation at Griffith University, where he completed his PhD. After his doctoral studies he moved to Scotland, where he lectured in sport management and research methods at the University of Edinburgh. John currently lectures in research methods and organizational psychology at the University of Southampton, Southampton, UK. His research is located in the fields of social psychology and organizational psychology.

Narelle F. Smith has a Bachelor of Economics with First Class Honours in Economic Statistics from the University of Sydney. After several years working in market research and education she joined the University of Technology Sydney (UTS) as part of the lecturing staff in mathematical sciences. During her time at UTS she has developed a special interest in two particular areas: education and the design and analysis of questionnaire surveys. Narelle completed her PhD with a thesis titled 'The Use of Balanced Incomplete Block Designs in Designing Randomized Response Surveys' and is involved in many projects involving statistical analysis, particularly of surveys.

Sten Söderman is Professor of International Business at Stockholm University, School of Business, Stockholm, Sweden and a Visiting Professor at the University of Luxembourg. Previously he was a Professor at Luleå University of Technology and a business consultant specializing in startups (in Manila, Geneva and Brussels). His research has focused on market strategy development and implementation and is currently on the international expansion of European firms in Asia and the global entertainment economy. He is the author and editor of many books, case studies and articles. His most recent publications include 'Mega-sporting Events in Asia: Impacts on Society, Business & Management' (*Asian Business & Management*, June 2008, with Dolles); 'Developing International Sport' (*International Journal for Sport Marketing and Sponsorship*, October 2008, with Dolles); 'Sponsoring the Beijing Olympic Games – Patterns of Sponsor Advertising' (*Asia Pacific Journal of Marketing & Logistics*, January 2010, with Dolles), 'Addressing Ecology and Sustainability in Mega-sporting Events: The 2006 Football World Cup in Germany' (*Journal of Management and Organization*, September 2010, with Dolles) and 'Skills and Complexity in Management of IJVs: Exploring Swedish Managers' Experiences in China' (*International Business Review*, 2007, with Demir). Together with Harald Dolles he is currently editing the *Handbook of Research on Sport and Business* (Edward Elgar, 2012). Sten co-chairs the European Academy of Management (EURAM) Strategic Interests Group on 'Sport as a Business'.

Alexandre Vernhet graduated in business law and in accounting from the Faculty of Law at the University of Montpellier 1, Montpellier, France. Alexandre is currently Associate Professor at the Institute of the Sciences of Enterprise and Management and a member of the Research Team on Firms and Industry – Finance, Accounting, Control and Strategy Group, at Montpellier. He is the author of works on accounting, auditing, governance and sports management. His research work deals with the control and the assessment of the performances, the governance of public sector and sports organizations.

Pamela Wicker is Research Assistant and Lecturer at the Chair for Sport Management at the German Sport University Cologne, Cologne, Germany. She has specialized in research on sport demand and sport organizations. Her research mostly relates to willingness-to-pay and price elasticity of sport demand, factors influencing sport participation and identifying key drivers of viability of sport organizations (particularly non-profit sport clubs). Pamela has published several articles in journals such as *Research Quarterly for Exercise and Sport*, *European Sport Management Quarterly*, *Sport Management Review* and *European Journal for Sport and Society*.

Sport as a Business: Introduction

Harald Dolles and Sten Söderman

The role of sport is concrete in business terms, quotes Eric Falt, United Nations (UN) Director of Communications (2004):

> It is an industry with unparalleled global reach and power. Globally, sport-related turn-over amounts to three per cent of world total economic activity. In the United Kingdom, for example, sport-related turn-over equals that of the automotive and food industries. Major events such as the soccer World Cup or Formula One Grand Prix are watched around the world.... At the same time, the corporate practices of this worldwide industry can and do have widespread impact, socially and environmentally.

Some sports have achieved a global status; there are more members of the Fédération Internationale de Football Association (FIFA) than of the UN. Football (or 'soccer' as it is known in America) is a growth sport; however, its commercial representation can only be considered strong in certain world regions. For example, in 2009, the German Bundesliga overtook the English Premier League to be ranked as the world's most profitable football league, stacking up €172 million of operating profits, whilst the Premier League more than halved their revenues from €224 million to €96 million in the same year.[1] In total, the big five European football leagues (England's Premier League, Germany's Bundesliga, Italy's Serie A, Spain's La Liga and France's Ligue 1) generated revenues of €7,900 million in 2008/09 (€6,300 million in 2004/05 (Jones, Parkes and Houlihan, 2006)).[2] The combined revenue of the top 20 European football clubs broke the €3 billion barrier after growing by 6 per cent annually in recent years. Nonetheless, football is not as popular in the USA when viewed in comparison to the four other most popular team sports, namely, baseball, American football, basketball and ice hockey. The professional major leagues of each of these sports in the USA enjoy massive, however, mainly domestic, media exposure and are considered the pre-eminent competitions in their respective sports in the world. The big four major leagues in the USA – MLB, NFL, NBA and NHL – created total revenues of €15,070 million in 2009/10, seeing the NFL (€5,400 million) closely followed by MLB (€4,700 million).[3]

To take another case, one could consider Formula One to be an extremely popular international sport due to the season on season investment in the sport in terms of sponsorship income and sporting achievements as racing in China, the Middle East and elsewhere around the world every year. However, in the USA the TV coverage and interest in Formula One is, at best, minimal (Dolles and Söderman, 2008a). Cricket, as another example, attracts huge interest in South Asia. This is amply illustrated by comparing an international benchmark in this sport, such as the English ECB Premier Leagues in cricket, which are valued at €8,900 million (2010) to the Indian Premier League (IPL) in cricket, which, in a short span of three years since its inaugural season in 2008, is valued at €3,010 million and has the potential to grow further.[4] In 2009, security concerns forced the IPL organizers to seek an alternative host for the 59 matches. Six venues were found in South Africa for this purpose. It was said that this relocation of a complete cricket season will serve to strengthen the ties between South African and Indian cricket even further, as well as binding the nations closer together.[5]

Beyond the sporting and political aspects, mega events such as the final round of the FIFA Football World Championships or the Olympic Games also rank amongst the largest international marketing events in the world, reaching billions of people in over 200 countries around the globe and generating millions worth of revenues in merchandising and sponsorship (Dolles and Söderman, 2008b). The broadcasting giant NBC, in an act of foresight prior to Vancouver 2010 where it achieved success, paid €1,750 million in 2003[6] for TV and online media rights to retain the privilege of associating its brand with the Olympic Games until the London Olympics in 2012. This was nearly 50 per cent more than it paid for prior games. Despite the presence of numerous sporting events and brands, the Olympic Games command total attention in terms of corporate marketing. Overall revenues generated by the International Olympic Committee (IOC) in the past four Quadrennials amount to €11,190 billion (IOC, 2010). China made an operating profit of over Yuan 1 billion (about €104 million) from the 2008

Summer Olympics as reported by the Beijing Organizing Committee.[7] The Games' tracking audit recorded income by the Chinese National Audit Office of Yuan 20.5 billion (€2,331 million) with expenses of Yuan 19.34 billion (€2,198 million) in respect to the finances and construction costs of venues for the 2008 Beijing Olympics in comparison. The overriding source of income for the Games came from sales of broadcasting rights, souvenirs and tickets, assets sales and sponsorship (Söderman and Dolles, 2008, 2010). The Vancouver Organizing Committee for the 2010 Olympic and Paralympic Winter Games announced that it will exceed its sponsorship target, quoted to be €151 million (from the IOC TOP sponsorship programme), through domestic sponsorship reaching €580 million and €151 million in marketing royalties.[8]

In the 1950s and 1960s, most sports goods were produced and consumed in developed countries, generating significant trade amongst themselves, but only a tiny flow of international trade with developing countries (Andreff and Andreff, 2009). The sports goods industry today shows a completely different picture as a result of the rise of the emerging economies, coupled with the changing focus of firms' strategies towards accessing foreign markets and relocating labour-intensive production. In addition, sports goods producers like Nike, the Adidas-Salomon-Reebok-Group, Puma and others have increasingly contracted production modules to domestic sports goods producers in the emerging economies by means of subcontracting and outward processing trade. The sports goods industry today is bound up in a global network of interdependency chains marked by various cross-border transactions; as such, new competitors from the emerging economies like LiNing are challenging established producers.

The trade of goods and equipment around the globe, as well as the construction of sports complexes, racecourses and arenas, has also developed into a multi-billion dollar business as well. For example, German architects designed the World Cup arenas in Durban, Cape Town and Port Elizabeth which were built to host the FIFA World Cup in South Africa.[9] A German engineer named Hermann Tilke[10] designed nearly half of the current Formula One circuits, such as the Sepang Circuit in Malaysia, the Shanghai International Circuit and the Yas Marina Circuit in Abu Dhabi – a €995 million investment. The new circuit to be introduced to the Formula One calendar in 2010 – the Korean International Circuit in Yeongam – in addition to the new Moscow Raceway, are also designed by him. A German-Russian joint venture is responsible for the construction of the Moscow Raceway, with an estimated investment cost of RUB 5.5 billion (€13.5 million). In the future, it should become the first circuit in Russia suitable for hosting world-class motorsports including Formula One and MotoGP.[11]

Sport clubs build global brands and, increasingly, develop modes of international operation. These include international franchises and strategic alliances, such as that between Manchester United and New York Yankees, between Chelsea FC and the Chinese Olympic football team or between the Japanese Urawa Reds and Bayern Munich. The proliferation of information technology has made it possible to serve the needs of fans all over the world. They can consume an event either real-time or recorded from virtually anywhere. As a result of this, the opportunities for the promotion of sport, and the benefits for sport and its partners, are significant. Surprisingly the financial crises and even doping scandals appear to have had only limited impact on the sports industry.

Mainstream academic literature often suggests that sport should be studied in specialist niches on the grounds that it is 'not generalisable'. Indeed, sport does have a number of distinctive characteristics which may influence the way in which it internationalizes, professionalizes and commercializes. Sport events have uncertain outcomes and evoke strongly emotional responses from consumers which often result in an intense, sometimes unexpected, loyalty. It is the distinctive characteristics of sports which merit discussion in this volume on sport as business. This book seeks to provide a deeper understanding of sport's unique development, its governance and its logic of value co-creation, as well as the advancement of the sports industry towards internationalization, professionalization and commercialization.

We explored these critical issues during two workshops on 'Sport as a Business' at the German Graduate School of Management and Law (formerly Heilbronn Business School) in Heilbronn, Germany in 2007 and 2008. Chapters presented in this book were initially selected by the workshop committee on the basis of an extended abstract. The selected papers were then presented in full at the workshop. Comments and suggestions were provided to the attendees after which time a blind review was conducted. The papers were later rewritten for the purpose of this publication. Further double blind reviewed chapters to be included in this volume where chosen from our track on 'Sport as a Business' at the annual meeting of the European Academy of Management 2009 in Liverpool, UK.

The book is structured in three parts, each comprised of chapters addressing the three major themes that run through this volume – internationalization, professionalization and commercialization. Part I takes a look at the industry from the perspective of the sport consumer. Part II is based on sports events and facility management, while Part III focuses on the challenges for sport organizations and governance structures in sports.

Part I: Sport consumers perspective

Chapter 1: ' "As American as mom, apple pie and Dutch soccer?": The team identification of foreign Ajax FC supporters' by Anthony K. Kerr, Narelle F. Smith and Alastair Anderson

Globalization and advances in communications technology, notably satellite television and broadband internet, have greatly expanded the potential marketplace for professional sport teams. As a result, many team brands profit from millions of satellite supporters worldwide. This study is the second in a series that explores why, and how, the foreign consumer supports their chosen team, in this instance, AFC Ajax of Amsterdam. Respondents highlighted the importance of team reputation and/or tradition; the presence of a particular player(s); team success; and media coverage in their decision to support Ajax FC. Furthermore, satellite supporters expressed intense loyalty for, and appeared to derive psychological benefit from their support of, the foreign-based team. As such, satellite supporters present an opportunity for sport marketers to tap into a potentially lucrative fan base and enhance their own team brands.

Chapter 2: 'Decision-making styles in purchasing sport products: An international comparison between American and Korean college students' by Sungwon Bae

A consumer's decision-making style is a very important area to consider when attempting to identify and understand the consumer's shopping behaviour and motivation, especially in the sports apparel market. Thus, the author applies a consumer decision-making model to consider specific shopping styles involving athletic apparel and to examine specific shopping pattern differences between selected university students in the USA and South Korea. A quantitative research design was performed to analyse the effect of seven factors: brand, quality, recreation, confusion, fashion, impulse and price consciousness. A total of 1,720 college students (822 American and 841 Korean) enrolled in the Lifetime Activity Programme at a university in the south-east of the USA and South Korea participated in the study. The analysis of variance revealed that there were significant differences between nations across all seven dimensions. Overall, the South Korean college-aged consumers had higher mean scores than the American college-aged consumers regarding the following factors: quality, recreation, fashion, impulse, price and brand consciousness. Conversely, American college-aged consumers scored significantly higher than the Korean on confusion consciousness.

Chapter 3: 'Travel time elasticities in recreational sports: Empirical findings for the professionalization in sports facility management' by Tim Pawlowski, Christoph Breuer and Pamela Wicker

Given the increasing scarcity of public funds, measures to allocate public money efficiently are becoming more and more important. Since most public funds in the sports sector are spent on the construction and operation of sports facilities, strategies to reallocate public money more efficiently, particularly in the recreational sports facility sector, are auspicious for all public authorities. Efficiency could be improved by increasing the number of people practising sport, for example, via facilitating access to public sports facilities. In this regard, sports managers need to know about the degree of demand sensitivity to the distance or time involved in travelling to sports facilities. Therefore, this chapter is focused on the analysis of sport consumers' travel time sensitivity. Based on survey data from Cologne and Stuttgart in Germany the authors found significant differences in travel time sensitivity for different sports and between the cities. Their findings suggest that, with the objective of increasing efficiency, one could consider a more centralized sports facility allocation for sports with less travel time elastic consumers such as apparatus gymnastics, dancing and fitness. On the contrary, a more decentralized allocation of handball gyms and swimming pools might actually increase efficiency through an increased number of consumers.

Part II: Sport events and sport facilities

Chapter 4: 'Perceptions of the impacts of major commercial sport events' by Christopher J. Auld, Kathleen M. Lloyd and Jennifer Rieck

This chapter examines community perceptions about the potential outcomes from major sport events. Bidding and staging a major sport event attracts significant costs and this use of public funds also incurs considerable opportunity costs by taxpayers. Because of this substantial government expenditure, it might be expected that community opinions would be seen as an important part of the event planning and bidding process. Using data from a sample of 281 university students, the results indicated that respondents recorded moderately high levels of agreement with a series of government statements regarding the potential economic benefits of staging and, adversely, the costs resulting from major sport events. The results suggest there is some basis for assumptions regarding positive public perceptions about the benefits derived from sport events and also that governments are likely to continue to feel little pressure to consult with the public about event bidding and stadia development. However, it is argued by the authors that the public is largely informed on the basis of information supplied by event organizers and government agencies.

Chapter 5: 'Gender, race and nationality: An examination of print media coverage of the 2006 Winter Olympics' by Andrea N. Eagleman and Erin L. McNary

The mass media today serves an important role in bringing every aspect of an event to their readers and subscribers. Media coverage of the Olympic Games in the USA has traditionally been biased. Due to this history of coverage, the purpose of this chapter is to examine multiple print media to determine if differences exist in the amount of coverage granted to athletes of differing gender, race and nationality. A content analysis methodology is used by the authors to examine US newspapers' coverage of the 2006 Winter Olympic Games, as well as the top three general-interest sport magazines in the USA. A total of 958 newspaper articles and 25 magazine articles were examined. Chi square analysis revealed statistically significant differences in coverage of gender in magazines, revealing that more coverage was devoted to women than expected. Additionally, newspapers provided statistically significant coverage based on race, providing more coverage of different races than expected. Both newspapers and magazines provided statistically significant amounts of coverage to US athletes over their international counterparts.

Chapter 6: 'Enhancing public sports facilities: A representation of the global value' by Bernard Augé, Arnaud Pedenon and Alexandre Vernhet

With the development of sports practices, public actors have become aware of the necessity to modernize sports facilities. Faced with this observation, this study aims to provide an assessment of the performance of public sports facilities, more specifically based on the value attributed to the facilities by individuals practising sport. The authors firstly consider the global value of a sports facility, working from the model developed by Aurier, Evrard and N'Goala, which integrates both transactional and relational marketing approaches of value. Secondly, they show to what extent a cognitive approach can be considered as a relevant methodology to permit exploration of the main actors' mental representations regarding sports equipment's global value (by main actors the authors refer to the elected town councillors in charge of sport and the town sports service directors). The objective of this chapter is to provide an assessment of the performance management of these practices based on value and to gain an understanding of the representation of the value of such equipment by individuals practising sport.

Part III: Sport organizations and governance

Chapter 7: 'Sports organizations, professionalization and organizational conflict: A review of the literature' by John Schulz

One of the most common issues facing managers these days is the management of conflict. While conflict has been studied exhaustively within the public and private sectors, when it comes to sport there has been limited research. This chapter provides an overview of the theoretical and empirical research on conflict in sports organizations and how that relates to changes currently occurring in sport. The consensus of the sport literature suggests that it is the structural arrangements of sports organizations that make them an environment for the emergence of sport. However, this review argues that, although it was possible to adopt new organizational designs to reduce conflict, the process of change in itself creates conflict and, furthermore, new conflicts emerge in the new design. The continuing issue is that the interaction of individuals within these structures causes conflict; hence, the real problem is how to manage that conflict.

Chapter 8: 'International and professional dimensions of national governing bodies: Insights from the Gaelic Athletic Association' by Anne Bourke

This chapter highlights the key characteristics of sports' national governing bodies (NGBs), describes their organizational structure and governance arrangements and identifies the factors which facilitate them to gain and sustain a competitive edge. NGB's international activities normally refer to hosting events or participating in competitions (Champions League, 6 Nations), while their professional dimensions generally refer to player/athlete salaries, contracts and conditions. Using the Gaelic Athletic Association (GAA) (a leading sport NGB in Ireland) as a case study in this chapter, insights on governance, recent policy developments and changes are provided. The GAA is not just a form of recreation but an expression of the people and their culture. Stemming from the strategic plans, the GAA and its structure has evolved, with two resources being considered vital – its 'amateur status' and voluntary input together with the need for financial acumen – also with developing further the international dimension of its own games and elite players.

Chapter 9: 'The role of central brokers and their influence on effectiveness in an intentionally created sports professionalization network' by Simon G. Martin, Maureen Benson-Rea and Nitha Palakshappa

The primary aim of this chapter is to demonstrate how the role of the central broker influences the effectiveness of an intentionally created network in an elite sports sector professionalization context. The authors contribute to network literature, as prior research shows that the central broker role in networks that are intentionally created by governments is only temporary, with power and control being handed back to network actors. Such networks have been found not to be durable. This research finds networks that are intentionally created and managed can be durable and effective, greatly contributing to overall professionalization, but that their effectiveness is dependent on the ability of the central broker to add value. The authors develop a deeper understanding of causal events for the effectiveness of networks, discovering conditions under which these events occurred and how they were related to network effectiveness. A new network type, a *structured* network is identified.

Chapter 10: 'Business ecosystem co-evolution: The Ultimate Fighting Championships' by Simon Ford and Clive Kerr

This chapter analyses the growth and present success of the Ultimate Fighting Championships (UFC), a US organization that promotes mixed martial arts (MMA) events and programming. The authors do so through the lens of the 'business ecosystem', seeking insight by studying the actors and co-evolutionary complex dynamics that operate in this ecosystem. Drawing primarily on online media sources, they observe how the UFC has positioned itself as the premier MMA organization and how its recruitment and retention policy enables it to build its product around highly talented and improving fighters. These policies have created an evolutionary trajectory within the business ecosystem that, in combination with the increase in free-to-air events and sponsorship exposure, has embedded the UFC at the core of the North American MMA ecosystem. This chapter contributes to our understanding of how new sports and sports governing organizations emerge and evolve.

Chapter 11: 'Learning from failure: Is Major League Soccer repeating the mistakes of the North American Soccer League?' by John D. Francis

The signing of David Beckham in 2007 by Major League Soccer is considered by many to be a watershed moment for the league. However, critics contend that this strategy is similar to the signing of Pelé by the North American Soccer League in the 1970s, a move which ultimately contributed to its demise. Using American professional soccer as a focal case, the chapter explores how organizations learn vicariously through the failure of others. As the growth of sports as business intensifies, learning from the failure of others remains a key basis for overall organizational learning and performance. By comparing the similarities and differences of the leagues' attributes in this chapter, broader lessons are presented by the author for sports leagues as they seek to grow their organizations in challenging environments.

Chapter 12: 'Learning from success: Implementing a professional football league in Japan' by Harald Dolles and Sten Söderman

By considering the implementation as well as the immediate and sustainable success of the Japanese professional football league (J-League) during its first two decades as a neglected research example, the authors apply the "network of value captures" research framework to the Japanese context. This research framework identifies and describes the business parameters of professional football (soccer) by the following dimensions: (1) the product and its features; (2) various customer groups; and (3) the future vision of the club as central to different levels of strategy aggregation. This chapter provides insights into the management of football in Japan by revealing different practices compared to Europe, for example, in target customer groups, in associated product marketing and merchandising or in distribution of media revenues. The success story of the J-League also contributes to an increasing international awareness of Japanese football, its players and its fans.

Acknowledgements

Finally, we would like to thank the contributors to this volume, who have been most cooperative. We also want to thank the many reviewers who provided critical and thoughtful reviews of the manuscripts – without their help this book would not have been possible. The editors gratefully acknowledge financial support from the German Graduate School of Management and Law (formerly Heilbronn Business School) in hosting the two workshops in Heilbronn and providing substantial travel funding to the speakers.

Notes

1. 'England's Premier League Top European Football Earnings in 2009 but Wages at 67% of Revenues Threaten Profitability', http://www.finfacts.ie/irishfinancenews/European_3/article_1019860_printer.shtml, retrieved 10.09.2010.
2. *Annual Review of Football Finance 2010* (Manchester: Deloitte, Sport Business Group), http://www.deloitte.com/view/en_GB/uk/industries/sportsbusiness group/sports/football/0a4be867d38f8210VgnVCM200000bb42f00aRCRD.htm, retrieved 10.09.2010.
3. 'Sports Industry Overview', http://www.plunkettresearch.com/Industries/Sports/SportsStatistics/tabid/273/Default.aspx, retrieved 12.09.2010.
4. 'IPL Brand Value Doubles to $4.13 Billion: Study', *The Times of India*, 22.03.2010, http://timesofindia.indiatimes.com/iplarticleshow/5713042.cms, retrieved 10.09.2010.
5. 'IPL Confirms South Africa Switch', *BBC Sport Cricket*, 24.03.2009, http://news.bbc.co.uk/sport2/hi/cricket/7958664.stm, retrieved 13.09.2010.
6. 'OLYMPICS; NBC's Olympic Run is Extended to 2012 with $2 Billion Bid', *New York Times*, 07.06.2003, http://www.nytimes.com/2003/06/07/sports/olympics-nbc-s-olympic-run-is-extended-to-2012-with-2-billion-bid.html, retrieved 18.07.2010.
7. 'Beijing Olympics' Profit Exceeds 1b yuan', *China Daily*, 19.06.2009, http://www.chinadaily.com.cn/business/2009-06/19/content_8302950.htm, retrieved 10.09.2010.
8. 'VANOC Business Plan and Games Budget', http://www.vancouver2010.com/more-2010-information/about-vanoc/business-plan-and-games-budget/, retrieved 10.09.2010.
9. 'Deutsche Architeken entwerfen 3 WM Stadien in Südafrika', *Afrika Wirtschaft*, http://www.afrikawirtschaft.de/_uploads/media/635_AW-2006-4-Kultur-WM-Stadien.pdf, retrieved 12.09.2010.
10. http://www.tilke.de/, retrieved 12.09.2010.
11. 'F1 Circuit to be Built in Moscow Suburbs Soon', http://en.motonews.ru/news.moto?id=3548&sort_cat=, retrieved 12.09.2010.

References

Andreff, M. and Andreff, W. (2009) 'Global Trade in Sports Goods: International Specialisation of Major Trading Countries', *European Sport Management Quarterly*, 9(3): 259–294.

Dolles, H. and Söderman, S. (2008a) 'Formula One in the US. Interview with Joie Chitwood III President and Chief Operating Officer Indianapolis Motor Speedway LLC', *International Journal of Sports Marketing and Sponsorship*, 10(1): 11–14.

Dolles, H. and Söderman, S. (2008b) 'Mega-sporting Events in Asia: Impacts on Society, Business and Management – An Introduction', *Asian Business and Management*, 7(1): 1–16.

Falt, E. (2004) 'UNEP Presentation for the Global Forum for Sports and Environment', Presentation for the Global Forum for Sports and Environment, 24–26 November 2004 (Lahore, Pakistan), http://www.unep.org/Documents.Multilingual/Default.asp?DocumentID=413&ArticleID=4671&l=en, retrieved 09.09.2010.

International Olympic Committee (IOC) (ed.) (2010) *Olympic Marketing Fact File 2010* (Lausanne: International Olympic Committee), http://www.olympic.org/Documents/fact_file_2010.pdf, retrieved 20.7.2010.

Jones, D., Parkes, R. and Houlihan, A. (2006) *Football Money League: Changing of the Guard* (Manchester: Deloitte, Sports Business Group), http://www.deloitte.com/assets/Dcom-UnitedKingdom/Local%20Assets/Documents/UK_SBG_DeloitteFootballMoneyLeague2006.pdf, retrieved 09.09.2010.

Söderman, S. and Dolles, H. (2008) 'Strategic Fit in International Sponsorship – The Case of the Olympic Games in Beijing 2008', *International Journal of Sports Marketing and Sponsorship*, 9(2): 95–110.

Söderman, S. and Dolles, H. (2010) 'Sponsoring the Beijing Olympic Games – Patterns of Sponsor Advertising', *Asia Pacific Journal of Marketing and Logistics*, 22(1): 8–24.

Part I
Sport Consumers' Perspective

1
'As American as Mom, Apple Pie and Dutch Soccer?': The Team Identification of Foreign Ajax FC Supporters

Anthony K. Kerr, Narelle F. Smith and Alastair Anderson

1. Introduction

Professional team sport, like other forms of popular culture, is attractive and highly marketable. Furthermore, technological advances and globalization have greatly expanded the potential marketplace for professional sport organizations. For instance, Barcelona FC is believed to have 70 million supporters worldwide[1] and English rival, Manchester United, has seen its fan base double in the past five years to 139 million.[2] Real Madrid could have a potential fan base of nearly half a billion.[3] However, foreign interest extends beyond Association football, and the success of home-grown players such as Suzuki, Matsui and Matsuzaka has boosted the popularity in Japan of a number of Major League Baseball (MLB) teams. Similarly, 30 million Chinese regularly watch the National Basketball Association's (NBA) Houston Rockets to cheer on their countryman, Yao Ming (Larmer, 2005).

Ben-Porat (2000: 344) claimed that a foreign team often becomes "an 'overseas sweetheart,' far away but close to the heart". Kerr (2008, 2009a) describes these individuals as 'satellite supporters' and they have become increasingly critical in a global marketplace since they often generate significant revenue. For instance, sport organizations such as the NBA (India), Australian and New Zealand rugby union (Japan), the J-League's Urawa Reds (Europe) and the Australian Football League's Hawthorn (New Zealand),[4] are actively targeting foreign markets (Dolles and Söderman, 2005, 2011). Real Madrid now earns 60 per cent of merchandise revenue from international markets, up from 10 per cent at the beginning of the decade (Jones, Parkes and Houlihan, 2006). Moreover, in a bid to garner more revenue they have even argued for earlier kick-off times in the Spanish league so that more Chinese fans can watch matches.[5] Although satellite supporters might prove to be the future lifeblood of a sport franchise, their psychological attachment to a foreign-based team has received relatively little attention.

2. Team identification

Wann et al. (2001: 3) describe team identification as "the extent to which a fan feels psychologically connected" to a particular team or player. Professional sports, given their importance in modern society, often benefit from the identification that develops between the team and its fans. Indeed, team identification is based upon social identification (Fink, Trail and Anderson, 2002; Madrigal, 2004; Wann and Branscombe, 1993). Consequently, fans that identify strongly with their team tend to invest more time and money in support (Milne and McDonald, 1999; Murrell and Dietz, 1992; Sutton et al., 1997; Wann and Branscombe, 1990, 1993, 1995).

Although fandom is intrinsically personal, reasons have been identified which may explain why an individual develops an identification with a team. In addition, for those with high levels of identification, the role of fan is an important component of their identity. According to Wann (2006a), individuals identify with their chosen team due to three important factors: psychological, environmental and team-related.

A key psychological factor is the supporter's need for belonging and affiliation, and the opportunity to affiliate with others is a common reason given for team identification (Wann, Tucker and Schrader, 1996). Sutton et al. (1997: 19) argued that community affiliation, derived from "common symbols, shared goals, history, and a fan's need to belong" is the most significant element in the creation of team identification.

Environmental factors, in particular the process of socialization, also contribute to identification with a team (Wann, 2006a). The socialization process, whereby one learns and internalizes "the attitudes, values, knowledge and behaviors that are associated with fans of a team" (Kolbe and James, 2000: 25), is critical to team identification. Common socialization agents include the family (Dimmock and Grove, 2006; Donavan, Janda and Suh, 2006; Funk and James, 2001; Greenwood, Kanters and Casper, 2006; Jacobson, 2003; Jones, 1997; Kolbe and James, 2000; Melnick and Wann, 2004; Wann, Tucker and Schrader, 1996) and friends or peers (Crawford, 2003; Dimmock and Grove, 2006; Donavan, Janda and Suh, 2006; Jacobson, 2003; Kolbe and James, 2000; Melnick and Wann, 2004; Wann, Tucker and Schrader, 1996). The introduction of satellite television and the Internet has prompted others to suggest the media as a viable agent (Jacobson, 2003; Mahony et al., 2002; Melnick and Wann, 2004; Sutton et al., 1997; Wann, Tucker and Schrader, 1996). These environmental factors can influence team identification through people and place or via "physical proximity to the entity" (Donavan, Janda and Suh, 2006: 125). Socialization through geographic proximity is such a powerful force because living or growing up close to a team increases opportunities for socialization (Wann, 2006a). Therefore, geographic proximity, or support for a 'hometown team', has typically featured as an important determinant in a supporter's identification with their team (Greenwood, Kanters and Casper, 2006; Kolbe and James, 2000; Wann, Tucker and Schrader, 1996).

The third factor in the development of team identification relates to issues such as team performance, player attributes and organizational characteristics (Wann, 2006a). Fink, Trail and Anderson (2002) found vicarious achievement to be the primary driver of team identification, while it has also been shown that the degree of identification accounts for the 'die-hard' and 'fair-weather' fan. Die-hard fans remain loyal irrespective of on-field performance, while the latter associate with a team only when it performs well (Wann and Branscombe, 1990). Organizational characteristics encompass the 'off-field' image of the organization, including managerial decisions, reputation and tradition, and the quality of their conference or league (Sutton et al., 1997).

Team identification has a positive impact upon psychological health because it can facilitate social connections with others (Melnick, 1993; Wann et al., 2001). However, some argue that fans who identify with geographically distant teams (or, for our purpose, satellite supporters), do not usually receive the same psychological benefits (Wann, 2006a, 2006b; Wann and Pierce, 2005; Wann et al., 1999, 2004). Identification with distant teams is unlikely to provide significant psychological benefit because supporters are usually isolated from, and find it difficult to interact with, likeminded fans (Wann, 2006b, 2006c). However, should satellite supporters be able to enjoy the company of fellow fans, their shared identification with the team might enhance their psychological well-being (Wann, 2006c; Wann et al., 1999, 2004).

The global popularity of certain teams has seen the rise of fan communities. For instance, the English Premier League's (EPL) Liverpool FC has more than 150 international supporter branches and the National Football League's (NFL) Cleveland Browns has a worldwide network of 'Browns Backers'. Kolbe and James (2000) found that Browns' fans felt a 'connective bond' with a community of likeminded supporters. Although research suggests that fans of geographically distant teams are unlikely to accrue the same psychological benefits as local fans, it is apparent that under certain circumstances they might accrue psychological benefits from their fandom. This might explain the existence, and growth, of online (and physical) foreign fan communities.

Wann, Tucker and Schrader's (1996) landmark study on the origins of team identification suggested their effort should be considered "the first step in understanding the factors involved in identification with sport teams" (ibid.: 1001). In recent years there has been increased attention paid to team identification (see, for example, Greenwood, Kanters and Casper, 2006; Gwinner and Swanson, 2003; Jacobson, 2003; Jones, 1998; Kerr, 2009a, 2009b; Kolbe and James, 2000; Sutton et al., 1997). Furthermore, Richardson and O'Dwyer (2003) welcomed research as to why fans adopted their favourite team.

Sport marketers need to understand the satellite supporter as a valuable consumer and adopt a different strategy to reach these 'international fans' and to enhance their team's global brand profile (Dolles and Söderman, 2008). However, research has been largely confined to domestic or local fans. This chapter reports the results of preliminary research on the team identification of satellite supporters and is the second in a series designed to foster a better understanding of these consumers. An earlier study (Kerr, forthcoming) was an exploratory examination of the team identification of Australian Football League (AFL) American supporters. This chapter examines satellite supporters and their identification with the Dutch football giant, AFC Ajax of Amsterdam (Ajax FC).

Founded at the turn of the twentieth century, Ajax FC has been crowned European champion four times and has dominated the Dutch football league, the Eredivisie. Since their first national championship in 1918, the red and whites have won an additional 28 league titles.[6] Ajax FC is famous for their youth academy which has produced superstars such as Johan Cruijff, Frank Rijkaard, Marco van Basten, Patrick Kluivert and Dennis Bergkamp.[7] It was under the leadership of Cruijff in 1972 that the club had one of the best seasons ever by a professional football team as Ajax FC dominated the Dutch and European competitions. In an effort to exploit international opportunities and expand its brand, it has also established a South African franchise, Ajax Cape Town (Browne, 1999).

3. Method

The Internet has been successfully used to engage with distant sport fans: online surveys (Kerr, 2009a, 2009b; Nash, 2000), online message boards (End, 2001; Lewis, 2001; Mitrano, 1999) and online 'interviews' (Heinonen, 2002; Kerr, 2009a, 2009b; Mitrano, 1999). The existence of online communities also makes it possible to target specific and difficult to reach populations (Hoyle, Harris and Judd, 2002). The popularity of the Internet for fan research reflects the increased access to, and acceptance of, electronic media as a means of communication and the increased availability of broadband connections (Alreck and Settle, 2004). According to Bailey (1994: 205), the online survey might prove "the ideal method for studying respondents in remote locations all over the world".

Since our interest was in satellite supporters of Ajax FC and given the advantages of administration over the Internet we chose to develop an online questionnaire. Officially launched in January 1996, www.ajaxusa.com, an online forum for supporters of Ajax FC, pre-dates the club's official website, www.ajax.nl. As founder, Jim McGough explained, "In those days we provided a service that was badly needed. At our height, we could occasionally have more than ten thousand unique site visitors in a single day."[8] With more than a 1000 registered members, Ajax USA agreed to act as the vehicle for the administration of the survey.

3.1. Respondents

One hundred and eighty seven visitors to www.ajaxusa.com voluntarily filled in the questionnaire. However, 59 cases were removed from the sample: 34 individuals completed only the demographic questions and 25 others were Dutch or had an immediate family member from the Netherlands. The primary purpose of this study was to research satellite supporters and so these latter individuals, perhaps better categorized as 'expatriate fans', were outside its scope. Therefore, the final sample comprised 128 satellite supporters of Ajax FC. All of the respondents in the sample were male and nearly three-quarters were aged between 18 and 35 years. Furthermore, although most of the respondents (36.7%) were American, which was consistent with a US supporter organization, the sample represented 44 countries. However, only five other countries (UK, England, India, Slovenia, Canada and Denmark) had more than three representatives.

3.2. Materials and procedure

Respondents followed a link on the Ajax USA website that led them to the survey hosted by www.surveymonkey.com, an independent third party which specializes in the creation and management of online surveys. The questionnaire was available for two weeks and contained five sections. The first section described the purpose of the study while the second asked supporters to complete demographic details such as age, gender, country of residence and nationality. Respondents were asked whether they had a personal connection to the Netherlands, the home of Ajax FC (as described earlier, these individuals were excluded from the study).

The third section asked respondents to rate the importance of the 14 items related to their original decision to support Ajax FC. The study's purpose was to explore supporter identification with a specific sport team; however, the term 'team identification' is a psychological definition most likely unknown to many potential participants. They were instead asked about their 'support' for the team. The items were derived from an exploratory examination of satellite supporter team identification (Kerr, forthcoming) and Kerr and Gladden's (2008) brand equity model in a global sport marketplace. The brand equity items were included due to the assertion that brand equity and team identification are likely to share common antecedents (Kerr, 2008, 2009b). An additional item probed team loyalty. The items were scored on a five-point Likert scale, ranging from 1, not important, to 5, extremely important.

The team-specific questionnaire was based on an earlier pilot study (Kerr, forthcoming). The questionnaire allowed participants to explain in their own words why they supported their favourite sport team. The use of open-ended questions was advantageous since it was an exploratory examination of their team support and many of the responses mirrored antecedents of team identification found in the fan literature. The survey instrument measured what it was designed to measure, notably those items responsible for their identification with the team. The potential drivers of team identification unearthed from this study were able to be easily modified to explore the satellite supporter's identification with any specific team. The online questionnaire was therefore a valid and reliable research instrument to examine a satellite supporter's identification with a foreign-based team and was consequently used as the basis for this Ajax FC study.

As discussed earlier, team identification is based upon social identification. Tajfel and Turner (1979, 1986) developed social identity theory to understand the behaviour of individuals in group situations. They concluded that individuals identify with groups they perceive they belong to, and then compare these groups with others to reflect positively upon themselves. In the context of this chapter, satellite supporters chose to categorize themselves as fans of Ajax FC, identified with the club and fellow fans, and compared themselves to rival team fans.

Social identity theory has often been used to examine team identification (Dimmock, Grove and Eklund, 2005; Dimmock and Gucciardi, 2007; Donavan, Janda and Suh, 2006; Gwinner and Swanson, 2003; Jacobson, 2003; Jones, 1998; Wann, 2006a). Donavan, Carlson and Zimmerman (2005: 33) argued that social identity theory is an appropriate perspective to understand fan behaviour since this behaviour "involves interpersonal and group relationships, it is socially observable, it often revolves around the distinctions that exist between opposing groups, and it is heavily affected by the level of identification with a team". Social identity theory is a proven and popular framework to explore issues regarding the sport fan.

The fourth section was structured to collect data about consumption behaviour. Section five thanked respondents for their time and invited them to participate in further discussions regarding their support of a foreign team.

The data were coded and entered into SPSS 15. Frequency tables and descriptive statistics were produced for all variables. Differences between means on quantitative variables according to age categories were tested. Chi-square tests were used to test for significant relationships between categorical variables.

4. Results and discussion

4.1. Identification with Ajax FC

The responses in relation to the 14 items pertaining to the decision to support a club were ranked from the highest to the lowest based on the percentage of respondents who indicated that the item was at least 'moderately important' in their initial decision to support Ajax FC. The ranking revealed the importance of four reasons: reputation and/or tradition; the presence of a particular player(s); team success; and the ability to watch Ajax FC play due to media coverage. The salience of these reasons is shown in Table 1.1.

By far the most important reason in their original decision to support Ajax FC was its reputation and tradition: more than 60 per cent

Table 1.1 Importance of reasons in original Ajax FC support (N = 128)

Reasons for support	% Important	% Not important	Mean[a,b]	SD
Team reputation and/or tradition	96.2	3.1	4.40	0.93
They had a particular player(s) I liked	79.0	9.4	3.65	1.31
They were (and possibly still are) a successful team	77.3	8.6	3.33	1.19
Ability to watch them play due to media coverage	60.1	24.2	3.00	1.51
They belonged to the highest division, the Eredivisie	53.8	33.6	2.57	1.37
A personal/emotional 'connection' to the Netherlands	49.2	40.6	2.60	1.55
Liked their logo design and/or name	37.5	39.8	2.26	1.31
They had a particular manager I liked	37.5	49.2	2.12	1.30
Liked the stadium they called 'home'	34.4	46.9	2.15	1.33
The broadcast quality of their games	31.3	57.0	1.95	1.27
A fellow countryman played for them	20.3	71.9	1.63	1.16
My family or friends supported them	13.3	76.6	1.48	1.01
They had high-profile and/or quality sponsors	12.5	75.8	1.43	0.88
They had famous or celebrity fans	11.0	78.9	1.38	0.86

[a] Lower scores indicate lower salience for each variable.
[b] Scale range 1–5 for each variable.

rated the item as extremely important. Respondents were informed that this item could include the team's history of success, its style of play and ethical behaviour as these are features often found in discussions of team reputation and tradition in the fan literature (Gladden, Milne and Sutton, 1998; Kolbe and James, 2000; Sutton et al., 1997; Underwood, Bond and Baer, 2001). For instance, an American fan said, "at the time they were the top team in the world and I wanted to cheer against them since they were often the favorite to win. However, their fluid, attacking style of play won me over not only to the team, but also the sport of football." Other supporters agreed, claiming that "Ajax are innovators of the modern game" (Evan, USA) and that their "style of play was highly attractive when I first began watching them (1993–94), and they were entering their most successful period in the modern era" (Jim, USA).

The second most important reason was the presence of particular player(s) and that Ajax FC was successful. A third of respondents said that having a particular player they liked at the club was extremely important. Indeed, for some, the fact that Ajax FC boasted a number of Dutch superstars from the famous 1974 World Cup side fuelled their support. One Finnish fan said, "I actually got 'the Ajax fever' from Oranje 74 [the 1974 Dutch World Cup team]" while Ben, an American, explained that the "backbone of the Clockwork Orange Dutch World Cup side were the Ajax players, i.e. Cruijff, Neeskens, Suurbier, Hulshof, Rep, Keizer, Krol, etc. I so enjoyed watching them play in the national side that I decided to learn about the club side they played for." A fifth of respondents said that the club's success at the time they became a supporter was extremely important. For instance, "the year I started watching football was in 1995, in wich [sic] Ajax won the champions league. Most probably because they won the cup…" (Edward, Lebanon).

As can be seen in Table 1.1, these three reasons were almost universally regarded as important in the original decision to support Ajax FC. Cialdini et al. (1976) claimed that fans would publicly announce their association with successful teams, or tend to 'bask in reflected glory' (BIRG). As a result, spectators often choose to follow successful teams rather than those which perennially struggle (Branscombe and Wann, 1991; End et al., 2002; Mahony, Howard and Madrigal, 2000; Wann, Tucker and Schrader, 1996). It was little surprise, therefore, that the club's success featured prominently.

The next most important influence regarded media coverage. A quarter of respondents said the ability to watch Ajax FC play due to media coverage was extremely important. The fan literature consistently claims that socialisation agents are instrumental in the development of team identification, however, satellite supporters cannot benefit from geographic proximity, a key socialization agent. Instead, their attendance is largely virtual via the radio, television or Internet (Söderman, Dolles and Dum, 2010). Moreover, in the absence of international media exposure, teams are unlikely to develop significant brand awareness outside their domestic markets.

The majority of Ajax USA's members live thousands of kilometres from the Netherlands and so international media arrangements ensure that Ajax FC games are available to supporters who are abroad. For instance, one Finnish fan explained that he became "an Ajax fan in the 80's when I started to see Ajax's games via Sky Channel". Indeed, the increased accessibility to Ajax football has led to the ultimate demise of www.ajaxusa.com. As its founder explains: "Ajax USA has been there, in one form or another, since 1995. Thousands of 'Ajax starved' supporters from across the globe relied on us: they couldn't watch Ajax games. But times have changed. Almost every Ajax match is available online these days."[9] However, the importance of media coverage is not as compelling as it might seem since one-quarter of the respondents rated it as 'not important'. There were no significant differences between age groups in relation to the salience of media coverage in their decision to support Ajax FC.

Expatriate fans were excluded from the sample since the aim of this research was to understand satellite supporters and their identification with a foreign-based sport team. However, their involvement provided an opportunity to compare their responses to their foreign counterparts. A number of reasons were clearly important to the expatriate Ajax fan, that is, they were at least 'moderately important' in their original identification. A comparison of these supporters can be seen in Table 1.2.

Both groups were similar in terms of the relative importance of the items proposed as motivators of team support. However, two key differences emerged. For expatriate fans, a personal or emotional 'connection' to the Netherlands was the second most important item: 92 per cent of them considered this 'connection' at least moderately important in their decision to adopt Ajax FC (compared to less than half of satellite supporters). For instance, "I love Holland and that love tides over to Ajax... They are kind of a simble [sic] of my love for the Netherlands, and give me an outlet to express that love" (Matthew, Australia). Indeed, a third of expatriate fans said their connection to the Netherlands was extremely important in their choice. Furthermore, 40 per cent of

Table 1.2 Mean scores of the important reasons in original Ajax FC support (satellite supporters versus expatriate fans)

Reasons for support	Mean[a,b]	SD
Satellite supporters ($N = 128$)		
Team reputation and/or tradition	4.40	0.93
They had a particular player(s) I liked	3.65	1.31
They were (and possibly still are) a successful team	3.33	1.19
Ability to watch them play due to media coverage	3.00	1.51
Expatriate fans ($N = 25$)		
Team reputation and/or tradition	4.12	1.05
I had a personal/emotional 'connection' to the Netherlands	3.88	1.09
They had a particular player(s) I liked	3.28	1.10
They were (and possibly still are) a successful team	3.08	1.22

[a] Lower scores indicate lower salience for each variable.
[b] Scale range 1–5 for each variable.

expatriate fans said that because their family or friends supported Ajax FC was at least moderately important in their team choice. As such, family or friends (although a distant seventh with a mean of 2.32) were more influential upon their choice of team than for satellite supporters. These results are consistent with the expatriate fan being Dutch or having an immediate family member from the Netherlands.

Wann (2006a) claimed that individuals would identify with their team due to psychological, environmental and team-related factors. However, as discussed later, opportunities for satellite supporters to share the company of fellow Ajax fans was somewhat limited. On the other hand, the importance of environmental factors, especially the media, was evident for satellite supporters (in contrast to the importance of another socialization agent, family or friends, for the expatriate fan). In addition, team-related factors (such as reputation, tradition, success or a notable player) were instrumental in making the Ajax FC an attractive product for foreign-based fans.

4.2. The loyalty of Ajax FC satellite supporters

Support for a 'hometown team' consistently features in the team identification literature yet, in the absence of geographic ties, one might expect foreign consumers to be more fickle and their support for overseas teams less stable. This was, however, not the case and some supporters were quite adamant about their devotion. A Finnish fan explained that "once you got the 'Ajax fever', you will never 'recover' so I still follow Ajax and Oranje".

When asked, 'Is it possible you would ever stop supporting Ajax FC?', only 17 of the 128 respondents (13.3%) said 'yes'. Although one might expect satellite supporters to resemble 'fair-weather' rather than 'die-hard' fans, this was not reflected in the study. Three of the 17 were aged over 55, representing 60 per cent of the five respondents aged over 55. Thus, older respondents were more likely to consider switching teams, however, the small numbers represented from this age group make it unwise to generalize.

4.3. Consumption behaviour of Ajax FC satellite supporters

Respondents were asked how often they participated in a number of consumption activities related to their support of Ajax FC (during, or out of, season) For instance, they could purchase licensed merchandise, watch games on television, visit official websites or purchase a sponsor's product.

Table 1.3 Behaviour to support Ajax FC (during season) (N = 126)

Supporter behaviour	% Weekly	% Monthly	% Seasonally	% Never
Visit unofficial club supporter websites	91.3	4.8	1.6	2.4
Visit the official club website	67.5	19.8	7.1	5.6
Watch online video highlights	57.9	26.2	6.3	9.5
Watch club games on television	17.5	38.1	27.8	16.7
Get together with other club fans	7.1	4.8	21.4	66.7
Purchase team-related merchandise	4.0	5.6	69.0	21.4
Purchase products from companies that support the club	1.6	6.3	30.2	61.9
Purchase tickets to the club's Eredivisie games	1.6	2.4	22.2	73.8
Purchase additional club items	1.6	0.8	4.8	92.9
Purchase shares in the club	1.6	0.0	1.6	96.8
Purchase tickets to the club's overseas games	0.0	1.6	15.1	83.3

As shown in Table 1.3, three activities were the most popular. More than 90 per cent of respondents visit unofficial Ajax FC supporter websites, the official club website (www.ajax.nl), and watch online video highlights at least once per season. More than 90 per cent of respondents visit unofficial supporter websites (such as www.ajaxusa.com) weekly. As noted earlier, it has been argued that fans who identify with geographically distant teams might not receive the same psychological benefit as traditional fans (Wann, 2006a, 2006b; Wann and Pierce, 2005; Wann et al., 1999, 2004), since they find themselves isolated from fellow fans. However, should they be able to interact with such fans they might receive psychological benefits (Wann, 2006c). This might explain the propensity of respondents to visit unofficial supporter sites in a bid to interact with this community. However, it does not explain why respondents rarely 'got together' with fellow fans, although opportunities for face-to-face interaction might be limited.

Although the Dutch league, the Eredivisie, is not as popular (or accessible) as the major European leagues, 83 per cent of respondents watched televised club games at least once per season, while more than half did so at least once per month. The absence of geographic proximity may have reinforced the importance of the media to these consumers and influenced their behaviour. In addition, nearly 80 per cent of respondents said they purchase licensed merchandise at least once per season. This appeared logical since clubs regularly re-design their jerseys to maximize revenue.

Several activities were particularly unpopular. For instance, nearly two-thirds of respondents said that they never purchased products from club sponsors. This would be a worrying sign for those companies that financially support the Ajax FC as a means to drive sales. Current sponsors include financial services and insurance provider, Aegon, ABN-AMRO, Adidas and brewery, Amstel. This may be because not all of these products are readily available in the satellite supporter's home market. In addition, nearly three-quarters of respondents said that they never purchased tickets to Ajax FC Eredivisie games. This most likely reflected their willingness to purchase tickets to an overseas sport contest, hence the significance of the media.

The final question asked whether respondents pursued any of these activities outside of the football season. The 11 earlier proposed activities were reduced to 9 for their out-of-season consumption because, although it was no longer possible to watch live televised club games, supporters could still watch video highlights of previously completed matches. Furthermore, the question regarding the purchase of tickets no longer differentiated between Eredivisie and foreign exhibition fixtures. Responses were rated dichotomously as a yes/no question and the results can be seen in Table 1.4.

Those activities most popular outside of football season mirrored those pursued during the season. Visiting unofficial Ajax FC supporter websites was the most common activity followed by visiting the club's official website. Supporters in the youngest age group (18–25) were less likely than others to visit the official website although this was still a

Table 1.4 Behaviour to support Ajax FC (out of season) ($N = 126$)

Popularity of behaviour highest- to lowest-grouped	%
Visit unofficial club supporter websites	94.4
Visit the official club website	87.3
Watch video highlights on the Internet or television	73.0
Purchase team-related merchandise	49.2
Purchase products from companies that support the club	23.0
Get together with other club fans	19.8
Purchase tickets to club games for the upcoming season	12.7
Purchase additional club items	4.0
Purchase shares in the club	3.2

very popular activity with 77.6 per cent of these individuals participating in this activity compared with 95.6 per cent of those aged older than 25 ($p = 0.002$). Furthermore, nearly three-quarters of respondents watched video highlights online or on television.

5. Limitations and future directions

This preliminary study is the second in a series designed to research the reasons why satellite supporters choose to support a foreign-based sport team. While an earlier exploratory study examined satellite supporters and their support for AFL teams, the study reported here extends the research to satellite supporters of a specific team, AFC Ajax of Amsterdam. Although it has pointed to significant evidence as to why, and how, these consumers support the club, there are opportunities to strengthen an understanding of the satellite supporter and their identification with a chosen team.

The worldwide popularity of football has seen a number of its team brands become internationally recognized. Although the objective of this study was not to make broad generalizations of other teams, it would be useful to compare the results to other football teams. The Ajax FC has a proud and distinguished history, has dominated its domestic league and has nurtured potential superstars for the famous Oranje. As a result, perhaps the factors that lead satellite supporters to identify with a less distinguished, or popular, football team might be different. Furthermore, due to its universal appeal, football was chosen for this study, yet the identification of supporters from other sports might differ significantly from the football fan.

The respondents in this study exhibited high levels of loyalty and could be said to have a high degree of identification with Ajax FC. As earlier explained, highly identified fans are more inclined to support their team and being a fan is an important component of their identity. An analysis of satellite supporters with lower levels of identification would prove an interesting comparison; however, they are less likely to join an organized supporter group and so locating a large number of these individuals is a challenge.

6. Conclusion

The media's reach and influence has allowed fans to have unprecedented access to their favourite teams and players regardless of geographic location. Although advances in communications technology and globalization have greatly enhanced the popularity of many professional sport teams, there has been very little research undertaken on the satellite supporter. In a competitive global sport marketplace, there is a need to understand who these consumers are and why they identify with a foreign-based team.

This study sought to understand the origins of team identification for the satellite supporter and explored their identification with the Dutch dynamo, Ajax FC. It generated valuable insights into the psychology of these supporters and their consumption behaviour. Three items were almost universally accepted as important in their original decision to support Ajax FC: team reputation and/or tradition; the presence of particular player(s); and team success. Their ability to watch the team play was also salient and highlighted the importance of international media arrangements as team brands seek to exploit foreign opportunities.

The emergence of these primary antecedents has important implications for sport marketers whose teams battle for market share in a competitive global environment. Although the Ajax FC satellite supporters highlighted the importance of team success, both in a particular season and over time, marketers of professional sport teams are largely unable to control their core product, that is, on-field competition. As a result, sport marketers cannot guarantee team success and are cautioned against focusing on winning in their marketing campaigns. There were, however, a number of other antecedents which marketers can manipulate in order to attract a larger international fan base, notably the team's international exposure, its style of play or player personnel. For instance, although its importance was minimal in this particular case, teams have aggressively signed key foreign players in order to appeal to certain geographic markets.

Although international media arrangements are usually negotiated at the league level, marketers should embrace every opportunity to create broader awareness for their brand in global markets. In addition, improved accessibility to broadband and mobile Internet services provides a golden opportunity for team marketers to cultivate satellite supporters. While www.ajax.nl, the club's official website, proved popular with supporters, unofficial supporter websites were a more attractive destination, especially for the youngest fans in this study. It is conceivable that fans welcomed the opportunity to interact with each other in a user-mediated environment rather than one controlled by the organization, and so an opportunity exists to target a new generation of fans through these and other unofficial media channels such as www.facebook.com, www.myspace.com or www.twitter.com.

Sport organizations could even encourage the development of these channels – for instance, the Liverpool FC enjoys a 'close working relationship' with more than 200 official supporter branches – through exclusive content or offers for members. As such, the opportunity exists for sport teams to develop a worldwide brand community or a "specialized, non-geographically bound community, based on a structured set of social relationships among admirers of a brand" (Muniz and O'Guinn, 2001: 412). Once engaged through this medium, the opportunities to strengthen an individual's connection, or identification with the team, is enhanced and thus offers a potentially lucrative revenue stream.

In conclusion, the satellite supporters in this study expressed intense team loyalty and relied heavily on the media, especially the Internet, to express their support. However, given that they live outside the Netherlands, and that they belong to an online fan organization, it was logical that the media might prove a critical conduit for their fandom. They actively seek opportunities to support Ajax FC (and engage with the club and fellow fans) throughout the year, not solely during football season. Satellite supporters most likely receive psychological benefit from their support of an 'overseas sweetheart'. As such, these consumers present an opportunity for sport marketers to tap into a potentially lucrative fan base and enhance their own team brands.

Notes

1. 'Nike Extends FC Barcelona Sponsorship in $189M deal', http://soccernet.espn.go.com/news/story?id=388101&cc=5901, retrieved 09.05.2007.
2. 'Reds Fans Double', http://www.manchestereveningnews.co.uk/sport/football/manchester_united/s/1031105_reds_fans_double, retrieved 17.06.2008.
3. 'Lure of United dims as Real reels in Fans', http://www.realmadrid.dk/news/article/default.asp?newsid=5194, retrieved 07.08.2006.
4. 'Australia and New Zealand Rugby Looks to Asia to Halt Decline', http://www.sportbusiness.com/news/170856/australia-and-nz-rugby-looks-to-asia-to-halt-decline, retrieved 18.11.2009; 'NBA Launches Indian New Media Drive', http://www.sportbusiness.com/news/171191/nba-launches-indian-new-media-drive, retrieved 18.12.2009; 'Hawthorn Goes Back to School to Plant AFL in New Zealand', *The Australian* (23.11.2009), http://www.theaustralian.com.au/news/sport/hawthorn-goes-back-to-school-to-plant-afl-in-new-zealand/story-e6frg7mf-1225801844010, retrieved 18.12.2010.
5. 'Real Madrid Calls for Early Kick-offs for Chinese Fans', http://www.sportbusiness.com/news/170550/real-madrid-calls-for-early-kick-offs-for-chinese-fans?utm_source=sbinsl&utm_medium=email&utm_campaign=sep28, retrieved 28.09.2009.
6. 'The Club', http://english.ajax.nl/The-Club/The-club.htm, retrieved 12.10.2010.

7. 'Youth Academy', http://english.ajax.nl/Youth-Academy.htm, retrieved 12.01.2010.
8. 'Obituary for a Fansite: AJAX USA (1995–2008)', http://www.ajaxusa.com/ajax-usa-calling-it-quits.html, retrieved 15.12.2009.
9. 'Obituary for a Fansite: AJAX USA (1995–2008)', http://www.ajaxusa.com/ajax-usa-calling-it-quits.html, retrieved 15.12.2009.

References

Alreck, P.L. and Settle, R.B. (2004) *The Survey Research Handbook*, 3rd edn (Boston, MA: McGraw-Hill Irwin).
Bailey, K.D. (1994) *Methods of Social Research*, 4th edn (New York: The Free Press).
Ben-Porat, A. (2000) 'Overseas Sweetheart: Israeli Fans of English Football', *Journal of Sport and Social Issues*, 24(4): 344–350.
Branscombe, N.R. and Wann, D.L. (1991) 'The Positive Social and Self Concept Consequences of Sports Team Identification', *Journal of Sport and Social Issues*, 15(2): 115–127.
Browne, K. (1999) 'The Branding of Soccer', *Finance Week* (29.01.1999): 26.
Cialdini, R.B., Borden, R.J., Thorne, A., Walker, M.R., Freeman, S. and Sloan, L.R. (1976) 'Basking in Reflected Glory: Three (Football) Field Studies', *Journal of Personality and Social Psychology*, 34(3): 366–375.
Crawford, G. (2003) 'The Career of the Sport Supporter: The Case of the Manchester Storm', *Sociology*, 37(2): 219–237.
Dimmock, J.A. and Grove, J.R. (2006) 'Identification with Sport Teams as a Function of the Search for Certainty', *Journal of Sports Sciences*, 24(11): 1203–1211.
Dimmock, J.A. and Gucciardi, D.F. (2007) 'The Utility of Modern Theories of Intergroup Bias for Research on Antecedents to Team Identification', *Psychology of Sport and Exercise*, 9(3): 284–300.
Dimmock, J.A., Grove, J.R. and Eklund, R.C. (2005) 'Reconceptualizing Team Identification: New Dimensions and Their Relationship to Intergroup Bias', *Group Dynamics: Theory, Research, and Practice*, 9(2): 75–86.
Dolles, H. and Söderman, S. (2005) Implementing a Professional Football League in Japan – Challenges to Research in International Business, *DIJ Working Paper*, No. 05/6 (Tokyo: German Institute for Japanese Studies).
Dolles, H. and Söderman, S. (2008) 'The Network of Value Captures: Creating Competitive Advantage in Football Management', *Austrian Economic Papers*, 55(1): 39–58.
Dolles, H. and Söderman, S. (2011) 'Learning from Success: Implementing a Professional Football League in Japan', in H. Dolles and S. Söderman (eds), *Sport as Business: International, Professional and Commercial Aspects* (Houndmills, Basingstoke: Palgrave Macmillan): 228–250.
Donavan, D.T., Carlson, B.D. and Zimmerman, M. (2005) 'The Influence of Personality Traits on Sports Fan Identification', *Sport Marketing Quarterly*, 14(1): 31–42.
Donavan, D.T., Janda, S. and Suh, J. (2006) 'Environmental Influences in Corporate Brand Identification and Outcomes', *Journal of Brand Management*, 14(1/2): 125–136.

End, C.M. (2001) 'An Examination of NFL Fans' Computer Mediated BIRGing', *Journal of Sport Behavior*, 24(2): 162–181.

End, C.M., Dietz-Uhler, B., Harrick, E.A. and Jacquemotte, L. (2002) 'Identifying with Winners: A Reexamination of Sport Fans' Tendency to BIRG', *Journal of Applied Social Psychology*, 32(5): 1017–1030.

Fink, J.S., Trail, G.T. and Anderson, D.F. (2002) 'An Examination of Team Identification: Which Motives are Most Salient to its Existence?', *International Sports Journal*, 6(2): 195–207.

Funk, D.C. and James, J.D. (2001) 'The Psychological Continuum Model: A Conceptual Framework for Understanding an Individual's Psychological Connection to Sport', *Sport Management Review*, 4(2): 119–150.

Gladden, J.M., Milne, G.R. and Sutton, W.A. (1998) 'A Conceptual Framework for Assessing Brand Equity in Division I College Athletics', *Journal of Sport Management*, 12(1): 1–19.

Greenwood, P.B., Kanters, M.A. and Casper, J.M. (2006) 'Sport Fan Team Identification Formation in Mid-level Professional Sport', *European Sport Management Quarterly*, 6(3): 253–265.

Gwinner, K. and Swanson, S.R. (2003) 'A Model of Fan Identification: Antecedents and Sponsorship Outcomes', *Journal of Services Marketing*, 17(3): 275–294.

Heinonen, H. (2002) 'Finnish Soccer Supporters Away from Home: A Case Study of Finnish National Team Fans at a World Cup Qualifying Match in Liverpool, England', *Soccer and Society*, 3(3): 26–50.

Hoyle, R.H., Harris, M.J. and Judd, C.M. (2002) *Research Methods in Social Relations* (Fort Worth, TX: Wadsworth).

Jacobson, B.P. (2003) 'Rooting for Laundry: An Examination of the Creation and Maintenance of a Sport Fan Identity', Doctoral dissertation thesis (Storrs: University of Connecticut).

Jones, I. (1997) 'A Further Examination of the Factors Influencing Current Identification with a Sports Team, A Response to Wann, et al. (1996)', *Perceptual and Motor Skills*, 85: 257–258.

Jones, I. (1998) 'Football Fandom: Football Fan Identity and Identification at Luton Town Football Club', Doctoral dissertation thesis (Luton: University of Luton).

Jones, D., Parkes, R. and Houlihan, A. (2006) *Football Money League: Changing of the Guard* (Manchester: Deloitte, Sports Business Group).

Kerr, A.K. (2008) 'Team Identification and Satellite Supporters: The Potential Value of Brand Equity Frameworks', in *Papers from the 6th Annual Sport Marketing Association Conference* (Toowoomba: University of Southern Queensland): 48–66, http://www.usq.edu.au/sma08/conference/callforpapers/default.htm, retrieved 19.07.2008.

Kerr, A.K. (2009a) 'Online Questionnaires and Interviews as a Successful Tool to Explore Foreign Sports Fandom', in N.K.L. Pope, K.L. Kuhn and J. Forster (eds), *Digital Sport for Performance Enhancement and Competitive Evolution: Intelligent Gaming Technologies* (Hershey, PA: IGI Global): 228–244.

Kerr, A.K. (2009b) '"You'll Never Walk Alone". The Use of Brand Equity Frameworks to Explore the Team Identification of the "Satellite Supporter"', Doctoral dissertation thesis (Sydney: University of Technology).

Kerr, A.K. (forthcoming) 'Australian Football Goes for Goal: The Team Identification of American A.F.L. Sports Fans', *Football Studies*.

Kerr, A.K. and Gladden, J.M. (2008) 'Extending the Understanding of Professional Team Brand Equity to the Global Marketplace', *International Journal of Sport Management and Marketing*, 3(1/2): 58–77.

Kolbe, R.H. and James, J.D. (2000) 'An Identification and Examination of Influences that Shape the Creation of a Professional Team Fan', *International Journal of Sports Marketing and Sponsorship*, 2(1): 23–37.

Larmer, B. (2005) 'The Center of the World', *Foreign Policy*, 150: 66–74.

Lewis, M. (2001) 'Franchise Relocation and Fan Allegiance', *Journal of Sport and Social Issues*, 25(1): 6–19.

Madrigal, R. (2004) 'A Review of Team Identification and Its Influence on Consumers' Responses Toward Corporate Sponsors', in L.R. Kahle and C. Riley (eds), *Sports Marketing and the Psychology of Marketing Communication* (Mahwah, NJ: Lawrence Erlbaum Associates): 241–255.

Mahony, D.F., Howard, D.R. and Madrigal, R. (2000) 'BIRGing and CORFing Behaviors by Sport Spectators: High Self-monitors Versus Low Self-monitors', *International Sports Journal*, 4(1): 87–106.

Mahony, D.F., Nakazawa, M., Funk, D., James, J.D. and Gladden, J.M. (2002) 'Motivational Factors Influencing the Behaviour of J-League Spectators', *Sport Management Review*, 5(1): 1–24.

Melnick, M.J. (1993) 'Searching for Sociability in the Stands: A Theory of Sports Spectating', *Journal of Sport Management*, 7(1): 44–60.

Melnick, M.J. and Wann, D.L. (2004) 'Sport Fandom Influences, Interests, and Behaviors Among Norwegian University Students', *International Sports Journal*, 8(1): 1–13.

Milne, G.R. and McDonald, M.A. (1999) *Sport Marketing: Managing the Exchange Process* (Sudbury, MA: Jones and Bartlett Publishers).

Mitrano, J.R. (1999) 'The "Sudden Death" of Hockey in Hartford: Sports Fans and Franchise Relocation', *Sociology of Sport Journal*, 16(2): 134–154.

Muniz, A.M. and O'Guinn, T.C. (2001) 'Brand Community', *Journal of Consumer Research*, 27(4): 412–432.

Murrell, A.J. and Dietz, B. (1992) 'Fan Support of Sport Teams: The Effect of a Common Group Identity', *Journal of Sport and Exercise Psychology*, 14(1): 28–39.

Nash, R. (2000) 'Globalised Football Fandom: Scandinavian Liverpool FC Supporters', *Football Studies*, 3(2): 5–23.

Richardson, B. and O'Dwyer, E. (2003) 'Football Supporters and Football Team Brands: A Study in Consumer Brand Loyalty', *Irish Marketing Review*, 16(1): 43–53.

Söderman, S., Dolles, H. and Dum, T. (2010) 'Managing Football: International and Global Development', in S. Hamil and S. Chadwick (eds), *Managing Football: An International Perspective* (Amsterdam: Elsevier): 85–101.

Sutton, W.A., McDonald, M.A., Milne, G.R. and Cimperman, J. (1997) 'Creating and Fostering Fan Identification in Professional Sports', *Sport Marketing Quarterly*, 6(1): 15–22.

Tajfel, H. and Turner, J. (1979) 'An Integrative Theory of Intergroup Conflict', in S. Worchel and W.G. Austin (eds), *The Social Psychology of Intergroup Relations* (Monterey, CA: Brooks/Cole Publishing Company): 33–47.

Tajfel, H. and Turner, J.C. (1986) 'The Social Identity Theory of Intergroup Behaviour', in S. Worchel and W.G. Austin (eds), *Psychology of Intergroup Relations*, Vol. 2 (Chicago, IL: Nelson-Hall Publishers): 7–24.

Underwood, R., Bond, E. and Baer, R. (2001) 'Building Service Brands via Social Identity: Lessons from the Sports Marketplace', *Journal of Marketing Theory and Practice*, 9(1): 1–13.

Wann, D.L. (2006a) 'The Causes and Consequences of Sport Team Identification', in A.A. Raney and J. Bryant (eds), *Handbook of Sports and Media* (Mahwah, NJ: Lawrence Erlbaum Associates): 331–352.

Wann, D.L. (2006b) 'Examining the Potential Causal Relationship Between Sport Team Identification and Psychological Well-being', *Journal of Sport Behavior*, 29(1): 79–95.

Wann, D.L. (2006c) 'Understanding the Positive Social Psychological Benefits of Sport Team Identification: The Team Identification – Social Psychological Health Model', *Group Dynamics: Theory, Research, and Practice*, 10(4): 272–296.

Wann, D.L. and Branscombe, N.R. (1990) 'Die-hard and Fair-weather Fans: Effects of Identification on BIRGing and CORFing Tendencies', *Journal of Sport and Social Issues*, 14(2): 103–117.

Wann, D.L. and Branscombe, N.R. (1993) 'Sports Fans: Measuring Degree of Identification with Their Team', *International Journal of Sport Psychology*, 24(1): 1–17.

Wann, D.L. and Branscombe, N.R. (1995) 'Influence of Identification with a Sports Team on Objective Knowledge and Subjective Beliefs', *International Journal of Sport Psychology*, 26: 551–567.

Wann, D.L. and Pierce, S. (2005) 'The Relationship Between Sport Team Identification and Social Well-being: Additional Evidence Supporting the Team Identification Social Psychological Health Model', *North American Journal of Psychology*, 7(1): 117–124.

Wann, D.L., Tucker, K.B. and Schrader, M.P. (1996) 'An Exploratory Examination of the Factors Influencing the Origination, Continuation, and Cessation of Identification with Sports Teams', *Perceptual and Motor Skills*, 82(3): 995–1001.

Wann, D.L., Dunham, M.D., Byrd, M.L. and Keenan, B.L. (2004) 'The Five-factor Model of Personality and the Psychological Health of Highly Identified Sport Fans', *International Sports Journal*, 8(2): 28–36.

Wann, D.L., Melnick, M.J., Russell, G.W. and Pease, D.G. (2001) *Sport Fans: The Psychology and Social Impact of Spectators* (New York, NY: Routledge).

Wann, D.L., Inman, S., Ensor, C.L., Gates, R.D. and Caldwell, D.S. (1999) 'Assessing the Psychological Well-being of Sport Fans Using the Profile of Mood States: The Importance of Team Identification', *International Sports Journal*, 3: 81–90.

2
Decision-making Styles in Purchasing Sport Products: An International Comparison Between American and Korean College Students

Sungwon Bae

1. Introduction

Sports globalization is impacting the importation and exportation of sports apparel and equipment on a national and international scale. According to reported Street & Smith's *Sports Business Journal*, the sport industry ranked as a top fourth industry in the United States which equaled approximately US$300,000 million in sales during 2006.[1] In comparison, it revealed that South Korea had nearly US$130,000 million of sports business in 2002 (Park et al., 2004). Of the entire amount about US$26,000 million, representing 17 percent were derived from sales of sport apparel and equipment in 2002. Thus, it appears that the sports industry represents a significant and expanding consumer product market for both the United States and South Korea.

Sports consumers participate in many different sports including basketball, volleyball, skiing, golf, tennis, scuba diving and numerous others. Each sport has a specific apparel and equipment market and participants can either rent or purchase the various needs. Some consumers are willing to rent their need equipment from sports facilities such as bowling shoes and balls or ski shoes, poles or helmets. Other consumers elect to purchase their products (for example, scuba diving, golf, tennis, jogging and so on). Many consumers devote a great deal of time and effort researching the various products and brands of apparel and equipment prior to purchase to ensure that they are making an informed purchase and that they are receiving the best value for the purchase. These consumers use social agents, shopping malls or the Internet to research selected products and develop consumer preferences (for example, brand, design, color, price, quality and so on).

The formation of consumer preferences relies on many diverse experiences, needs and preferences. Thus, an expanded understanding regarding shopping behaviors, motivations for where people shop and what they buy is essential. Shopping centers and mall developments provide consumers with increased shopping alternatives within a localized central business district. Consumers may be expected to derive greater utility from larger areas because of greater product classification, even though they are likely to spend more money and incur increased indisposition by traveling to more distant shopping areas (Bell, 1999).

During the 1980s, three-fourths of the US national consumer population visited a shopping mall at least once a month (Stoffel, 1988). The development of dual income families increased discretionary spending while reducing the time for shopping (Kotler and Amstrong, 2001). Today, consumers shop in malls while many others elect to access online shopping sites to buy or sell products. For example, today almost 50 percent of consumers are interested in purchasing brand-name clothing online especially through outlet, direct import and discount sites.[2] For the twenty-first century, increased access to retail stores, shopping malls and Internet technology will provide many new shopping opportunities for consumers driving changes in shopping patterns and selection processes.

Consumer shopping characteristics are an important area in marketing research because each consumer develops and uses different shopping patterns (Walsh et al., 2001). Further, consumer's decision-making styles are based on previous purchasing experiences which allow the consumer to employ unique decision-making styles when shopping. Specifically, research has shown that most consumers have a different kind of shopping consciousness relating to such factors as quality, fashion, price, brand, recreation, confusion and habit when shopping (Sproles and Kendall, 1986). Therefore, a consumer's decision-making style is an extremely important area to consider when attempting to identify and understand the consumer's shopping behavior and motivation, especially as related to the sports apparel market.

2. Consumer decision-making styles

The model of consumer decision-making styles has been used, since 1986, as a worldwide measurement of consumer decision-making styles in textile and other business markets. Sproles and Kendall (1986) tested the reliability and validity of the Consumer Style Inventory (CSI) using only a sample of US high school students to find consumer decision-making styles. Due to consumers' different individual decision-making styles, therefore, Sproles and Kendall suggest validating the instrument across other populations in order to establish generality.

The consumer decision-making styles are described as "a mental orientation characterizing a consumer approach to making choices" (ibid.: 268). To identify a consumer's decision-making style, they focus on three different approaches. The first is the consumer characteristics approach, that focuses on consumers' decision-making in cognitive and affective directions, the second is the psychographic/lifestyle approach that shows consumers' different personality characteristics, attitudes, opinions, values, choices and general styles that describe activities, interests and opinions and the last approach is the consumer typology that describes general consumer types: economic, personalizing, ethical and apathetic. These approaches are powerful components in making a decision about a product.

From the aforementioned three approaches, Sproles and Kendall (1986) created a more parsimonious scale with 40 items, under the following eight characteristics of consumers' decision-making styles: (1) perfectionistic (high-quality) conscious shopper; (2) brand (price equals quality) conscious shopper; (3) novelty (fashion) conscious shopper; (4) recreation (hedonic) conscious shopper; (5) price (value for money) conscious shopper; (6) impulsiveness/carelessness conscious shopper; (7) confusion by overchoice conscious shopper; and (8) habit (brand loyalty) conscious shopper (ibid.: 268).

Research topics in the area of consumer decision-making styles are becoming more popular in recent years (Hafstrom, Chae and Chung, 1992; Lysonski, Durvasula and Zotos, 1996; Tai, 2005). Moreover, because the process of consumer decision-making styles is a complex phenomenon, there is a need to better understand consumers' decision process and shopping behavior. By understanding these processes, advertisers and marketers can employ appropriate strategies in marketing segmentation and product positioning. However, the majority of these studies were aimed at investigating consumer decision-making styles in general products such as cereal, grocery and casual apparel; and there were very few studies devoted to the comparison of shopping behaviors between different cultures (Fan and Xiao, 1998; Hafstrom, Chae and Chung, 1992; Hiu et al., 2001; Jenkins, 1973; King and

Ring, 1980; Lysonski, Durvasula and Zotos, 1996; Sproles and Kendall, 1986; Sproles and Sproles, 1990; Tai, 2005; Walsh and Vincent, 2001). Additionally, studies have identified the basic characteristics of an individual's decision-making style about shopping and treated cross-cultural issues between or among countries such as the United States (Sproles and Kendall, 1986), South Korea (Hafstrom, Chae and Chung, 1992), China (Fan and Xiao, 1998; Tai, 2005) and Greece, India and New Zealand (Lysonski, Durvasula and Zotos, 1996) with respect to general shopping styles.

Regarding the many different shopping characteristics used by consumers, Sproles and Kendall (1986) recommend that consumer decision-making styles should not only be used for other youth and adult groups, but also for ascertaining consumer preferences by country. Even though a consumer decision-making style for shopping is a critical issue for market segmentation, previous studies have not investigated specific shopping patterns for sports apparel. Therefore, the purpose of this study was to apply a consumer decision-making style model to analyse specific shopping pattern differences between select college-aged populations in the United States and South Korea. The specific questions that were addressed in this investigation were:

1. Were there any different shopping patterns in shopping frequency, shopping day, shopping hour, store preference, shopping information, shopping companion and brand preference between college-aged consumers in the United States and South Korea?
2. Were there significantly different shopping patterns in brand, quality, recreation, confusion, fashion, impulse and price consciousness between college-aged consumers in the United States and South Korea?

3. Methodology

3.1. Samples and procedures

The total sample size of this study was approximately 1720 undergraduate students, enrolled in Lifetime Activities Program (LAP) classes at universities in both the United States and South Korea. A total of 1663 students (94%) completed the survey. Demographically, 822 (49%) were university students in the United States and 841 (51%) were Korean students. Moreover, 929 (56%) were males while 734 (44%) were females. The sample size adequately represents the given populations, according to Krejcie and Morgan (1970); the recommended minimum sample size for this study is 331, for a 95 percent confidence level. This study was conducted using a non-probability sampling method, also known as a convenient sample. This sampling method is "useful for exploratory research, to get a feel for what's going on out there" (Bernard, 1988: 97).

Prior to distribution of the questionnaires, the researchers informed students about the purpose of this study and explained how to complete the survey. The surveys were administered concurrently at each site. Informed consent was obtained and participation was completely voluntary. All questionnaires were administered to students at the beginning of classes in each country and all researchers had been thoroughly trained to standardize the process.

3.2. Instrumentation

The questionnaire consisted of two sections. The first section consisted of revised and modified questionnaire from the original CSI (Sproles and Kendall, 1986) and the second section was composed of demographic questions. The original CSI measures consumer shopping styles for general products based on 40 items addressing the eight factors. Cronbach's alphas of the eight factors of the CSI were: perfectionistic (0.69), brand conscious (0.63), novelty-fashion conscious (0.76), recreational shopping conscious (0.71), price-value conscious (0.48), impulsive (0.41), confused by overchoice (0.51) and habitual/brand-loyal (0.54).

To determine reliability, a pilot study was conducted. The pilot study verified that researchers can correctly manage the test and treatments for this study, using appropriate subjects (Thomas and Nelson, 1996). After a pilot study was performed, an eight-factor model clearly identified a seven-factor model: (1) brand consciousness, (2) quality consciousness, (3) recreation consciousness, (4) confusion consciousness, (5) fashion consciousness, (6) impulse consciousness and (7) price consciousness (Table 2.1). The Cronbach's alpha coefficients for factor 1 to factor 6 were between 0.66 and 0.91, indicating satisfactory levels of reliability. However, factor 7 showed low reliability with the alpha coefficient 0.45, indicating an unsatisfactory level of reliability on consumer shopping characteristics. Even though factor 7 resulted in low reliability, it was decided that the factor could be used in the test of the shopping characteristic because impulsive characteristics have marginal reliability. So, it reflects the psychological nature of impulsiveness and the youth of the subjects (Sproles and Kendall, 1986).

Table 2.1 Factor loadings and Cronbach's alpha coefficients

No.	Items	Factor loading
	Brand consciousness ($\alpha = 0.87$)	
1.	I choose the well-known, national or designer brands.	0.83
2.	I usually choose expensive brands.	0.83
3.	I think that the higher the price of the product, the better the quality.	0.85
4.	I prefer buying the best-selling product.	0.84
5.	Advertised athletic clothing displayed in window or catalog is usually a good choice.	0.85
6.	I buy my favorite brands over and over.	0.86
	Quality consciousness ($\alpha = 0.91$)	
1.	When it comes to purchasing athletic clothing, I try to get the highest quality.	0.90
2.	I usually try to buy the best quality athletic clothing.	0.91
3.	I make a special effort to choose the best quality athletic clothing.	0.90
4.	My expectations for athletic clothing I buy are very high.	0.93
	Recreation consciousness ($\alpha = 0.85$)	
1.	I shop just for fun.	0.81
2.	Going shopping is one of the fun activities in my life.	0.80
3.	I do my shopping quickly.	0.83
4.	I don't waste my time just shopping.	0.83
5.	Shopping is not a pleasurable activity.	0.83
	Confusion consciousness ($\alpha = 0.76$)	
1.	Sometimes, it's hard to choose which store to shop.	0.62
2.	All of the information I get on different products confuses me.	0.63
3.	The more I learn about athletic clothing, the harder it seems to choose the best.	0.76
	Impulse consciousness ($\alpha = 0.45$)	
1.	I am impulsive when I purchase athletic clothing.	0.39
2.	I take the time to shop carefully for best buys.	0.28
3.	I carefully look for damages on the clothing.	0.40
	Fashion consciousness ($\alpha = 0.79$)	
1.	I usually keep my wardrobe up-to-date with the changing fashions.	0.69
2.	Fashionable, attractive athletic clothing is very important to me.	0.69
3.	I usually have one or more outfits of the very latest style.	0.69
4.	Nice department and specialty stores offer me the best product.	0.84
	Price consciousness ($\alpha = 0.66$)	
1.	I buy as much as possible at sale prices.	0.66
2.	I save money as much as I can when shopping.	0.66

3.3. Data analysis

In the first step, demographic analysis was performed to identify the descriptive statistics for college consumers in the United States and South Korea. They included the following: shopping frequency, shopping day, shopping hour, store preference, shopping information, shopping companion and brand preference. An analysis of variance (ANOVA) and mean comparison tests were performed to analyse the specific shopping pattern differences of shopping characteristics between college consumers in the United States and South Korea. According to Thomas and Nelson (1996), the analysis of variance, when a combination of seven dependent variables is made, will maximally separate the levels of the independent variables. Therefore, F ratio and p value were used in interpreting the statistically significant difference between male and female subjects on each shopping factor in the United States and in South Korea. An alpha level of 0.05 was set to test the research questions.

4. Results

4.1. Demographic description

The population of this study was undergraduate college students enrolled in LAPs at a public university in the United States as well as a public South Korean university The results indicated that American college-aged students preferred the weekends as 550 (66.9%) and 87 (10.6%) shopped on Saturdays and Sundays, respectively. Similarly, it was revealed that 87 percent of the South Korean college-aged students also preferred to shop either Saturdays (523) or Sunday (210) (see Table 2.2). Based upon these results, American and Korean college students usually shop for athletic apparel during the weekend.

4.2. Shopping hours per visit

American college students spent three hours or less shopping. In comparison, the majority of Korean college-aged students spent between 1 and 3 hours shopping (see Table 2.2). Thus, it appeared that Korean college-aged students shopped for at least one hour whereas their countertparts in the United States may not have even shopped at that minimum.

4.3. Shopping frequency for athletic apparel

Two hundred and eight (25.3%) American college students responded that they shopped twice per year, followed by 167 (20.3%) who shopped

Table 2.2 Frequency of distribution and percentage

		Frequency		Percent (%)	
Description		USA	SK	USA	SK
Day	Monday	11	8	1.3	1.0
	Tuesday	11	10	1.3	1.2
	Wednesday	30	7	3.6	0.8
	Thursday	15	10	1.8	1.2
	Friday	118	73	14.4	8.7
	Saturday	550	523	66.9	62.2
Hour(s)	0–1	324	82	39.4	9.8
	1–2	295	277	35.9	32.9
	2–3	149	254	18.1	30.2
	3–4	41	202	5.0	24.0
	Others	13	26	1.6	3.1
Shopping frequency	Once a year	157	360	19.1	42.8
	Two times a year	208	241	25.3	28.7
	Three times a year	165	61	20.1	7.3
	Four times a year	167	51	20.3	6.1
	Others	125	128	15.2	15.2
Store preference	Department store	230	204	28.0	24.3
	Discount store	140	489	17.0	58.1
	Specialty store	392	98	47.7	11.7
	Others	60	50	7.3	5.9
Shopping information	Television	250	171	30.4	20.3
	Radio	5	3	0.6	0.4
	Magazine	259	266	31.5	31.6
	Newspaper	52	24	6.3	2.9
	Others	256	377	31.1	44.8
Shopping companion	Parent	105	126	12.8	15.0
	Friend	398	622	48.4	74.0
	Alone	281	72	34.2	8.6
	Others	38	21	4.6	2.5
Favorite brand	Nike	407	335	49.5	39.8
	Adidas	108	160	13.1	19.0
	New balance	39	–	4.7	–
	Reebok	19	35	2.3	4.2
	Champion	13	–	1.6	–
	Others	236	259	28.8	28.5

Note: USA (The United States); SK (South Korea).

three times and 165 (20.1%) who indicated that they shopped four times annually (see Table 2.2). For South Korean students, the frequency of once a year category was the highest, at 360 (42.5%), while the remainder of responses indicated 241 (28.7%) twice a year, followed by 61 (7.3%) three times a year and 51 (6.1%) four times a year. On average, American and South Korean college students shop at least two times a year for athletic apparel.

4.4. Sport apparel store preference

The American respondents indicated the following store preferences: 392 (47.7%) specialty stores, 230 (28.2%) department stores, 140 (17.0%) discount stores and 60 (7.3%) others (such as Wal-Mart or Internet stores). In contrast, the South Korean respondents indicated the following store preferences: 489 (58.1%) discount stores, 204 (24.3%) department stores, 98 (11.7%) specialty stores and 50 (5.9%) others. Based upon these findings, American college students are more likely to use specialty stores, whereas South Korean college students prefer discount stores when shopping for athletic apparel (see Table 2.2).

4.5. Location of athletic apparel information

The finding indicated that college-age students in the United States obtained athletic apparel information from television 250 (30.4%), magazines 259 (31.5%), newspapers 52 (6.3%), radio 5 (0.6%) and other 256 (31.1%), such as the Internet, friends, word of mouth, at the store or family. In South Korea, college students reported that they received information about athletic apparel from magazines 266 (31.6%), television 171 (20.3%), newspapers 24 (2.9%), radio 3 (0.4%) and other 377 (44.8%) such as the Internet, friends, at the store or word of mouth. Based upon this finding, it appears that American and South Korean college students similarly obtain information about athletic apparel through magazines and television advertisements (see Table 2.2).

4.6. Shopping companion preference

In respect to shopping companions preferences, the American participants indicated that they shopped with friends 398 (48.4%), parents 105 (12.8%), by themselves 281 (34.2%) or with some other person 38 (4.6%), such as a sibling. Similarly, the Korean respondents indicated that they preferred to shop with friends 622 (74.0%), parents 126 (15.0%), by themselves 72 (8.6%) or with some other person (2.5%), such as a sibling. These findings indicate that both American and South

Korean college-aged consumers are more likely to shop with friends or parents. However, it should be noted that Americans were more likely to shop alone than Korean college-aged consumers (see Table 2.2).

4.7. Athletic apparel brand preference

In the United States, college-aged consumers indicated that their favorite brand was Nike 407 (49.5%) followed by New Balance 39 (4.7%), Adidas 108 (13.1%), Rebook 19 (2.3%), Champion 13 (1.6%) and others 236 (28.8%). Of the 236 American college-aged consumers, 132 (16.1%) responded that they are indifferent to brand and 104 (12.7%) prefer activity casual brands such as Nautica, Gap, Abercrombie and Fitch. However, college-aged consumers in South Korea responded that their favorite brand was Nike 335 (39.8%), Adidas 160 (19%), Puma 72 (8.6%), Reebok 35 (4.2%) and others 259 (28.5%). Of 259 college-aged consumers, 67 (8.0%) responded that they are indifferent to brand and 172 (20.5%) indicated that they prefer Korean national sport apparel brands, such as Head, Rapido, Pro-specs, Active, Head and EXR (see Table 2.2).

4.8. American and South Korean college consumers' different shopping patterns

To investigate American and South Korean college consumers' different shopping patterns, it was concluded that there were statistically significant differences in quality consciousness ($F(1, 1647) = 26.71, p < 0.001$), recreation ($F(1, 1647) = 144.81, p < 0.001$), confusion ($F(1, 1647) = 261.12, p < 0.001$), fashion ($F(1, 1647) = 78.90, p < 0.001$), impulse ($F(1, 1647) = 27.11, p < 0.001$), price ($F(1, 1647) = 268.11, p < 0.001$) and brand consciousness ($F(1, 1647) = 40.17, p < 0.001$) (Table 2.3).

Table 2.3 Nationality comparison of the United States and South Korea

Consciousness	SS	Df	MS	F	Sig.
Quality	11.730	1	11.730	26.705*	0.000
Recreation	31.267	1	31.267	144.811*	0.000
Confusion	146.22	1	146.22	261.120*	0.000
Fashion	64.436	1	64.436	78.899*	0.000
Impulse	8.360	1	8.360	27.107*	0.000
Price	150.785	1	150.785	268.107*	0.000
Brand	15.653	1	15.653	40.168*	0.000

Note: Wilks' Lambda = 0.64; $F = 129.89$; $p = 0.000$; *$p < 0.001$.

Table 2.4 The results of mean comparison for nationality

Consciousness	Nationality	N	Mean	Std. error
Quality	American	822	2.507	0.024
	Korean	841	2.690	0.026
Recreation	American	822	3.003	0.017
	Korean	841	3.303	0.018
Confusion	American	822	3.410	0.027
	Korean	841	2.762	0.030
Fashion	American	822	2.721	0.032
	Korean	841	3.151	0.036
Impulse	American	822	2.763	0.020
	Korean	841	2.918	0.022
Price	American	822	2.124	0.027
	Korean	841	2.782	0.030
Brand	American	822	2.782	0.022
	Korean	841	2.994	0.025

Additionally, it was revealed that Korean college-aged consumers placed more statistical emphasis on quality ($M = 2.69$ versus 2.51), recreation ($M = 3.30$ versus 3.00), fashion ($M = 3.15$ versus 2.72), impulse ($M = 2.92$ versus 2.76), price ($M = 2.78$ versus 2.12) and brand consciousness ($M = 2.99$ versus 2.78) than American college-aged consumers. However, American college-aged consumers were significantly higher than the Koreans on confusion consciousness ($M = 3.41$ versus 2.76) (Table 2.4).

5. Discussion

The results of this study indicated that there were several similarities and a few differences in shopping styles between American and South Korean college-aged students. Interestingly, there were significantly different shopping patterns in quality, recreation, confusion, fashion, impulse, price and brand consciousness between American and Korean college-aged consumers. A previous literature has shown that young American consumers are similar to young Korean consumers on brand, quality, recreation, confusion, fashion, impulse and price consciousnesses (Hafstrom, Chae and Chung, 1992). Reasons that have been put forth have included different cultural and economic reasons, lifestyle or business style (Fan and Xiao, 1998; Hiu et al., 2001). For example, weekday South Korean shopping mall hours are similar to those in the United States. However, weekend shopping mall hours differ in South Korea from those in the United States. Accordingly, it may be assumed that Korean customers go shopping more often on Saturday and Sunday than consumers in the United States. Moreover, Fan and Xiao (1998) stated that due to different economic environments and cultural backgrounds, the purchasing power of average Asian college students is probably much lower than that of the average Western college students. Thus, the purchasing power of college-aged students may depend substantially upon their country's economic growth.

The findings revealed that South Korean college students were more willing to pay for named brands' (brand) sport products. In fact, this is not highly surprising as it has been documented that well-known brand names such as Rolex watches, BMW vehicles, Sony electronics and GUCCI textiles often make a social statement about the individual's status (Wanke, Bohner and Jurkowitsch, 1997). This finding is important as it reflects a specific decision-making outcome for the consumers that purchase these items. Therefore, it may be stated that brand consciousness plays an important part in society, and breeds the belief that higher prices mean higher quality.

South Korean students enjoyed shopping (recreation) as well as buying products based on the spur of the moment (impulsiveness). For those shoppers who enjoy shopping or purchase on an impulse, store attractiveness is a significant contributor for return business. To do so, studies have shown that stores may appeal to the shoppers' senses through the use of aromas, light colors, signs and music (Alpert and Alpert, 1990; Areni and Kim, 1994; Blumenthal, 1988). How consumers view store image has long been considered an integral part of consumer decision-making (Baker, Lavy and Grewal, 1992; Bell, 1999; Martineau, 1958). The image influences the consumer's perceptions of goods and services purchased (Kunkel and Berry, 1968). Therefore, sports apparel companies need to make a campus visit promotion with giveaways and special events to inform South Korean students of their products.

South Korean college students also consider fashion, price, brand and quality when they go shopping in malls or discount stores. They tend to purchase (fashion) good quality sport products in an affordable and reasonable price (price). This finding supports a previous investigation which found that fashion conscious consumers of the late twentieth century measured both retailer quality and the value of their own time (Kim, 1988). However, American college-aged consumers were confused by overchoice. For many consumers, there appeared to be a feeling of confusion about product choices because of the proliferation of brands, stores and consumer information that existed (Sproles and Kendall,

1986). Because of the increased proliferation of brands in recent years, many companies are employing an imitation strategy to sell more products in different sizes, prices, qualities and colors (Fletcher, 1987; Foxman, Muehling and Berger, 1990). Even though each brand markets a variety of products, college-aged students are also a target for consumer age groups. When young consumers shop at stores, they might need to be assisted in finding the product as sometimes the products are not arranged clearly. Therefore, marketers need to develop better layout, arrangement and to have a guest service.

6. Conclusions and implications

As sports are globalized, sports products are being sold more often nationally and internationally rather than locally. Examining different decision-making styles for shopping is an important area of inquiry in the vast understanding of consumer behavior. Because consumer shopping patterns differed significantly in previous studies, this study has focused on the specific shopping pattern differences in relation to athletic apparel between Korean and American college-aged consumers.

Consumers' shopping characteristics are important factors when sports apparel companies develop promotional and distribution strategies. Consumers often exhibit different characteristics, market behaviors and shopping orientations, which may be based upon nationality. These differences are affected by culture, gender role, economic situations and environment according to previous research (Best and Williams, 1997; Buss, 1990; Low, 1989; Nisbett, 1990; Suzuki, 1991; Williams and Best, 1990). Athletic apparel companies must, therefore, learn more about the distinctive characteristics of sports consumers, especially the sports apparel wearing college-aged consumers.

In comparing nationality-based differences between the United States and South Korea, the results of this study demonstrated American and South Korean college-aged consumers reflect shopping pattern differences in relation to quality, recreation, confusion, fashion, impulse, price and brand consciousness. According to a recent study (Hiu et al., 2001), American and South Korean college-aged consumers may reflect different cultural or economic situations. Since culture has a substantial effect on consumer behavior (Best and Williams, 1993), the diversity of consumers' characteristics and preferences may manifest differently. For example, while American and Korean college-aged consumers are certainly conscious of brand, Korean college-aged consumers are more focused on price than brand.[3] Thus, it may be assumed that due to economic problems in South Korea many young consumers are more sensitive to price than brand. Based upon such examples, sports apparel companies should sufficiently examine the cultural background and economic situation before attempting to export products to other countries or developing target market strategies.

According to the aforementioned, it is assumed that college students from different countries may display some similar or different shopping preferences. In order to approach the accurate target market, international sports apparel marketers are able to develop a precise marketing strategy (product, price, promotion and place/distribution). Since this study focused on shopping styles for general sports products, the international marketers need to investigate different factors for specific target market consumers.

Most previous studies have been conducted with the aim of identifying a theoretical framework for measuring consumer decision-making styles in general business, as developed by Sproles and Kendall (1986). No study has been undertaken to measure consumer decision-making styles in relation to athletic apparel. This study, therefore, extended a specific consumer decision-making style, used in previous research, for sports apparel. The findings of this study have implications for developing consumer education in the United States and South Korea. The proposed model for this study consisted of seven shopping consciousnesses in consumer decision-making styles, in the specific area of athletic apparel, between two countries. The shopping consciousnesses in this model are important concepts in consumer decision-making styles; therefore, the proposed model may be used to develop better consumer decision-making style guidelines in consumer education. In addition, it can be used as a conceptual background in future studies relating to the shopping behaviors of athletic apparel consumers.

This study may also be used as a source for more detailed information when educating sport management students about consumer shopping behaviors, for athletic apparel, in the United States and South Korea. According to the results of this study, the similarities and differences between college-aged consumers in the two countries can be used to assist students, in consumer economics and marketing, in better understanding the commonalities and differences of consumer behavior from different cultures. As sports continue to become more globalized, consumers are not only interested in game outcome, but also in products. A study of consumer decision-making styles is an important area in sports marketing strategy. Information about consumers' decision-making styles can be useful for corporations when targeting Korean and American college-aged markets.

Profiling college consumers by combining their decision-making styles and demographic information between the two countries can provide more meaningful ways to identify and understand various consumer segments and to target each segment with more focused marketing strategies. According to this study, Korean college-aged consumers tend to stick with brand, price, quality and fashion when shopping. Brand conscious shoppers usually focus on higher quality with higher price; therefore, sports apparel marketers display diverse brands in stores. Price conscious shoppers are sensitive to price and attempt to find the lowest price with the best value; therefore, sports apparel marketers develop precise marketing strategies with diverse and reasonable prices introduced through advertising. Retailers can provide good value and present a variety of clothing in sports apparel stores. Fashion and quality conscious shoppers desire high quality with new styles. Therefore, sports apparel marketers focus on diverse designs, sizes and colors, and can introduce their products through fashion shows, magazines and television. Most Korean consumers have strong relationships with listening (word of mouth); therefore, sports apparel marketers can focus on word of mouth to build unique brand recognition and loyalty through promotions in South Korea.

In contrast to South Korean college-aged consumers, according to the findings of this study, American college-aged consumers were more confused when shopping. Due to diverse international sports brands displayed in sports apparel stores, most consumers of television and print magazine tend to be confused by overchoice. Because of problems with store arrangement and unclear price tags, the consumers are confused when selecting sports products. Therefore, sports marketers and retailers can build a unique store environment and better customer services so that college-aged consumers can be impressed and more likely to return to the store. Up to this point, Korean and American sports apparel marketers can position their brands as reputable and high quality through the use of word of mouth, fashion magazines, advertisements on television and special weekend promotions to make college consumers consider purchasing more sports apparel. Moreover, they can develop joint ventures with local companies so that they can emphasize more promotional programs.

Based on the results of this study, the following recommendations are offered primarily to sports apparel marketers and retailers. First, this study used a convenient sample rather than a random sample because it was difficult to collect a Korean random sample from the United States. If sports apparel marketers and retailers use the results of this study in the 'real world', subtle differences may exist. It is, therefore, recommended that randomly selected diverse and geographical samples should be used to find specific shopping patterns in each sports product. Second, this study used a revised instrument from an original instrument. It is recommended that a questionnaire be developed that addresses more shopping consciousness factors related to specific sports apparel. Third, differences were compared between American and South Korean college-aged consumers in relation to shopping consciousnesses for sports apparel. As sports are more globalized, most international sports consumers need and want to purchase international sports brand apparel. It is, therefore, recommended that a more cross-cultural study addressing shopping pattern differences among countries should be conducted. Fourth, while the choice of population is very important when sports apparel marketers attempt to sell products, different populations exhibit different shopping styles. It is, therefore, recommended that studies examining religion, race, job status and income level should be conducted in relation to specific target markets. Finally, the numbers of Internet users who are interested in sports products have been growing rapidly. Finding an Internet shopper's characteristics is very important when developing marketing strategies and marketing products, considering e-commerce growth. It is, therefore, recommended that a study of Internet consumers' shopping characteristics should be conducted in the future.

Acknowledgments

The author would like to express the deepest appreciation to Harald Dolles and Sten Söderman for their guidance and support of this chapter.

Notes

1. http://www.sportsbusinessjournal.com, retrieved 09.11.2007.
2. 'The Motivation for Purchasing Brand Clothes and Accessories Among Japanese', http://www.sjr.dk/brand.htm, retrieved 09.05.2003.
3. 'Consumer Profile Research 2000', http://www.adchannel.co.kr/other/cpr/1/1_2.htm, retrieved 25.07.2002.

References

Alpert, J.I. and Alpert, I.M. (1990) 'Music Influences on Mood and Purchase Intentions', *Psychology and Marketing*, 7(2): 109–134.

Areni, C.S. and Kim, D. (1994) 'Influence of In-store Lighting on Consumers' Examination of Merchandise in a Wine Store', *International Journal of Research in Marketing*, 11(2): 117–125.

Baker, J., Lavy, M. and Grewal, D. (1992) 'An Experimental Approach to Marketing Retail Store Environmental Decisions', *Journal of Retailing*, 68(4): 445–460.

Bell, S.J. (1999) 'Image and Consumer Attraction to Intraurban Retail Areas: An Environmental Psychology Approach', *Journal of Retailing and Consumer Services*, 6(2): 67–78.

Bernard, R.H. (1988) *Research Methods in Cultural Anthropology* (Newbury Park, CA: Sage).

Best, D.L. and Williams, J.E. (1993) 'Cross-Cultural Viewpoint', in A.E. Beall and R.J. Sternberg (eds), *Perspectives on the Psychology of Gender* (New York, NY: Guilford): 215–248.

Best, D.L. and Williams, J.E. (1997) 'Sex, Gender, and Culture', in J.W. Berry, M.H. Segall and C. Kagitcibasi (eds), *Handbook of Cross-cultural Psychology, Vol. 3: Social Behavior and Applications*, 2nd edn (Boston, MA: Allyn & Bacon): 163–212.

Blumenthal, D. (1988) 'Scenic Design for In-store Try-ones', *New York Times* (09.04.1988): N9.

Buss, D. (1990) 'Evolutionary Social Psychology: Prospect and Pitfalls', *Motivation and Emotion*, 14: 265–286.

Fan, X.J. and Xiao, J.J. (1998) 'Consumer Decision-making Styles of Young Adult Chinese', *The Journal of Consumer Affairs*, 32(2): 275–294.

Fletcher, K. (1987) 'Consumers' Use and Perceptions of Retailer-controlled Information Sources', *International Journal of Retailing*, 2(3): 59–66.

Foxman, E.R., Muehling, D.D. and Berger, P.W. (1990) 'An Investigation of Factors Contributing to Consumer Brand Confusion', *The Journal of Consumer Affairs*, 24(1): 170–189.

Hafstrom, J.L., Chae, J.S. and Chung, Y.C. (1992) 'Consumer Decision-making Styles: Comparison Between United States and Korean Young Consumers', *The Journal of Consumer Affairs*, 26(1): 146–158.

Hiu, S.Y., Siu, Y.M., Wang, C.L. and Chang, M.K. (2001) 'An Investigation of Decision-making Styles of Consumers in China', *The Journal of Consumer Affairs*, 35(2): 326–345.

Jenkins, M.C. (1973) 'Clothing and Textile Evaluative Criteria: Basis for Benefit Segmentation and Reflection of Underlying Values', Unpublished Doctoral dissertation (Columbus, OH: Ohio State University).

Kim, M.S. (1988) 'Segmentation of the Korean Apparel Market as Determined by the Life Style Differences of Korean College Women', Unpublished Doctoral dissertation (Columbus, OH: Ohio State University).

King, C.W. and Ring, L.J. (1980) 'Market Positioning Across Retail Fashion Institutions: A Comparative Analysis of Store Types', *Journal of Retailing*, 56(1): 37–55.

Kotler, P. and Amstrong, G. (2001) *Principles of Marketing*, 9th edn (Upper Saddle River, NJ: Prentice-Hall).

Krejcie, R.V. and Morgan, D.W. (1970) 'Determining Sample Size for Research Activities', *Educational and Psychological Measurement*, 30: 607–610.

Kunkel, J.H. and Berry, L.L. (1968) 'A Behavioral Concept of Retail Images', *Journal of Marketing*, 32(4): 21–27.

Low, B.S. (1989) 'Cross-cultural Patterns in the Training of Children: An Evolutionary Perspective', *Journal of Comparative Psychology*, 103: 311–319.

Lysonski, S., Durvasula, S. and Zotos, Y. (1996) 'Consumer Decision-making: A Multi-country Investigation', *European Journal of Marketing*, 30(12): 10–21.

Martineau, P. (1958) 'The Personality of a Retail Store', *Harvard Business Review*, 36(1): 47–55.

Nisbett, R.E. (1990) 'Evaluation Psychology, Biology, and Cultural Evaluation', *Motivation and Emotion*, 14: 255–263.

Park, Y., Joo, N., Hong, J., Kim, J., Kim, Y. and Kim, E. (2004) *The Investigation of Sports Industry in Korea* (Seoul: Korea Institute of Sport Science).

Sproles, E.L. and Sproles, G.B. (1990) 'Consumer Decision-Making Styles as a Function of Individual Learning Styles', *The Journal of Consumer Affairs*, 24(1): 134–147.

Sproles, G.B. and Kendall, E.L. (1986) 'A Methodology for Profiling Consumer's Decision-making Styles', *The Journal of Consumer Affairs*, 20(2): 267–279.

Stoffel, J. (1988) 'Where America Goes for Entertainment', *New York Times* (07.08.1988): 11–12.

Suzuki, A. (1991) 'Egalitarian Sex Role Attitudes: Scale Development and Comparison of American and Japanese Women', *Sex Roles*, 24: 245–259.

Tai, S.H. (2005) 'Shopping Styles of Working Chinese Females', *Journal of Retailing and Consumer Services*, 12(3): 191–203.

Thomas, J.R. and Nelson, J.K. (1996) *Research Method in Physical Activity*, 3rd edn (Champaign, IL: Human Kinetics).

Walsh, G. and Vincent, W. (2001) 'German Market Mavens' Decision Making Styles', *Journal of Euro-Marketing*, 10(4): 83–108.

Walsh, G., Hennig-Thurau, T., Wayne-Mitchell, V. and Wiedmann, K. (2001) 'Consumers' Decision-making Style as a Basis for Market Segmentation', *Journal of Targeting, Measurement and Analysis for Marketing*, 10(2): 117–131.

Wanke, M., Bohner, G. and Jurkowitsch, A. (1997) 'There are Many Reasons to Drive a BMW: Does Imagined Ease of Argument Generation Influence Attitudes?', *Journal of Consumer Research*, 24(September): 170–177.

Williams, J.E. and Best, D.L. (1990) *Sex and Psyche: Gender and Self Viewed Cross Culturally* (Newbury Park, CA: Sage).

3
Travel Time Elasticities in Recreational Sports: Empirical Findings for the Professionalization in Sports Facility Management

Tim Pawlowski, Christoph Breuer and Pamela Wicker

1. Introduction

Regarding the increasing scarcity of public funds, measures to allocate public money efficiently are becoming more and more important. In the sports sector, most of the public funds are spent on the construction and operation of sports facilities in professional spectator sports as well as recreational sports. Since all public authorities are faced with recreational sports while the number of public authorities faced with professional spectator sports is restricted, strategies to (1) save public money and/or (2) reallocate public money more efficiently, particularly in the recreational sports facility sector, are auspicious for all public authorities.

First, a commonly used strategy to save public money is privatization through commercialization and/or outsourcing. The central idea of commercialization in the sports facility sector is the increase of private funding to reduce public construction costs. In this context public private partnership (PPP) approaches are often discussed in the literature. Second, efficiency in the context of recreational sports facility planning could be increased by increasing the number of people practising sport while the total budget allocated to sports facilities remains constant. In general, a political consensus exists to allocate sports facilities locally so that 'time taken to reach the sports facility' is reduced for each consumer. The central argument for this political decision is that a 'small distance to sports facilities' (hence 'short individual travel time') influences the consumers' decision to practise sport positively.

Although the relationship between sports consumption and time has already been subject to several studies in different areas of sport economics (for example, Cawley, 2004; Downward and Riordan, 2007; Humphreys and Ruseski, 2007), there is very limited empirical evidence (Pawlowski et al., 2009) for the above-mentioned argumentation. Furthermore, since centralization also contains efficiency potential (for economies of scale, see Samuelson and Nordhaus, 2001) and this way could increase sports demand (for example, through favourable pricing), sports managers need to know about the degree of demand sensitivity to the distance or time involved in travelling to sports facilities. Therefore, the purpose of this chapter is to investigate the degree of sensitivity of (active) sports consumers to changes in time taken to reach the sports facility. In detail, this chapter explores the following questions: If a 'small distance to sport facilities' does indeed influence the consumer decision in favour of practising sport (a) are there differences between sports? (b) are there differences between organizations (non-profit versus for-profit organizations)? (c) to what extent are sports consumers time sensitive? (d) are there demographic, socio-cultural or economic variables that influence the consumers' time sensitivity? and (e) is there potential for reallocating sports facilities more efficiently?

The findings are expected to provide important information to sports facility planners and managers concerning the efficient allocation of sports facilities.

The chapter is organized as follows: Section 2 discusses the theoretical background of the study; Section 3 discusses the applied methodology; Section 4 presents the major results of our study; and Section 5 discusses the practical implications as well as some aspects regarding further research topics.

2. Theoretical background

Regarding consumption decisions, 'time' was comprehensively modelled in the household production theory developed by Gorman (1956), Becker (1965), Lancaster (1966) and extended by Stigler and Becker (1977). According to their approaches, households actively maximize their utility function of commodities. Therefore consumption activities (for example, practising a sport like basketball) are produced by means of the input of market goods (for example, basketball shoes), time (for example, time to reach the sports facility), human capital (for example, knowledge of tactics) and other inputs (for example, team-mates). With Humphreys and Ruseski's (2007) theoretical 'Model of Participation in

Physical Activity', the individual time allocation decision was recently comprehensively implemented in sports economics. Summing up, the argument that a 'small distance to sport facilities' influences the consumers' decision to practise sport positively could theoretically be derived by the 'new' consumer theory.

Regarding the theoretical background of factors influencing the amount of time sports consumers are willing to spend on travelling, we could primarily revert to general economic demand theory. Following this theory, prices of a good or service, disposal of complement and substitute goods and income have a major impact on the extent of consumption (for example, Frank, 2003; Samuelson and Nordhaus, 2001). In general, the price is often stated to play a minor role in the sports participation decision (for example, Coalter, 2004; Késenne and Butzen, 1987) and therefore is not a major barrier to sports participation (Lera-López and Rapún-Gárate, 2005). However, we think that sports consumers' expenditures might have an impact on their willingness to spend travel minutes since this way the approximated cost of sport might be a correlate of involvement in sport. Our intuition is that the sports consumers' expenditure is higher the more they are involved in their sport. We also think that sports consumers are more willing to spend travel minutes the more they are involved in sport.

In addition, the original extent of sports consumers' involvement might be observed with characteristics such as the frequency, the duration or the number of years a sport is practised. Complement/substitute goods are originally defined according to the fact that an increase in the price of one good will tend to decrease/increase the demand for another one (Frank, 2003). In the context of our study disposable leisure time might be a complement good to travel time since the more leisure time is disposable, the more time (theoretically) can be spent in reaching the sports facility. In addition, working time per week might be a substitute good to travel time since the more time people spend working, the less time for leisure activities is at their disposal. Since, in general, a trade-off between possible income and disposable leisure time is considered (for example, Douglas, 1934; Hicks, 1932), our intuition is that the higher a person's income, the less disposable travel time they have. Following Socioeconomic Demand Theory (Lavoie, 2004), we suggest that there might be various socio-demographic factors such as household size, age and gender as well as socio-cultural background variables such as nationality or education level that influence the travel time decision.

3. Methodology

3.1. Data

The relevant data were collected in two of the six biggest German cities: Cologne (written survey) and Stuttgart (Computer-Assisted Telephone Interviewing: CATI). Inter alia, we inquire about (1) the time people need to reach the sports facility of their most practised sport(s) (CTIME) (2) their maximum willingness to spend travel time if necessary (MTIME) and (as mentioned above) different factors that are supposed to influence the sports consumers' travel time spending. Due to the fact that no travelling-cost data were collected in our study, we try to approximate the impact with inclusion of (3) sports consumers' expenditure (in € per year) (EXP). Our intuition is that sports consumers' expenditure is higher, the more they are involved in their sport. Also we think that sports consumers are more willing to spend travel time, the more they are involved in sport. To cover a wider range of involvement in sport, we additionally include (4) the frequency (times per week) (FREQ) (5) the duration (time in minutes per session) (DUR) and (6) the number of years (YEAR), sport is practised as potential factors to explain sports consumers' travel time spending.

To approximate the impact of possible travel time complements and substitutes we include (7) disposable leisure time per week (LEIS) (intuition: leisure time is a complement good to travel time since the more leisure time is disposable, the more time (theoretically) can be spent on reaching the sports facility) as well as (8) working time per week (WORK) (intuition: working time per week is a substitute good to travel time since the more time people spend on working, the less time for leisure activities is at their disposal) in our research. Additionally (9) net income (INC) is analysed as an economic variable. Our intuition is that INC is also a substitute good to MTIME since the higher the income, the more time people spend on working, and the less time for leisure activities is at their disposal. Furthermore we assume that there might be various socio-demographic factors that influence the travel time spending decision. Moreover, since these factors provide a demand segmentation possibility with direct management purpose, we include demographic variables such as (10) household size (PERS) (11) age (AGE) and (12) gender (SEX) as well as socio-cultural background variables such as (13) nationality (NAT) and (14) level of education (EDU) in our research.

More than 100 different sports are practised by the 3725 respondents in Stuttgart and the 5158 respondents in Cologne. By reason of the reliability of results we only focus on the 14 most popular sports which are practised by a minimum number of 30 respondents in each city. We eliminated observations with internal invalidity (for example, cases where individuals mentioned MTIME is less than CTIME). On the other hand, we could enlarge the Stuttgart data set by aggregating observations of individuals practising two sports. Therefore, if we mention most practised sports in the following, we revert to the most practised sports in Cologne as well as the first and second most practised sports in Stuttgart. All in all $n = 2558$ cases in Stuttgart and $n = 4031$ cases in the Cologne data are accessible for this research.

Since we analysed two data sets of two different projects, not all variables appear in both data sets. While NAT was not asked in Cologne, YEAR was not asked in Stuttgart. Additionally, we have data on LEIS only in Cologne and data on WORK only in Stuttgart.

3.2. Methods

With the objective of measuring the degree of demand sensitivity to the distance or time to sports facilities, we make use of the elasticity concept (see Cooke, 1994; Samuelson and Nordhaus, 2001). This way we get to know how sports consumers respond to changes in 'time taken to reach the sports facility' and if there are differences between different sports. Therefore we simulate different scenarios where we measure the quantity of demanded different sports services evoked by increasing 'time taken to reach the sports facility'. This results in the ability to derive the sport-specific travel time elasticities (ε).

To detect possible covariates of time sensitivity, we apply correlation and regression analysis with MTIME as the dependent variable.

4. Results

4.1. Descriptive statistics

The most popular sports practised in Stuttgart are running ($n = 523$), swimming ($n = 460$), fitness ($n = 428$), soccer ($n = 348$) and gymnastics ($n = 165$). This preference pattern differs from Cologne where most of the people questioned practise soccer ($n = 1057$), running ($n = 555$), fitness ($n = 475$), handball ($n = 344$) and tennis ($n = 311$). Regarding the organization of their sport, inhabitants of both cities reveal more or less similar patterns. Handball (87.8% in Stuttgart; 95.1% in Cologne), track and field (86.7% in Stuttgart; 90.0% in Cologne) and tennis (77.8% in Stuttgart; 86.2% in Cologne) are examples of sports primarily practised in sports clubs (non-profit organizations) with a

Table 3.1 Descriptive statistics data set Stuttgart and Cologne

Sport	Stuttgart (1st and 2nd sport)				Cologne (1st sport)			
	n	(%) club	(%) com	(%) else	n	(%) club	(%) com	(%) else
Running	523	3.1	1.1	**95.8**	555	6.3	2.3	**91.4**
Swimming	470	12.8	21.1	**66.1**	257	**38.5**	11.7	49.8
Fitness	428	8.4	**78.0**	13.6	475	9.7	**77.7**	12.6
Soccer	348	**57.5**	0.3	42.2	1057	**79.3**	2.5	18.2
Gymnastics	165	**52.7**	14.5	32.8	34	**50.0**	20.6	29.4
Tennis	126	**77.8**	11.1	11.1	311	**86.2**	5.1	8.7
Dancing	112	36.6	**43.8**	19.6	101	**35.5**	31.7	32.7
Apparatus gymnastics	94	**89.4**	1.1	9.5	80	**66.3**	7.5	26.2
Volleyball	60	**60.0**	1.7	38.3	232	**84.5**	0.0	15.5
Badminton	55	**36.4**	27.3	36.3	78	**62.8**	16.7	20.5
Basketball	51	37.3	0.0	**62.7**	235	**83.0**	0.9	16.1
Handball	49	**87.8**	0.0	12.2	344	**95.1**	0.0	4.9
Bodybuilding	47	4.3	**74.5**	21.2	161	1.9	**68.9**	29.2
Track and field	30	**86.7**	6.7	6.6	111	**90.0**	0.9	9.1

Note: Most frequent organizational type in bold letters.

similar proportion in both data sets. Fitness (78.0% in Stuttgart; 77.7% in Cologne) as well as bodybuilding (74.5% in Stuttgart; 68.9% in Cologne) are mostly practised in commercial fitness centres (for-profit organizations). Additionally there are sports that are practised primarily without any organization or that are self-organized like running (95.8% in Stuttgart; 91.4% in Cologne) or swimming (66.1% in Stuttgart; 49.8% in Cologne) (see Table 3.1).

In both cities minimum values of CTIME and MTIME amount to zero. While CTIME = 0 implies that some people questioned do not have to spend any time reaching the sports 'facility' of their most practised sport, MTIME = 0 implies that some people are not willing to spend any time reaching their sports location. With $n = 292$ (Stuttgart) and $n = 244$ (Cologne) for CTIME as well as $n = 63$ (Stuttgart) and $n = 20$ (Cologne) for MTIME, most of the zero observations could be assigned to running. This seems to be quite intuitive since running can be practised almost anywhere without a facility. The number of zero observations for other sports in Cologne is rather low with a maximum for soccer (CTIME: $n = 5$; MTIME: $n = 1$). In Stuttgart we could detect a significant number of zero observations for fitness (CTIME: $n = 47$;

MTIME: $n = 23$) and gymnastics (CTIME: $n = 22$; MTIME: $n = 11$). The maximum values of CTIME and MTIME are between 90 minutes (CTIME in Cologne) and 180 minutes (MTIME in Cologne). The arithmetical mean of CTIME for all sports amounts to 11.8 minutes in Stuttgart (standard deviation: 10.9 minutes) and 13.7 minutes in Cologne (standard deviation: 12.3 minutes). With 24.3 minutes (standard deviation: 14.7 minutes) in Stuttgart and 29.7 minutes in Cologne (standard deviation: 17.1 minutes), the arithmetical mean of MTIME for all sports is more than twice as much as the arithmetical mean for CTIME. Regarding descriptive statistics, we could detect some significant differences in sports with similar characteristics in both cities (see Table 3.2).

4.2. Travel time elasticities of sports demand

For small changes in time all sports in both cities have a highly time elastic demand ($\varepsilon > 1$), although interesting differences between different sports and the two cities exist (see Table 3.3). The most reasonable simulation results could be summarized as follows:

1. A look at the five sports with the highest time elastic demand in Stuttgart shows that a simulated 1 per cent increase in time yields a 25.1 per cent decrease in quantity demanded swimming, a 24.5 per cent decrease in quantity demanded playing handball, a 23.3 per cent decrease in quantity demanded practising track and field, a 19.6 per cent decrease in quantity demanded playing basketball and a 17.0 per cent decrease in practising bodybuilding. Regarding Cologne, the five sports with the highest time elastic demand are gymnastics ($\varepsilon = 11.8$), bodybuilding ($\varepsilon = 9.3$), swimming ($\varepsilon = 8.6$), volleyball ($\varepsilon = 8.6$) and handball ($\varepsilon = 8.4$).
2. In both cities, the sport with the lowest time elastic demand is running (Stuttgart: $\varepsilon = 7.5$; Cologne: $\varepsilon = 3.1$).
3. No organization-specific elasticity pattern exists. For example, handball (which is most frequently played in sports clubs) is one of the sports with the highest travel time elasticity while demand for apparatus gymnastics (which is also most frequently practised in sports clubs) is less time elastic in both cities.
4. With the exception of gymnastics, all elasticities simulated with Stuttgart data are exceedingly high compared to Cologne data. The sport with the highest city-specific elasticity spread is track and field (Stuttgart: $\varepsilon = 23.3$; Cologne: $\varepsilon = 4.5$).

5. Regarding further simulation results (for example, 5 and 10 per cent increases in time), the above-derived demand pattern shows hardly any significant change. The city-specific elasticity spread is nearly the same for all simulated time changes.

The city-specific elasticity spread might be the result of different questioning techniques and different sample selections. As already mentioned, in Stuttgart we inquire about the first and second most practised sport. To increase the data sample, we simply aggregated cases, which means that sports consumers practising at least two sports appear twice in the sample. Our intuition is that people are more time elastic regarding their second sport since their second sport is less important to them than their first (hence more often) practised sport. Therefore, we simulate time elasticities for Stuttgart data with data of sports consumers practising the relevant sport as the first as well as the second sport separately. Indeed we find proof for this hypothesis in some sports (for example, swimming, apparatus gymnastics, bodybuilding, gymnastics, fitness and running) since the travel time elasticity of sports consumers who practise swimming as their first sport is significantly lower compared to the estimated time elasticity of both consumer types together. Surprisingly, sports consumers practising the remaining sports are even more elastic if the relevant sport is their first sport.

Summing up, the methodological difference between analysing only the most practised sport (Cologne) and the first and the second most practised sports together (Stuttgart) might be an explanation for different time elasticities in the samples. Furthermore, in Cologne we questioned sports service consumers in sports clubs, fitness centres and parks. Therefore, the likelihood of questioning highly involved sports consumers is disproportionately higher in Cologne compared to Stuttgart where we interviewed a random sample of the total population. In general we expect involvement to influence the consumers' maximum willingness to spend travel time and (hence) the sport-specific travel time elasticity positively. Since we questioned sports consumers in both cities only about FREQ and DUR, we have access to two proxy variables indicating the extent of involvement (see Table 3.4). The most frequently practised sports per week are bodybuilding in Stuttgart (mean: 2.38 times per week) and track and field in Cologne (mean: 3.80 times per week). With an average duration of around 106 minutes per training session in Stuttgart and around 114 minutes per training session in Cologne, volleyball is the sport with the biggest time investment in Stuttgart and Cologne (in Cologne apparatus gymnastics

Table 3.2 Descriptive statistics time variables Stuttgart and Cologne

Sport	Var.	Stuttgart (1st and 2nd sport)				Cologne (1st sport)			
		Mean	S.D.	Min.	Max.	Mean	S.D.	Min.	Max.
Running	CTIME	4.24	6.62	0.00	60.00	4.37	6.04	0.00	60.00
	MTIME	16.23	12.07	0.00	120.00	19.02	11.61	0.00	100.00
Swimming	CTIME	17.28	11.86	0.00	90.00	13.73	8.47	0.00	45.00
	MTIME	29.11	15.14	0.00	120.00	28.58	13.31	7.00	60.00
Fitness	CTIME	10.44	8.49	0.00	60.00	11.51	8.07	0.00	50.00
	MTIME	20.64	11.01	0.00	60.00	22.77	11.61	0.00	90.00
Soccer	CTIME	13.91	11.69	0.00	90.00	15.35	13.87	0.00	120.00
	MTIME	29.20	16.73	5.00	120.00	33.78	19.09	1.00	120.00
Gymnastics	CTIME	10.36	9.51	0.00	60.00	11.16	5.95	0.00	20.00
	MTIME	23.47	13.43	0.00	60.00	24.74	18.31	0.00	100.00
Tennis	CTIME	11.95	8.90	1.00	45.00	14.23	9.82	2.00	60.00
	MTIME	25.38	13.69	2.00	90.00	30.43	13.78	10.00	100.00
Dancing	CTIME	17.13	11.65	0.00	60.00	17.62	12.12	1.00	60.00
	MTIME	31.92	14.68	5.00	60.00	34.43	16.65	10.00	120.00
Apparatus gymnastics	CTIME	11.65	10.20	3.00	75.00	14.16	11.89	1.00	60.00
	MTIME	22.39	12.46	5.00	75.00	30.59	17.64	5.00	120.00
Volleyball	CTIME	15.73	8.76	3.00	40.00	17.38	13.97	0.00	90.00
	MTIME	28.35	12.13	10.00	60.00	32.61	15.96	10.00	120.00
Badminton	CTIME	15.73	11.22	5.00	60.00	15.31	10.70	1.00	45.00
	MTIME	26.53	11.13	7.00	60.00	30.96	15.75	10.00	90.00
Basketball	CTIME	14.25	8.68	2.00	45.00	17.18	10.80	1.00	70.00
	MTIME	32.16	19.83	5.00	120.00	34.06	15.21	10.00	120.00
Handball	CTIME	16.59	14.64	2.00	60.00	19.57	16.59	1.00	110.00
	MTIME	29.49	14.41	10.00	60.00	39.40	21.50	7.00	180.00
Bodybuilding	CTIME	13.28	12.73	0.00	60.00	13.00	10.54	0.00	105.00
	MTIME	20.64	11.01	0.00	60.00	24.43	12.38	4.00	120.00
Track and field	CTIME	13.20	8.84	2.00	45.00	15.05	11.11	3.00	90.00
	MTIME	25.17	12.00	10.00	60.00	33.25	15.15	10.00	100.00

Note: In minutes.

Table 3.3 Simulated time elasticities in Stuttgart and Cologne

Stuttgart

Simulated time steps (%)	Swimming	Handball	Track & field	Basketball	Bodybuilding	Volleyball	Badminton	Soccer	Apparatus gymnastics	Tennis	Fitness	Dancing	Gymnastics	Running
1	25.11	24.49	23.33	19.61	17.02	16.67	16.36	16.38	15.96	15.87	14.02	13.39	9.09	7.46
5	5.11	4.90	4.67	3.92	3.40	3.67	3.27	3.33	3.19	3.17	2.85	2.68	1.82	1.49
10	2.55	2.45	2.33	1.96	1.70	1.83	1.64	1.70	1.60	1.59	1.45	1.34	0.91	0.75
15	1.72	1.63	1.56	1.31	1.13	1.22	1.09	1.13	1.06	1.22	0.98	0.89	0.73	0.51
20	1.32	1.22	1.17	0.98	0.85	0.92	0.82	0.85	0.80	0.91	0.74	0.71	0.55	0.38
25	1.12	1.06	0.93	0.86	0.68	0.80	0.80	0.74	0.64	0.76	0.65	0.61	0.51	0.33
30	0.97	0.88	0.78	0.72	0.57	0.72	0.67	0.61	0.57	0.63	0.58	0.51	0.42	0.28
35	0.95	0.82	0.67	0.73	0.55	0.71	0.78	0.57	0.61	0.63	0.59	0.59	0.42	0.27
40	0.84	0.71	0.58	0.64	0.48	0.63	0.68	0.50	0.53	0.56	0.51	0.51	0.36	0.23
45	0.75	0.63	0.52	0.57	0.43	0.56	0.61	0.45	0.47	0.49	0.47	0.48	0.35	0.21
50	0.68	0.57	0.47	0.51	0.38	0.50	0.55	0.40	0.43	0.44	0.43	0.43	0.32	0.19

Cologne

Simulated time steps (%)	Swimming	Handball	Track & field	Basketball	Bodybuilding	Volleyball	Badminton	Soccer	Apparatus gymnastics	Tennis	Fitness	Dancing	Gymnastics	Running
1	8.56	8.43	4.50	5.08	9.32	8.62	7.70	7.60	3.75	7.40	7.00	4.95	11.76	3.06
5	1.71	1.69	1.08	1.11	1.86	1.81	1.54	1.51	0.75	1.48	1.43	0.99	2.35	0.61
10	0.86	0.84	0.54	0.60	0.99	0.99	0.77	0.76	0.38	0.74	0.74	0.50	1.18	0.32
15	0.62	0.60	0.36	0.45	0.75	0.72	0.60	0.54	0.25	0.51	0.58	0.40	0.98	0.22
20	0.47	0.45	0.27	0.38	0.59	0.58	0.45	0.41	0.25	0.39	0.43	0.35	0.74	0.16
25	0.40	0.42	0.43	0.41	0.52	0.50	0.46	0.38	0.40	0.35	0.36	0.44	0.59	0.14
30	0.40	0.39	0.39	0.40	0.48	0.43	0.51	0.35	0.42	0.31	0.36	0.36	0.49	0.13
35	0.50	0.51	0.41	0.51	0.41	0.50	0.44	0.42	0.50	0.39	0.48	0.45	0.76	0.14
40	0.44	0.45	0.36	0.45	0.57	0.44	0.38	0.37	0.44	0.34	0.42	0.40	0.66	0.12
45	0.41	0.40	0.32	0.41	0.52	0.44	0.34	0.34	0.39	0.31	0.38	0.35	0.59	0.11
50	0.37	0.36	0.29	0.37	0.47	0.40	0.31	0.31	0.35	0.28	0.35	0.32	0.53	0.10

Table 3.4 Descriptive statistics involvement variables Stuttgart and Cologne

Sport	Var.	Stuttgart (1st and 2nd sport)				Cologne (1st sport)			
		Mean	S.D.	Min.	Max.	Mean	S.D.	Min.	Max.
Running	FREQ	2.00	1.44	0.00	7.00	2.73	1.19	1.00	8.00
	DUR	53.48	22.37	15.00	240.00	65.40	29.74	15.00	240.00
Swimming	FREQ	1.17	1.09	0.00	8.00	2.39	1.31	1.00	9.00
	DUR	69.48	39.38	10.00	320.00	82.40	31.74	27.00	270.00
Fitness	FREQ	2.32	1.29	0.00	7.00	2.79	1.10	1.00	7.00
	DUR	82.54	42.69	10.00	453.00	96.51	33.34	0.00	360.00
Soccer	FREQ	2.05	1.49	0.00	9.00	2.80	1.14	0.00	10.00
	DUR	98.46	41.90	20.00	400.00	103.72	24.23	0.00	480.00
Gymnastics	FREQ	1.99	1.82	0.00	7.00	2.26	1.46	1.00	6.00
	DUR	57.80	23.07	1.00	120.00	89.38	33.47	24.00	180.00
Tennis	FREQ	1.59	1.00	0.00	5.00	2.18	1.16	1.00	10.00
	DUR	83.04	30.25	5.00	180.00	97.04	24.45	60.00	180.00
Dancing	FREQ	1.65	1.198	0.00	7.00	2.24	1.11	1.00	6.00
	DUR	95.63	52.951	1.00	300.00	116.73	59.95	30.00	420.00
Apparatus gymnastics	FREQ	1.32	0.83	0.00	6.00	2.53	1.137	1.00	5.00
	DUR	67.39	37.60	30.00	360.00	114.38	36.38	60.00	300.00
Volleyball	FREQ	1.25	0.82	0.00	4.00	2.22	0.94	1.00	6.00
	DUR	106.15	30.62	60.00	180.00	114.31	25.06	30.00	360.00
Badminton	FREQ	1.15	1.21	0.00	8.00	1.76	0.90	1.00	6.00
	DUR	87.62	27.72	30.00	150.00	112.88	33.47	60.00	240.00
Basketball	FREQ	1.80	1.50	0.00	9.00	2.84	1.24	1.00	10.00
	DUR	91.89	33.34	30.00	180.00	107.36	21.06	60.00	240.00
Handball	FREQ	1.82	1.15	0.00	6.00	2.88	1.03	1.00	7.00
	DUR	81.78	25.99	2.00	120.00	101.30	19.23	60.00	180.00
Bodybuilding	FREQ	2.38	1.30	0.00	7.00	2.96	1.10	1.00	6.00
	DUR	76.63	32.88	20.00	150.00	91.86	40.00	21.00	240.00
Track and field	FREQ	1.80	1.27	1.00	7.00	3.80	1.84	1.00	11.00
	DUR	76.00	23.87	5.00	120.00	113.38	24.08	45.00	180.00

Note: In minutes.

is practised with an average duration of 114 minutes per training session as well). Regarding the above-derived hypothesis it is interesting to note that average FREQ as well as average DUR are significantly higher in Cologne compared to the Stuttgart sample. Hence involvement might be an additional factor in explaining city-specific differences in time elasticities.

4.3. Factors influencing MTIME

Bivariate correlations give a first overview about factors influencing sports consumers' MTIME. Regarding Cologne, EXP as well as the FREQ show significant positive correlation with MTIME in most sports. Additionally, the DUR and the YEAR show some positive correlation with MTIME. Considering these variables, involvement or value of sport seems to have a considerably positive impact on MTIME. It is interesting to note that LEIS and INC are significant at least for two sports. Socio-demographic factors have rather low explanatory power for differences in MTIME. Nevertheless the more PERS and the AGE, the less they are willing to spend travel time. A significant correlation for (dummy variable: men = 1) SEX could be detected only for soccer (here: women tend to spend more MTIME).

Regarding Stuttgart, people are questioned about EXP considering membership fees only. We could detect a significant (positive) correlation with MTIME only for swimming and dancing. The FREQ is often significant correlated with MTIME. In contrast to all sports in Cologne and most of the sports in Stuttgart, this correlation is significantly negative for fitness and gymnastics. Significant correlations between DUR and MTIME are always positive. While Stuttgart inhabitants were not asked about the YEAR nor about their LEIS, we could revert to working time per week WORK. Regarding WORK we could detect only one, but highly significant, correlation with MTIME for swimming. Since this correlation is positive, empirical results are in contradiction to our intuition that WORK is a substitute for MTIME. Although we have access to INC in 1,543 cases, we could not detect any significant correlation between income and MTIME. Therefore, we dropped income from the factor list for further research with Stuttgart data. Again socio-demographic factors have rather low explanatory power for differences in MTIME. While PERS again tends to have a negative impact on MTIME, all significant correlations with Stuttgart data between AGE, SEX and MTIME indicate a contrary effect compared to

Cologne data. Maximum willingness to spend time to reach the sports facility tends to be higher for men and older people. With (dummy variable: German = 1) NAT and (dummy variable: final secondary school examination and higher education = 1) EDU we could revert to additional possible factors influencing MTIME in Stuttgart data. While MTIME tends to be lower for sports consumers with higher ranked levels of education, the direction of nationality effect on MTIME is ambiguous.

Our regression models with ordinary least squares (OLS) estimates can confirm (most of) the above-described relationships even within the multivariate context (see Tables 3.5 and 3.6). Since some people questioned are not willing to spend any time getting to their most often-practised sport, MTIME amounts to zero. Therefore, we might be faced with the so-called censored sample problem (see Deaton and Muellbauer, 1999; Long, 1997; Philips, 1983) in models of running (Cologne data and Stuttgart data) as well as fitness and gymnastics (Stuttgart data) when the share of zeros is significant. However, since some experiments with Tobit models (Tobin, 1958) did not yield sensible estimation results, we simply focus on OLS estimates for all sports below.

Models with the best-estimated fit are apparatus gymnastics in Stuttgart ($R^2_{corr.}$ = 0.708) and gymnastics in Cologne ($R^2_{corr.}$ = 0.412). Regarding Stuttgart, models for handball ($R^2_{corr.}$ = 0.226), basketball ($R^2_{corr.}$ = 0.159), gymnastics ($R^2_{corr.}$ = 0.124) and swimming ($R^2_{corr.}$ = 0.122) are acceptable while models for all other sports show a rather low variance explanatory power for MTIME ($R^2_{corr.}$ < 0.100) or are even impossible to be estimated (for example, track and field). Regarding Cologne, models for badminton ($R^2_{corr.}$ = 0.293), handball ($R^2_{corr.}$ = 0.163), swimming ($R^2_{corr.}$ = 0.147) and tennis ($R^2_{corr.}$ = 0.112) show variance explanatory power for MTIME with more than 10 per cent. This indicates that the disposable factors seem to be appropriate for analysing MTIME in gymnastics, swimming and handball in both cities.

Regarding the apparatus gymnastics model in Stuttgart we are faced with a serious multicollinearity problem. To detect multicollinearity among independent factors, we applied Variance Inflation Factor (VIF). Regarding the apparatus gymnastics model in Stuttgart, VIF is higher than 10 for nearly all variables. This indicates potential multicollinearity and yields biased estimates (see Hair et al., 1998). Regarding all other models VIF is rather low (<3) for all variables.

Table 3.5 Multiple regression between MTIME and factors in Cologne

Sport	Intercept		Sex (men = 1)		Age		PERS		INC		LEIS		EXP		Year		FREQ		DUR	
	b	p	b	p	b	p	b	p	b	p	b	p	b	p	b	p	b	p	b	p
Running	18.26	***	−1.38		−0.079		0.330		−0.001	*	−0.031		0.006	***	0.178	**	−0.137		0.023	
Swimming	32.36	***	−0.443		−0.347	***	−1.49	**	−0.000		−0.003		−0.003		0.265	**	3.47	***	−0.007	
Fitness	18.21	***	−1.35		−0.098		0.945	*	0.000		0.089	*	−0.002		0.053		0.825		0.018	
Soccer	32.39	***	−7.67	***	−0.326	**	−1.08	**	0.072		0.005	**	0.326	**	0.326	***	3.85	***	0.004	
Gymnastics	22.38	*	−0.099		−0.335	**	−2.63		−0.003		−0.044		0.019	**	0.588	**	0.198		0.088	
Tennis	25.28	***	−1.60		−0.259	**	0.143		−0.000		0.028		0.004	***	−0.038		1.46	**	0.073	**
Dancing	4.65		9.61		0.632		0.027		−0.004		0.164		−0.002		0.178		5.78	**	0.007	
Apparatus gymnastics	6.93		3.61		−0.059		0.765		−0.001		0.078		0.006		−0.172		4.64	**	0.080	
Volleyball	36.82	***	−0.091		−0.437	*	−0.696		−0.000		−0.060		0.003		0.326		3.37	**	−0.007	
Badminton	44.18	***	−3.98		−0.816	**	−3.72	**	−0.001		−0.535	**	0.011	**	0.832	**	4.68	**	0.108	**
Basketball	8.70		−6.86	**	0.820	*	0.129		−0.001		−0.029		0.006		0.065		0.482		0.082	
Handball	29.00	**	2.36		−0.840	**	−3.11	***	0.000		0.025		0.010	**	0.253		6.40	**	0.108	*
Bodybuilding	19.54	***	−4.23		0.131		2.53	**	−0.002	**	0.160	**	−0.004		0.363		−1.56		0.027	
Track and field	51.15	***	2.32		−0.259		−1.28		−0.002		−0.110		0.000		−0.324		0.055		−0.025	

b ≡ coefficient; p ≡ significance level; * $p < 0.1$; ** $p < 0.05$; *** $p < 0.01$.

Table 3.6 Multiple regression between MTIME and factors in Stuttgart

Sport	Intercept b	p	Sex (men = 1) b	p	Age b	p	PERS b	p	WORK b	p	FREQ b	p	DUR b	p	NAT (German = 1) b	p	EDU (final second. - school exam. = 1) b	p
Running	4.53		-0.849		0.151	***	-0.735	*	-0.009	*	0.121		0.078	***	3.93	*	0.065	
Swimming	20.82	***	3.69	**	0.101	*	-0.513		-0.042	***	2.08	**	0.033		3.16		-5.58	***
Fitness	24.65	***	0.823		-0.046		-0.322		-0.007		-1.04	**	0.042	***	-2.10		-1.17	
Soccer	48.74	***	-0.913		-0.187		-1.86	*	0.004		3.06	***	-0.021		-7.02	**	-3.46	
Gymnastics	45.60	***	-0.804		-0.136		-4.92	***	-0.041		-1.08		0.069		-5.57		1.31	
Tennis	44.61	**	10.52	***	-0.114		0.349		-0.006		0.722		-0.020		-16.30		-3.05	
Dancing	36.35	***	-0.539		0.006		-1.13		-0.012		0.276		0.026		0.266		-0.348	
Apparatus gymnastics	22.36		48.57		-0.350		-0.290		-1.15		19.55	***	-0.318	**	18.31		-12.07	
Volleyball	18.51		9.02	*	-0.077		-3.28	**	-0.043		4.87		0.045		7.96		-3.74	
Badminton	35.21		3.77		-0.297		0.237		-0.001		3.42		-0.068		Dropped		2.03	
Basketball	9.55		-2.87		0.182		-2.50		-0.036		3.59		0.347	**	1.05		-10.65	
Handball	48.27	*	5.48		-0.356		0.600		0.002		4.80		-0.033		Dropped		-20.05	**
Bodybuilding	21.95	**	-5.88		0.085		0.948		-0.011		-0.429		0.073		-6.70		7.26	*
Track and field	Dropped		Dropped		Dropped		Dropped		Dropped		Dropped		Dropped		Dropped		Dropped	

b ≡ coefficient; p ≡ significance level; $^* p < 0.1$; $^{**} p < 0.05$; $^{***} p < 0.01$.

5. Conclusion and discussion

Regarding the above-derived results we could state that consumers do indeed care about the extent of time they need to reach their sports facilities. Our findings indicate the following:

1. Some significant differences in travel time elasticities for different sports exist. The sport-specific elasticity spread (1% increase in time) amounts to 17.6 in Stuttgart and 6.2 in Cologne. Furthermore, we could detect some city-specific elasticity differences that we could explain with different questioning techniques and different sample selections.
2. We could not detect any organization-specific elasticity patterns since some high travel time elastic sports are primarily practised in sports clubs (non-profit organizations) and others in fitness centres (for-profit organizations).
3. Swimmers, handball players and people practising track and field in Stuttgart as well as bodybuilders, volleyball and handball players in Cologne show the highest travel time elastic demand. In both cities, the sport with the lowest time elastic demand is running.
4. We could detect several demographic, socio-cultural or economic factors that influence MTIME and (hence) the sports consumers' time sensitivity. First of all, involvement (operationalized with EXP, the FREQ, the DUR and the YEAR) has a major and positive impact on MTIME. Surprisingly neither LEIS nor WORK could be clearly detected as a consistent complement and substitute good to MTIME. Socio-demographic factors reveal an inter-city consistent but intra-city inconsistent influence pattern. While AGE is positively correlated with MTIME in Stuttgart, we were able to detect primarily negative correlations in the Cologne data set. A possible explanation could be traced back to different questioning techniques. PERS tends to have a negative impact on MTIME. This seems to be quite intuitive since time is scarce in big families. Additionally we were able to detect some sports with significant negative and others with significant positive effect of SEX, NAT and EDU on MTIME. All in all we must state that differences in involvement are a consistent explanation for differences in MTIME. Nevertheless, socio-demographic factors exist with a sport-specific impact on MTIME.

Based on these results, we see potential for reallocating sports facilities more efficiently. With the objective of increasing efficiency, one could think about a more centralized sports facility allocation for sports with less travel time elastic consumers such as apparatus gymnastics, dancing and fitness. On the contrary, a more decentralized allocation of handball gyms and swimming pools might rather increase efficiency through an increased number of consumers. Hence, with the objective of maximizing efficiency, we advise against a generalized approach to sports facility allocation (similar to the proclaimed political consensus for general decentralization). To generate the appropriate efficiency-maximizing allocation pattern, a demand-oriented sports facility planning concept should take the appropriate sport-specific travel time elasticities into account. Moreover, the managers responsible for the operation of the sports facilities should consider the socio-demographic status of their target group. For instance, the maximum willingness to spend time for travelling to soccer gyms is significantly higher for women compared to men in Cologne. This means that, with the objective of attracting female soccer players, managers of soccer gyms might develop farther reaching communication campaigns for women while their drawing potential for men as target group is rather local.

Finally, we have three remarks regarding the limitations of our research and some brief ideas for further research. (1) In analogy to research and measurement of willingness to pay we have various possibilities to measure the maximum willingness to spend travel time. It is not unlikely that other methods such as scenario simulations ('Would you keep on practising your sport if you had to travel 10 minutes more?') or choice-models ('Would you practise swimming if a swimming pool could be reached in 15 minutes?') would yield slightly different results. In particular, the latter would increase the researchers' understanding of the travel time spending pattern in recreational sports since travelling to sports facilities might also be seen as a potential barrier to participation in terms of its time and financial cost aspects. (2) In order to increase the understanding of sports consumers' willingness to spend travel minutes, we should realize further research projects. By collecting and analysing data from different cities and different countries, it might be possible to detect more general travel time spending patterns. In this regard, it might be of great interest to analyse and compare the findings with the travel time spending patterns in rural areas since both Stuttgart and Cologne are metropolitan areas. In order to increase the comparability of the research data, we should focus on identically operationalized questions. (3) To get a detailed understanding of general time spending behaviour in sports, we propose a method analogous to expenditure research (demand system estimation).

With access to detailed leisure time information, it would be possible to apply multiple equation estimations such as seemingly unrelated regressions (SUR; Zellner, 1962). In doing so, we could model complex interaction effects of time spending patterns between different sports.

References

Becker, G.S. (1965) 'A Theory of the Allocation of Time', *Economic Journal*, 75(299): 493–517.
Cawley, J. (2004) 'An Economic Framework for Understanding Physical Activity and Eating Behaviors', *American Journal of Preventive Medicine*, 27(3 Suppl.): 117–125.
Coalter, F. (2004) 'Reference Pricing: Changing Perceptions of Entrance Charges for Sport and Recreation', *Managing Leisure*, 9(2): 73–93.
Cooke, A. (1994) *The Economics of Leisure and Sport* (London: Routledge).
Deaton, A. and Muellbauer, J. (1999) *Economics of Consumer Behavior*, 17th edn (Cambridge: Cambridge University Press).
Douglas, P.H. (1934) *The Theory of Wages* (New York, NY: Macmillan).
Downward, P. and Riordan, J. (2007) 'Social Interactions and the Demand for Sport: An Economic Analysis', *Contemporary Economic Policy*, 25(4): 518–537.
Frank, R.H. (2003) *Microeconomics and Behaviour*, 5th edn (Boston, MA: Irwin/McGraw-Hill).
Gorman, W.M. (1956) 'A Possible Procedure for Analysing Quality Differentials in the Egg Market, Iowa State University', reprinted in *Review of Economic Studies*, 1980, 47(5), 843–856.
Hair, J.F., Rolph, E.A., Tatham, R.L. and Black, W.C. (1998) *Multivariate Data Analysis* (Upper Saddle River, NJ: Pearson Prentice Hall).
Hicks, J.R. (1932) *The Theory of Wages* (London: Macmillan).
Humphreys, B.R. and Ruseski, J.E. (2007) 'Participation in Physical Activity and Government Spending on Parks and Recreation', *Contemporary Economic Policy*, 25(4): 538–552.
Késenne, S. and Butzen, P. (1987) 'Subsidizing Sports Facilities: The Shadow Price-elasticities of Sports', *Applied Economics*, 19(1): 101–110.
Lancaster, C. (1966) 'A New Approach to Consumer Theory', *Journal of Political Economy*, 74(2): 132–157.
Lavoie, M. (2004) 'Post Keynesian Consumer Theory: Potential Synergies with Consumer Research and Economic Psychology', *Journal of Economic Psychology*, 25(5): 639–649.
Lera-López, F. and Rapún-Gárate, M. (2005) 'Sports Participation Versus Consumer Expenditures on Sport: Different Determinants as Strategies in Sports Management', *European Sport Management Quarterly*, 5(2): 167–186.
Long, S.J. (1997) *Regression Models for Categorical and Limited Dependent Variables* (Thousand Oaks, CA: Sage).
Pawlowski, T., Breuer, C., Wicker, P. and Poupaux, S. (2009) 'Travel Time Spending Behavior in Recreational Sports: An Econometric Approach with Management Implications', *European Sport Management Quarterly*, 9(3): 215–242.

Philips, L. (1983) *Applied Consumption Analysis*, 2nd edn (Amsterdam, New York and Oxford: North-Holland Publishing Company).

Samuelson, P.A. and Nordhaus, W.D. (2001) *Economics*, 17th edn (New York, NY: McGraw-Hill).

Stigler, G.J. and Becker, G.S. (1977) 'De Gustibus Non Est Disputandum', *American Economic Review*, 67(2): 76–90.

Tobin, J. (1958) 'Estimation of Relationships for Limited Dependent Variables', *Econometrica*, 26(1): 24–36.

Zellner, A. (1962) 'An Efficient Method of Estimating Seemingly Unrelated Regressions and Test for Aggregation Bias', *Journal of the American Statistical Association*, 57(298): 348–368.

Part II
Sport Events and Sport Facilities

4
Perceptions of the Impacts of Major Commercial Sport Events

Christopher J. Auld, Kathleen M. Lloyd and Jennifer Rieck

1. Introduction

Governments worldwide have been encouraged to subsidize events, build stadia and arenas and engage in highly competitive and costly bidding processes by the expectation that benefits will accrue from major events (Bennett, 2006; Bull and Lovell, 2007; Crompton, 1995; Dolles and Söderman, 2008). There is a general belief amongst policy makers that hosting large-scale sporting events can realize substantial positive externalities (Bull and Lovell, 2007), and that the associated recognition effects are 'a major rationale for hosting such events' (Bob and Swart, 2009; Jones, 2001). Baade (2000: 24) argued that cities have used the "promise of increased economic activity to persuade citizens to lend financial support to an aggressive city strategy to remake their centres into cultural destinations". Such strategies are often manifested through the hosting of major sport events.

However, Austrian and Rosentraub (2002) indicated that much of the literature suggests that anticipated outcomes are frequently not realized and there is no clear evidence that the use of public funds results in sizable benefits to host communities. Gratton, Shibli and Coleman (2005) argued that the quantity and distribution of returns on government investment in sport events and associated infrastructure, particularly in relation to medium- and long-term returns, have been largely under-researched and remain uncertain. They identified three main issues relating to sport event outcomes. First, there is wide variety in the scale of economic impacts generated by different sport events and large events may generate relatively small returns;

second, for some events, social benefits can be far greater than the economic impacts; and third, it is difficult to accurately forecast the economic impact of any event prior to it being staged. The evidence suggests that while it is possible to assess expenditures during and immediately after the event, determination of the longer-term yield or 'legacy' of major sport events is more elusive (ibid.; Preuss, 2006).

Despite this evidence, interest by government in leveraging benefits from events has increased and most state governments in Australia have established agencies charged with the responsibility to attract, fund and facilitate major events (Whitford, 2009). For example, in Queensland these include the Queensland Events Corporation, Stadiums Queensland and Sport and Recreation Services, Department of Communities. Subsequently, a wide variety of sport events are managed and/or supported by the Queensland Government and to accommodate these, the government has invested heavily in sport facility infrastructure.

With such substantial expenditure by government it might be expected that community opinions would be seen as an important part of the event planning and bidding process. Bidding and staging a major sport event attracts significant costs and this use of public funds also incurs considerable opportunity costs by taxpayers. However, governments and sport authorities argue that the anticipated economic and social externalities resulting from major sport events justify the use of public resources (Baade, 2000). Such views are commonly reported in the media. In contrast, host communities in Australia are rarely provided with the opportunity to express their views on the public funding of major sport events and the anticipated outcomes. This lack of consultation is reflected in the dearth of literature related to community perceptions of events and their impacts.

Preuss and Solberg (2006: 393) suggested that literature focussing on "the role and importance of local residents when cities apply to host a major sport event is rare". It would therefore seem problematic for governments to know the extent to which host residents agree with this use of public funds or perceive that the 'promised' benefits are realized. With growing interest in sport events as a generator of economic and social outcomes (Preuss, 2006), and with the accompanying rise in expenditure on attracting and staging events, it would seem vital that policy makers better understand public attitudes about major sport events and the role they play in the lives of residents.

2. Literature

2.1. Funding sport events

An increased global focus on major sport events, partnered with the popular view that events promote positive economic activity (Bob and Swart, 2009; Chalip, 2006; Dwyer, Forsyth and Spurr, 2006), has resulted in competitive bidding processes between rival cities. Securing a major event can be a complex and expensive process, which involves cities 'selling' themselves to event organizers (Toohey and Veal, 2000) and the utilization of taxpayer funds to do so (Fulton, 1988; Preuss and Solberg, 2006). Furthermore, once secured, the infrastructure required to stage events is also "subsidized either directly or indirectly by investments from public sector funds" (Crompton, 1995: 14). The Australian Bureau of Statistics (ABS, 2003) reported that in 2001–02 the three levels of government in Australia (Federal, State and Local) invested just over AUD$2.1 billion in funding for sports and physical recreation. Of this amount, 60.8 per cent went towards venues, grounds and facilities.

Event operations also incur ongoing costs by government. The Australian and Victorian Governments together with Melbourne City Council spent approximately AUD$1.2 billion to host the 2006 Melbourne Commonwealth Games (Stewart, 2006) although Wood (2006) estimated the figure to be closer to AUD$1.5 billion. Both of these figures are somewhat disturbing given the original bid document indicated the cost would be AUD$146 million. In 2006, the Victorian Government invested AUD$21 million to host the Formula One Grand Prix (Robinson, 2007). This figure increased to AUD$35 million in 2007 and the government budgeted AUD$40 million for the event in 2008 (Davis, 2008). Furthermore, the Victorian Government also contributed AUD$63 million of the total cost of AUD$81 million of the 2007 World Swimming Championships (Australian Broadcasting Corporation (ABC), 2007). Similarly, the Queensland Government consistently funded the Gold Coast Indy from its inception in the late 1980s and by the mid-2000s was spending AUD$11 million per year to host the motor sport event (Australian Financial Review, 2006). Despite assertions to the contrary from policy makers, there has been increasing recognition amongst many economists that the expected returns from these investments are not forthcoming or fall significantly below expectations (Preuss and Solberg, 2006). More recently Downward, Dawson and Dejonghe (2009: 369) concluded "that, at best, hosting unique events or hosting post-season events adds nothing statistically to employment or the value of the economy, and at worst, can cost the locality".

According to Swindell and Rosentraub (1998), the data suggest some need for scepticism about the likely benefits. One of the key reasons is that costs of bidding for and hosting sport events, as well as the associated infrastructure costs, usually far exceed the original estimates (Quirk and Fort, 1992). Another fundamental concern is the estimated size of the television (TV) audiences for events and thus the financial value of worldwide 'free publicity' supposedly generated for the host city. Jones (2001: 242) suggested that "the commercialisation of major events and sport in general has increasingly drawn benefit away from host economies... and towards commercial sponsors". The size of the TV audience, for example, is a significant factor that influences sponsorship decisions. However, Harris (2007) argued that published TV audiences for sport events have been massively exaggerated in some cases and simply guessed in others. For example, Harris indicated that rather than the 715 million people reported to have watched the 2006 FIFA World Cup final, the actual audience was closer to 260 million.

2.2. Benefits and costs of major sport events

Benefits can be broadly categorized as either direct/tangible (for example, economic) or indirect/intangible (for example, social) impacts. There is a substantial amount of literature related to the economic impacts of major sport events (Chalip, 2006), including: direct expenditure during the event (Gratton, Shibli and Coleman, 2005); increased media coverage (Cashman, Toohey and Darcy, 2004; Owen, 2005); increased tourist visitation and expenditure (Crompton, 1995; Owen, 2005); increased employment for local residents (Austrian and Rosentraub, 2002; Cashman, Toohey and Darcy, 2004); and infrastructure investment, including sport facilities, transport and communications (Cashman, Toohey and Darcy, 2004; Owen, 2005). Hodur and Leistritz (2006) noted that most research dealing with the economic impacts of events has emerged since the 1990s and suggested this growing interest could be attributed "to a boom in the construction of publicly financed stadiums and arenas that took place between 1990 and 1998" (ibid.: 65).

Intangible benefits have been reported less frequently in event impact studies (Downward and Ralston, 2006). However, according to Swindell and Rosentraub (1998) and Crompton (2004) such benefits are becoming increasingly more valued by the community as doubts grow about predicted economic benefits. Social impact studies have focussed on national and community identity (Fredline and Faulkner, 1998; Hill,

1999; Richards and Wilson, 2004); social capital (Kim and Uysal, 2003; Wann et al., 2001); overall quality of life (Crompton, 2004); social cohesion (Zhang, Pease and Hui, 1996); and collective conscience (Eckstein and Delaney, 2002). Crompton (2004) argued that impact studies should concentrate more on the 'psychic income' generated by events. Psychic income is the "emotional and psychological benefit residents perceive they receive, even though they do not physically attend sport events, and are not involved in organising them" (ibid.: 49). It is not clear how widespread such benefits are although Swindell and Rosentraub (1998) noted that the civic pride effect was mainly confined to those who attend sport events, suggesting the potential for less support from those with lower levels of sporting engagement.

Although most event impact studies focus on event benefits, it is equally important to identify the potential economic and social costs associated with major sport events. Immediate costs prior to or at the time of the event may include excess traffic and pollution, noise, vandalism, environmental damage, an increase in crime and overcrowding and the removal (or relocation) of the socially excluded (Jones, 2001; Ritchie, 1984). Other costs with more long-term impacts include budget blowouts associated with event bids and/or staging the event and long-term ongoing facility costs. For example, Meyer (2009) reported that in the aftermath of the 2008 Beijing Olympics China was experiencing a 'hangover' with regards to the decaying infrastructure and limited noticeable positive outcomes for the community. As Meyer observed, "Beijing residents still cannot drink the tap water, or surf an unfiltered Internet, or exercise in safe air" (ibid.: 67).

2.3. Community perceptions of hosting major sport events

According to a number of authors (Hiller, 2006; Preuss and Solberg, 2006; Roche, 1994), decisions about hosting major events are essentially political. Roche argued that such decisions are not part of a rational planning process and include little or no democratic community input. Fort (2006: 380) extended this argument and asserted that many decisions about sport are political and the "groups that provide the most effective political support for politicians tend to gain from the political process". This suggests that the benefits of most sport-related decisions are relatively concentrated amongst those with political influence and power whereas the negative externalities are dispersed across the majority of less influential taxpayers. Gratton, Shibli and Coleman (2005) further reported that over the past 20 years community involvement was not even considered when governments made decisions about investments in sport events and infrastructure, although this situation has changed in relation to countries intending to bid for an Olympic Games (Sueur, 2006). However, community consultation has been shown to "add value to planning, policy and decision making processes" returning valuable information back to government (Cuthill, 2001: 190) and in Queensland, it is now a mandatory component of a legislated urban and regional planning process.

Research on community perceptions of hosting major sport events is limited but growing (Bull and Lovell, 2007; Jones, 2001). In Soutar and McLeod's (1993) study of resident perceptions relating to the 1986–87 America's Cup in Fremantle, Western Australia, respondents felt that overall the event had significantly improved their quality of life. Furthermore, expectations of both benefits and costs were more extreme than that actually realized. Fredline and Faulkner (1998) examined local residents' perceptions of the annual Gold Coast Indy and, on the one hand, found that the benefits residents perceived to be most important were tourism promotion, greater opportunities for socializing, increased self-esteem and increased employment and business opportunities. On the other hand, perceived costs included noise levels, traffic congestion, crowding and disruption to lifestyle. However, overall residents were "prepared to accept these negative impacts because they perceive that the event benefits the community at large" (ibid.: 202).

More recently, Andersson, Rustad and Solberg (2004) examined local resident's assessment of the World Skiing Championships in Trondheim, Norway, and found that the majority of residents were supportive of the event and the level of government subsidy. Interestingly, their positive attitudes related predominantly to the desire for a livelier and more social city life rather than any economic impacts. Furthermore, Solberg (2006) in a meta-analysis focussing on local resident attitudes towards the hosting of mega-events showed that the majority of people welcomed the idea of hosting such events and support increased as the event grew nearer. The study also revealed that a substantial proportion of people were willing for the event to be funded by dedicated taxes. Preuss and Solberg (2006) in an analysis of data from 117 public polls found that almost three-quarters of respondents supported hosting events. Strong resident support for the continued staging of the Tour de France was also reported by Bull and Lovell (2007). In their study, residents believed the event was primarily associated with "increasing tourism" and was "good for the local economy" (ibid.: 241).

There is little doubt that globally there is much interest in sport and sport events. For example, in Australia, seven million persons aged

18 years and over (48.2% of the adult population) attended at least one sporting event during 2001–02, with males (56%) attending more events than females (40.7%) (ABS, 2003). While it would be expected that attitudes within the community would vary, a key market segment for sport is the youth and young adult demographic. Young adults are significant consumers of sport and sport-related products/services, are frequently targeted for recruitment as sport event volunteers (Auld et al., 2000; Downward and Ralston, 2006) and a large proportion of advertising uses sport as a vehicle to penetrate this market segment. For example, in Australia in 2002, young people aged 18–24 years exhibited higher levels of participation in social activities outside the home than other adults and furthermore over two-thirds (69%) of this age group watched, attended or participated in sporting events in the preceding 12 months (ABS, 2006). More specifically, the ABS also reported that in 2003, 65 per cent of 18–24 year olds attended a sporting event and 73 per cent had actively participated in sport or physical recreation in the previous 12 months. The attitudes and perceptions of young adults towards sport events and their expected benefits and costs may be crucial to decision-makers as governments continue to focus on such events as a means of potentially leveraging significant returns.

In light of these statistics, this study examined the perceptions of university students in relation to the costs and benefits of hosting major sport events in South East Queensland, Australia. In order to address this overall issue, four research questions were developed:

1. To what extent do university students agree that a range of economic and social benefits are derived from hosting major sport events?
2. To what extent do university students agree that a range of economic and social costs result from hosting major sport events?
3. To what extent do university students agree that governments should invest in the infrastructure required to host major sport events?
4. What demographic and behavioural factors influence the perceptions of university students about the benefits and costs of hosting major sport events?

3. Method

3.1. Sample

Using convenience sampling, 281 students enrolled in a university research methods course participated in the study. Surveys were distributed at two campuses ($N = 135$) and ($N = 146$) and prior to participating, students were informed about the purposes of the research and voluntary nature of their involvement. Informed consent was acknowledged by completing and returning the survey to a collection box.

3.2. Instrument

The survey instrument was developed based on a literature review (Fredline, 2000; Soutar and McLeod, 1993; Swindell and Rosentraub, 1998; Turco, 1998), and consisted of four sections. The first section obtained demographic information including age, gender, postcode, marital status, employment status and annual personal income. The level and type of sport involvement and attendance at sport events were surveyed in the second and third sections. Questions included: hours per week participating in sport; hours per week watching sport events; and frequency of attendance at major sport events in the last 12 months. Section four elicited the level of agreement with 35 statements concerning the benefits and costs associated with major sport events. The items were distributed between four scales: economic benefits (eight items); infrastructure investment (eight items); social benefits (ten items); and, economic and social costs (nine items). Responses to the items were scored on a seven-point Likert scale, ranging from '1 = strongly disagree' to '7 = strongly agree'. Items included: 'I support the government spending funds to host major sport events'; 'The international profile of South East Queensland will be improved due to hosting major sport events'; and 'Traffic congestion increases too much when South East Queensland hosts major sport events'. Reliability analysis using Cronbach Alpha indicated that all scales were robust: infrastructure investment (0.84); social and economic cost (0.89); social benefits (0.91); and economic benefits (0.92).

3.3. Analysis of data

Data were analysed using SPSS. Individual item mean scores and overall scale mean scores were calculated. Subsequent analysis utilizing Pearsons Correlation Coefficient and ANOVA examined the influence of selected demographic and behavioural factors on perceptions of the benefits and costs of hosting major sport events.

4. Results

4.1. Demographic characteristics and sport involvement

The sample comprised 281 university students of whom 62.6 per cent were female. Just over two-thirds of respondents were aged 21 years or younger, and less than 10 per cent were aged 25 years or older. Almost 90 per cent of the sample had never been married. A significant proportion (45.2%) of respondents stated year 12 or equivalent as their highest completed education level, 38.9 per cent had either a trade certificate or diploma and 14.9 per cent had already completed an undergraduate degree. Two-thirds of respondents were employed, mostly on a part-time basis. The majority (57%) earned AUD$7799 or less per year, and only 11.5 per cent earned more than AUD$20,800 per year.

Table 4.1 indicates that more than two-thirds (69.4%) of respondents currently, or had previously, participated in organized competitive sport. Furthermore, 27.4 per cent were currently members of a sporting club, with an average length of membership of six years. More than two-thirds (67.4%) of respondents participated in sport and physical activity for between 1 and 6 hours per week (mean = 5 hours/week). Similarly, the majority of respondents (77.9%) spent up to 3 hours per week watching sporting events either live or on television (mean = 2.5 hours/week).

Considering the nature of the sample it was not surprising that only 6 per cent held a season ticket/pass for national league teams. However, almost 40 per cent of respondents reported that they had attended at least one major sporting event during the 12 months prior to the survey.

Table 4.1 Sporting involvement

Variable	Value	Frequency	Valid %
Participation in organized sport	Yes	195	69.4
	No	86	30.6
Sport participation – hours/week	Less than 1 hour	31	11.1
	1–3	111	39.8
	4–6	77	27.6
	7–10	40	14.4
	Over 10 hours	20	7.3
Current sporting membership	Yes	77	27.4
	No	204	72.6
Length of sporting club membership	Less than 1 year	7	9.1
	1–3 years	31	40.3
	4–6 years	10	13.0
	7–10 years	9	11.7
	Over 10 years	20	26.0
Sport watching – hours/week	Less than 1 hour	82	29.3
	1–3 hours	136	48.6
	4–6 hours	34	12.2
	7–10 hours	18	6.5
	Over 10 hours	10	3.7

4.2. Perceived economic and social benefits derived from hosting major sport events

Respondents indicated their level of agreement with a series of eight statements about the potential of economic benefits to result from staging major sport events (Table 4.2). Mean scores were calculated for each item, as well as for the overall scale. Respondents were in moderate to strong agreement about the potential for economic benefits to be realized from the hosting of major sport events (overall mean = 5.40) and indicated the highest level of agreement with outcomes such as the potential for events to: 'increase revenues for hotels, retailers, and restaurants'; 'attract investment in tourism infrastructure'; result in 'economic benefits'; and 'attract tourists'.

Respondents also recorded their perceptions about potential social benefits from hosting major sport events. Individual item means and the overall scale mean were calculated (Table 4.3). Overall, respondents were less certain about social benefits (overall mean = 4.91) derived from hosting sport events compared to the economic benefits. Respondents agreed that hosting events could increase the region's 'international'

Table 4.2 Perceived economic benefits agreement scores

Item	Mean	SD
Hosting major sport events in South East Queensland results in increased revenues for hotels, retailers and restaurants	5.77	1.24
Major sport events help attract investment in tourism infrastructure in South East Queensland	5.70	1.29
Hosting major sport events results in economic benefits to South East Queensland	5.65	1.29
Hosting major sport events attracts tourists to South East Queensland	5.51	1.38
Hosting major sport events injects a substantial amount of money into the local economy	5.27	1.28
Infrastructure construction, or renewal, will have a positive economic impact on South East Queensland	5.16	1.15
South East Queensland receives substantial media coverage when hosting major sport events	5.07	1.24
Hosting major sport events reduces unemployment in South East Queensland	5.02	1.40
Overall mean	5.40	–
Overall SD	1.03	–
Cronbach's Alpha	0.92	–

Table 4.3 Perceived social benefits agreement scores

Item	Mean	SD
The international profile of South East Queensland will be improved due to hosting major sport events	5.22	1.29
Hosting major sport events will improve the sporting culture in South East Queensland	5.22	1.32
South East Queensland's profile within Australia will be improved due to hosting major sport events	5.19	1.27
I feel a sense of pride when South East Queensland hosts major sport events	4.94	1.40
Hosting major sport events results in a bigger pool of community volunteers	4.90	1.17
More locals will participate in sport/physical activities due to South East Queensland hosting major sport events	4.90	1.27
I feel a sense of unity with other spectators at major sport events	4.89	1.31
I feel communities in South East Queensland become more united when hosting major sport events	4.85	1.25
Hosting major sport events creates trust within a community	4.57	1.17
Hosting major sport events increases my overall quality of life	4.42	1.47
Overall mean	4.91	–
Overall SD	0.97	–
Cronbach's Alpha	0.91	–

and 'national' profile and 'sporting culture'. However, they were in less agreement that hosting events increased their overall quality of life.

4.3. Perceived economic and social costs resulting from hosting major sport events

Participants also indicated their level of agreement with nine statements about perceived economic and social costs of hosting major sport events (Table 4.4). Respondents were either neutral or in moderate agreement about the statements (overall mean 4.42). There was a reasonable level of agreement that 'traffic congestion', 'crowding' and 'pollution' increased too much during major sport events. However, respondents were more ambivalent about the relationship between events and increased crime rates.

Table 4.4 Perceived economic and social costs agreement scores

Item	Mean	SD
Traffic congestion increases too much when South East Queensland hosts major sport events	5.25	1.28
Crowding increases too much when South East Queensland hosts major sport events	4.77	1.37
Pollution increases too much when South East Queensland hosts major sport events	4.55	1.39
Noise increases too much when South East Queensland hosts major sport events	4.30	1.47
Vandalism increases too much when South East Queensland hosts major sport events	4.23	1.31
It costs South East Queensland rate payers too much money to host major sport events	4.22	1.29
It costs Queensland taxpayers too much money to host major sport events	4.22	1.32
Environmental damage increases too much when South East Queensland hosts major sport events	4.20	1.36
Crime rates increase too much when South East Queensland hosts major sport events	4.03	1.35
Overall mean	4.42	–
Overall SD	0.99	–
Cronbach's Alpha	0.89	–

4.4. Support for investment in infrastructure to host major sport events

Analysis of the mean scores suggested a moderate to strong level of agreement about investment in event infrastructure (overall mean = 4.98). Respondents recorded the highest level of agreement with the statements concerning the provision of appropriate 'transportation' and 'telecommunication networks', the 'renovating and improvement of existing stadiums' and spending funds to 'host major sport events'. Respondents were relatively neutral when asked whether there were sufficient sport facilities to host major events (Table 4.5).

4.5. Factors influencing the perceptions of South East Queensland university students about the benefits and costs of hosting major sport events

In the second stage of the analysis, correlation and ANOVA were used to determine the extent to which factors related to selected demographic characteristics and sport behaviour influenced university

Table 4.5 Infrastructure investment agreement scores

Item	Mean	SD
Government should provide appropriate transportation and telecommunication networks to host major sport events	5.74	1.29
I support the government renovating and improving existing stadiums in order to host major sport events	5.27	1.35
I support the government spending funds to host major sport events	5.12	1.40
Government should invest more money in sport facilities	4.98	1.38
The private sector should invest more money in sport facilities	4.86	1.33
I support the government spending funds to build new sports stadiums	4.86	1.48
Government should build new stadiums to host major sport events	4.66	1.52
There are sufficient sport facilities in South East Queensland to host major sport events	4.33	1.26
Overall mean	4.98	–
Overall SD	0.95	–
Cronbach's Alpha	0.84	–

students' perceptions of the benefits and costs of hosting major sport events.

4.5.1. Income

Three broad income groups (less than AUD$7799; AUD$7800 to AUD$20,799; and AUD$20,800 and over) were used in the ANOVA analysis. The results indicated that a significant difference in agreement about overall economic benefits existed between income levels. *Post hoc* test analysis (Scheffe) indicated that respondents who earned less than AUD$7799 recorded a significantly lower agreement score than those in the other income groups (Table 4.6).

Furthermore, significant differences were also found between income categories in the level of agreement about support for necessary infrastructure investment. *Post hoc* analysis using Scheffe revealed that those earning AUD$7800–20,799 recorded a significantly higher level of agreement than those earning less than AUD$7799 but neither of these two groups varied significantly from those who earned more than AUD$20,800 (see Table 4.6). A significant difference also existed

Table 4.6 Differences in costs and benefits scales mean scores

	Mean scores				
Income levels	Less than AUD$7799	AUD$7800–20,799	Over AUD$20,800	F	P
Mean infrastructure investment	4.85	5.21	5.08	3.525	0.031
Mean social benefits	4.75	5.07	5.13	4.971	0.008
Mean economic/social costs	4.39	4.47	4.42	0.117	0.890

	Mean scores			
Gender	Male	Female	F	P
Mean economic benefits	5.72	5.20	17.679	0.000
Mean social benefits	5.18	4.74	14.261	0.000
Mean economic/social costs	4.29	4.49	2.425	0.121

	Mean scores			
Sport participation	Yes	No	F	P
Mean economic benefits	5.55	5.03	15.686	0.000
Mean social benefits	5.02	4.65	8.816	0.003
Mean economic/social costs	4.33	4.62	4.908	0.028

	Mean scores			
Club membership	Yes	No	F	P
Mean economic benefits	5.76	5.26	13.914	0.000
Mean infrastructure investment	5.38	4.82	20.391	0.000
Mean social benefits	5.23	4.78	11.855	0.001
Mean economic/social costs	4.16	4.51	6.897	0.009

	Mean scores			
Event attendance	Yes	No	F	P
Mean economic benefits	5.57	5.29	4.999	0.026
Infrastructure investment	5.22	4.83	11.440	0.001
Mean social benefits	5.08	4.80	5.386	0.021
Mean economic/social costs	4.28	4.51	3.475	0.063

between income levels on agreement about potential social benefits. Scheffe *post hoc* analysis found that respondents who earned less than AUD$7799 had a lower level of agreement than both of the other income categories.

4.5.2. Gender

One-way ANOVA analysis indicated that males recorded a higher level of agreement than did females concerning the potential economic and social benefits resulting from hosting sport events as well as the need for government and private sector investment in the infrastructure required to host such events (see Table 4.6).

4.5.3. Current/previous participation in organized competitive sport

One-way ANOVA was utilized to determine whether differences on the overall agreement scores existed between different levels of sport participation (see Table 4.6). A significant difference in agreement for both economic benefits and infrastructure support was evident between respondents who were current/previous participants in organized competitive sport, and those who had not played sport. Current and/or previous sport participants recorded higher mean scores than non-participants. Similar findings were evident for social benefits. However, respondents who were current and/or previous sport participants indicated lower levels of agreement about economic and social costs than those who had not participated.

4.5.4. Current sporting club membership

One-way ANOVA revealed significant differences in agreement about perceived economic benefits, infrastructure investment and social benefits between current members and non-members of sporting clubs. In all cases, current sport club members recorded higher mean scores than non-members. On the other hand, those who were not members of a sporting club were more likely to agree that costs accrued from hosting events (see Table 4.6).

4.5.5. Attendance at sport events

One way ANOVA indicated that respondents who had attended an event in the preceding 12 months recorded a higher level of agreement about economic and social benefits and the infrastructure investment required for major sport events than those who did not attend (see Table 4.6). However, event attendees recorded a lower level of agreement about economic and social costs than those who had not attended an event.

4.5.6. Participation in sport, watching sport and level of sport event attendance

Correlation was used to determine whether significant relationships existed between the overall agreement scale mean scores and the three sport engagement variables (Table 4.7). Significant positive relationships, although weak, were found between hours of participation in sport per week and overall mean scores for economic benefits, infrastructure investment and social benefits. Weak but positive significant relationships were found between hours spent watching sport per week and the overall agreement scores for economic benefits, infrastructure

Table 4.7 Correlations between sport participation, sport watching, attendance at events and agreement mean scores

	Hours per week participating in sport	Hours per week watching sport	Number of events attended over 12 months
Mean economic benefits	0.192**	0.245**	0.158**
Mean infrastructure investment	0.239**	0.289**	0.281**
Mean social benefits	0.179**	0.202**	0.178**
Mean economic/social costs	−0.065	−0.248**	−0.217**

**Correlation is significant at the 0.01 level (2-tailed).

investment and social benefits. Table 4.7 also illustrates the weak negative relationships found between watching sport and level of agreement about economic and social costs. The results further indicated that agreement about economic benefits, infrastructure investment and social benefits had weak positive relationships with the number of sport events attended in the preceding 12 months.

5. Discussion

Overall, the results indicated moderate to strong levels of agreement that economic and social benefits result from hosting sport events. However, respondents were more inclined to agree with statements regarding economic benefits than with those related to social benefits and males recorded higher levels of agreement than females. The results tend to reflect those of Fredline and Faulkner (1998) and Andersson, Rustad and Solberg (2004). In these studies the highest levels of agreement were recorded for statements indicating that hosting sport events would: increase revenue for hotels, retailers and restaurants, attract tourism infrastructure investment and produce overall economic benefits. Jeong and Faulkner (1996) indicated that perceived longer-term event benefits included urban and tourism infrastructure development and the acceleration of urban growth rates. King, Pizam and Milman (1993) also found that residents perceived that tourism contributed towards tax revenue, created employment and increased income and the standard of living. In the current study, economic benefit statements which recorded the lowest level of agreement were linked to increases in media exposure and reduced unemployment. A number of authors (Bull and Lovell, 2007; Gratton, Shibli and Coleman, 2005; Horne and Manzenreiter, 2004) also questioned the extent to which hosting sport events resulted in increased media coverage of event locations and a subsequent increase in tourist numbers and jobs.

In terms of perceived social benefits, respondents supported the view that hosting major sport events improved South East Queensland's international and national profile, increased its sporting culture and improved city image and identity. These results are consistent with Crompton's (2004) views about the 'psychic income' potential of sport events and also Turco (1998) who found that residents perceived that hosting events resulted in enhanced state and local image, and improved community spirit.

Economic and social costs were also seen to result from hosting major sport events. However, costs which recorded the highest agreement scores were mainly short term in nature, for example, increased traffic congestion, crowding and pollution, and tend to occur during the event itself. This finding reflects the results from Bull and Lovell's (2007) study of the impacts of the Tour de France which highlighted similar costs that were also predominantly limited to the duration of the event. Respondents in the present study were less likely to support the view that hosting sport events resulted in increased crime rates, environmental damage or were an economic burden for rate payers. These results are generally consistent with those of Fredline and Faulkner (1998), Soutar and McLeod (1993) and Turco (1998).

The study also sought to determine the extent to which respondents supported government investment in event infrastructure. The highest levels of agreement were associated with those statements concerning the provision of appropriate transportation and telecommunication networks, renovating and improving existing stadiums and supporting the use of public funds to host events. Respondents were less likely to agree that the government should build new stadiums in order to host events. These findings suggest that although respondents supported government investment in broad public infrastructure initiatives required for major sport events they were less inclined to support the use of public funds for the development of new major sport facilities. Soutar and McLeod (1993) also found that residents benefited from upgrading general social infrastructure facilities, rather than just investing in event-specific venues. The results of the present study suggest that long-term benefits or a tangible event legacy actually utilized by the majority of residents are more likely to find public support than major stadia developments utilized by a minority and promises of increased tourism numbers and financial returns.

Finally, a range of factors were examined to determine their influence on perceptions about the benefits and costs of hosting sport events. The results indicated that those who were more likely to agree about economic and social benefits and support government investment in infrastructure were: males; those who earn over AUD$20,000 per year; current/previous participants in organized competitive sport; current members of a sporting club; and those who attended an event during the preceding 12 months. However, respondents who were more likely to agree that economic and social costs resulted from sport events were those who were not current/previous participants in organized competitive sport and not current members of a sporting club. Swindell and Rosentraub (1998: 16) also found that those "who did not use an asset or attend an event did not derive as much pride from it as those who did". Thus, people who exhibit some level of sport involvement are more likely to perceive benefits as an outcome from events and support government expenditure on infrastructure than those who are not as engaged in sport. This result questions the 'trickle down' and positive externality arguments frequently used as a rationale for hosting large sport events.

Australia has a strong interest in sport and many observers agree that Australia has a vibrant sporting culture. This, in conjunction with the results of this study, suggests that the majority of residents are likely to support government investment in major sport events and the infrastructure required to successfully bid for and host such events. Bob and Swart's (2009) study of the FIFA World Cup produced similar findings, which showed that the increased social and economic opportunities resulting from investment in infrastructure were key factors contributing to resident's support for the event. In the current study, results also indicate that, in general, respondents perceive that economic and social benefits rather than costs will accrue from hosting major sport events. According to Crompton (2004), the concept of 'psychic income' is a frequently cited spillover benefit with which respondents may internally identify. Coupled with a strong interest in and emotional attachment to sport, this may explain why people are more positive about potential sport event benefits despite the lack of input into the decision to bid for and host the event. However, research has consistently shown that economic benefits are not always realized. Thus, government agencies and event organizers appear to have been very successful in influencing public perceptions to the extent that it seems a generally accepted proposition that sport events result in positive outcomes for communities.

Although there is widespread agreement about the need for community participation in the planning process (Bull and Lovell, 2007; Cuthill, 2001, 2002), in the context of major sport events and associated infrastructure, it seems this rarely occurs in Australia. Therefore, many such decisions appear to be made on the basis of assumed need and while this approach is frequently criticized, the results of this study provide support for such a pragmatic strategy on the part of government and event planners. Furthermore, the results indicate that there is some basis for the assumption of positive public perceptions about the benefits derived from major sport events and also imply that decision-makers are likely to continue to feel little pressure to fully consult with the public on event bidding and sport infrastructure development issues. Therefore, it seems that the results reinforce the rational actor view of politics which suggests that the benefits of the political process tend to accrue to politically connected interest groups while the costs of providing these benefits will be dispersed across those with less political influence and frequently those who also have less ability to pay such costs (Leeds and von Allmen, 2005). However, there are indications of change as Olympic Games bids must now demonstrate that public consultation is embedded in their planning processes (Sueur, 2006). But, as pointed out by Preuss and Solberg (2006: 397), it is somewhat surprising that the International Olympic Committee (IOC) "weights 'public opinion' as a sub-criterion out of 11 main topics by only 0.83 per cent in regards to all criterion of the 'Candidature Acceptance Procedure'".

Finally, the question arises as to the basis on which the public reaches its conclusions about economic and social benefits arising from sport events. It is argued here that the public is largely informed on the basis of media reports which tend to reflect the information supplied by event organizers, relevant government agencies and prominent decision-makers. However, the literature strongly suggests that actually realizing event benefits, especially long-term economic benefits, is problematic at best. Thus, future research should examine the degree of 'factual' and temporal congruity between community perceptions and the information distributed by pro-event stakeholders. While the results presented here provide some insights into community perceptions of the impacts of major sport events, they are limited by the nature of the student sample. Future studies should therefore seek to include a larger and more representative sample of residents. Furthermore, it would be useful to undertake longitudinal research on specific annual events measuring residents' level of agreement regarding event benefits and costs prior to, during and after the event over a number of years.

6. Conclusion

Involving communities in the planning process may result in improved event management, such as ongoing community support regarding sport events, increased goodwill to visitors, larger numbers of event volunteers and potentially greater community cohesion. This would be particularly important where government embarks on a sport event tourism strategy and actively pursues more and larger events in order to increase visitation and associated anticipated economic outcomes. Alternately, failure to undertake appropriate research and consultation prior to hosting an event may result in poor levels of local support and decreased goodwill especially if the promised benefits fail to materialize. Therefore, decision-making and policy making in relation to major sport events need to be informed to "ensure that the greatest good for the greatest number" is achieved (Baade, 2000: 45). This may ultimately be achieved by continuing to research resident perceptions regarding the benefits and costs of hosting major sport events.

References

Andersson, T., Rustad, A. and Solberg, H. (2004) 'Local Residents' Monetary Evaluation of Sports Events', *Managing Leisure*, 9(3): 145–158.
Auld, C.J., Hooper, S., Jobling, I. and Ringuet, C. (2000) 'A Model for Pre-Olympic Volunteer Involvement: A Case Study of Queensland', in M. Moragos, A. Moreno and N. Puig (eds), *Volunteers, Global Society and the Olympic Movement* (Lausanne, Switzerland: International Olympic Committee): 273–286.
Australian Broadcasting Corporation (ABC) (2007) 'Government Defends Swimming Championships' Cost', http://www.abc.net.au, retrieved 16.05.2007.
Australian Bureau of Statistics (ABS) (2003) *Sport and Recreation: A Statistical Overview*, Cat No. 4156.0 (Canberra: Commonwealth of Australia).
Australian Bureau of Statistics (ABS) (2006) *Australian Social Trends*, Cat No. 4102.0 (Canberra: Commonwealth of Australia).
Australian Financial Review (2006) *Race is On For A-G After Indy Party* (30.06.2006): 46.
Austrian, Z. and Rosentraub, M. (2002) 'Cities, Sports, and Economic Change: A Retrospective Assessment', *Journal of Urban Affairs*, 24(5): 549–563.
Baade, R. (2000) 'The Impacts of Sports Teams and Facilities on Neighbourhood Economies: What is the Score?', in W.S. Kern (ed.), *The Economics of Sports* (Kalamazoo, MI: W.E. Upjohn Institute for Employment Research): 21–49.
Bennett, D. (2006) 'Boston Globe', *New York Times* (19.05.2006): 15.
Bob, U. and Swart, K. (2009) 'Residential Perceptions of the 2010 FIFA World Cup Stadia Development in Cape Town', *Urban Forum*, 20(1): 47–59.
Bull, C. and Lovell, J. (2007) 'The Impact of Hosting Major Sporting Events on Local Residents: An Analysis of the Views and Perceptions of Canterbury Residents in Relation to the Tour de France 2007', *Journal of Sport and Tourism*, 12(3): 229–248.
Cashman, R., Toohey, K. and Darcy, S. (2004) 'When the Carnival is Over: Evaluating the Outcomes of Mega Sporting Events in Australia', *Sporting Traditions*, 21(1): 1–32.
Chalip, L. (2006) 'Towards Social Leverage of Sport Events', *Journal of Sport and Tourism*, 11(2): 109–127.
Crompton, J. (1995) 'Economic Impact Analysis of Sports Facilities and Events: Eleven Sources of Misapplication', *Journal of Sport Management*, 9(1): 14–35.
Crompton, J. (2004) 'Beyond Economic Impact: An Alternative Rationale for the Public Subsidy of Major League Sporting Facilities', *Journal of Sport Management*, 18(1): 40–58.

Cuthill, M. (2001) 'Developing Local Government Policy and Processes for Community Consultation and Participation', *Urban Policy and Research*, 19(2): 183–202.

Cuthill, M. (2002) 'Exploratory Research: Citizen Participation, Local Government and Sustainable Development in Australia', *Sustainable Development*, 10(2): 79–89.

Davis, M. (2008) 'Walker Says Time May Be Up for F1', *The Australian* (04.02.2008): 5.

Dolles, H. and Söderman, S. (2008) 'Mega-sporting Events in Asia: Impacts on Society, Business and Management – An Introduction', *Asian Business and Management*, 7(1): 1–16.

Downward, P., Dawson, A. and Dejonghe, T. (2009) *Sports Economics: Theory, Evidence and Policy* (Oxford: Elsevier).

Downward, P.M. and Ralston, R. (2006) 'The Sports Development Potential of Sports Events Volunteering: Insights from the XV11 Manchester Commonwealth Games', *European Sport Management Quarterly*, 6(4): 333–351.

Dwyer, L., Forsyth, P. and Spurr, R. (2006) 'Assessing the Economic Impacts of Events: A Computable General Equilibrium Approach', *Journal of Travel Research*, 45(1): 59–66.

Eckstein, R. and Delaney, K. (2002) 'New Sports Stadiums, Community Self-esteem, and Community Collective Conscience', *Journal of Sport and Social Issues*, 26(3): 235–247.

Fort, R.D. (2006) *Sports Economics*, 2nd edn (Upper Saddle River, NJ: Pearson Prentice Hall).

Fredline, E. (2000) 'Host Community Reactions to Hosting Major Sporting Events: The Gold Coast Indy and the Australian Formula One Grand Prix in Melbourne', Unpublished Honours thesis (Griffith University).

Fredline, E. and Faulkner, B. (1998) 'Resident Reactions to a Major Tourist Event: The Gold Coast Indy Car Race', *Festival Management and Event Tourism*, 5(4): 195–205.

Fulton, W. (1988) 'Politicians Who Chase After Sports Franchises May Get Less than They Pay For', *Governing* (March): 34–40.

Gratton, C., Shibli, S. and Coleman, R. (2005) 'Sport and Economic Regeneration in Cities', *Urban Studies*, 42(4/5): 985–999.

Harris, N. (2007) 'Why FIFA's Claim of One Billion TV Viewers Was a Quarter Right', http:www.sport.independent.co.uk, retrieved 13.08.2007.

Hill, J. (1999) 'Cocks, Cats, Caps and Cups: A Semiotic Approach to Sport and National Identity', *Culture, Sport, Society*, 2(2): 1–21.

Hiller, H.H. (2006) 'Post-event Outcomes and the Post-modern Turn: The Olympics and Urban Transformations', *European Sport Management Quarterly*, 6(4): 317–332.

Hodur, N. and Leistritz, F.L. (2006) 'Estimating the Economic Impact of Event Tourism: A Review of Issues and Methods', *Journal of Convention and Event Tourism*, 8(4): 63–79.

Horne, J. and Manzenreiter, W. (2004) 'Accounting for Mega-events: Forecast and Actual Impacts of the 2002 Football World Cup Finals on the Host Countries Japan/Korea', *International Review for the Sociology of Sport*, 39(2): 187–203.

Jeong, G. and Faulkner, B. (1996) 'Resident Perceptions of Mega-event Impacts: The Taejon International Exposition Cast', *Festival Management and Event Tourism*, 4(1/2): 3–11.

Jones, C. (2001) 'Mega-events and Host-region Impacts: Determining the True Worth of the 1999 Rugby World Cup', *International Journal of Tourism Research*, 3(3): 241–251.

Kim, K. and Uysal, M. (2003) 'Perceived Socio-economic Impacts of Festivals and Events Among Organizers', *Journal of Hospitality and Leisure Marketing*, 10(3/4): 159–171.

King, B., Pizam, A. and Milman, A. (1993) 'Social Impacts of Tourism Host Resident Perceptions', *Annals of Tourism Research*, 20: 650–665.

Leeds, M. and von Allmen, P. (2005) *The Economics of Sport*, 2nd edn (Boston, MA: Pearson/Addison Wesley).

Meyer, M. (2009) 'One World, One Dream, One Year Later', *Sports Illustrated*, 111(4): 66–72.

Owen, J.G. (2005) 'Estimating the Cost and Benefit of Hosting Olympic Games: What Can Beijing Expect from its 2008 Games?', *The Industrial Geographer*, 3(1): 1–18.

Preuss, H. (2006) 'Impact and Evaluation of Major Events', *European Sport Management Quarterly*, 6(4): 313–316.

Preuss, H. and Solberg, H.A. (2006) 'Attracting Major Sporting Events: The Role of Local Residents', *European Sport Management Quarterly*, 6(4): 391–411.

Quirk, J.P. and Fort, R.D. (1992) *Pay Dirt: The Business of Professional Team Sports* (Princeton, NJ: Princeton University Press).

Richards, G. and Wilson, J. (2004) 'The Impact of Cultural Events on City Image: Rotterdam, Cultural Capital of Europe 2001', *Urban Studies*, 41(10): 1931–1951.

Ritchie, J. (1984) 'Assessing the Impact of Hallmark Events: Conceptual and Research Issues', *Journal of Travel Research*, 23(1): 2–11.

Robinson, N. (2007) 'Grand Prix's Future in Doubt', *The Australian* (22.05.2007): 24.

Roche, M. (1994) 'Mega-events and Urban Policy', *Annals of Tourism Research*, 21(1): 1–19.

Solberg, H. (2006) 'Local Residents' Assessment of Hosting Major Sporting Events', Paper Presentation (Hangzhou: IX World Leisure Congress), 15–20 October.

Soutar, G. and McLeod, P. (1993) 'Residents' Perceptions on the Impact of the America's Cup', *Annals of Tourism Research*, 20(3): 571–582.

Stewart, B. (2006) 'A Lasting Investment?', *Australasian Leisure Management*, 55 (March/April): 24–26.

Sueur, R. (2006) 'Swiss Candidatures for the Olympic Winter Games: Why are there So Many Failures?', Paper Presentation (Olympia: The International Olympic Academy 14th International Seminar on Olympic Studies for Post Graduate Students), 6 July–6 August.

Swindell, D. and Rosentraub, M. (1998) 'Who Benefits from the Presence of Professional Sports Teams? The Implications for Public Funding of Stadiums and Arenas', *Public Administration Review*, 58(1): 11–20.

Toohey, K. and Veal, A.J. (2000) *The Olympic Games: A Social Science Perspective* (Oxon: CABI Publishing).

Turco, D. (1998) 'Host Residents' Perceived Social Costs and Benefits Towards a Staged Tourist Attraction', *Journal of Travel and Tourism Marketing*, 7(1): 21–30.

Wann D., Melnick, M., Russell, G. and Pease, D. (2001) *Sport Fans: The Psychology and Social Impact of Spectators* (New York, NY: Routledge).

Whitford, M. (2009) 'A Framework for the Development of Event Public Policy: Facilitating Regional Development', *Tourism Management*, 30(5): 674–682.

Wood, A. (2006) 'Dubious Benefits of an Expensive, Second Rate Circus', *The Australian* (08.03.2006): 9.

Zhang, J., Pease, D. and Hui, S. (1996) 'Value Dimensions of Professional Sport as Viewed by Spectators', *Journal of Sport and Social Issues*, 20(1): 78–94.

5
Gender, Race and Nationality: An Examination of Print Media Coverage of the 2006 Winter Olympics

Andrea N. Eagleman and Erin L. McNary

1. Introduction

The Olympics celebrate sport like no other event in the world. The uniqueness of this event recognizes a wide variety of sports and creates a sense of nationalistic pride. Billings and Eastman (2003: 569) stated, "the Olympics represents a mix of nationalism, internationalism, sport, and human drama unmatched by any other event". Olympism was represented at the 2006 Winter Olympic Games in Torino, Italy where Olympic organizers coined the theme 'Passion Lives Here'. This passion was broadcast internationally, bringing the culture and Olympic spirit to consumers' workplaces and homes. For more than two weeks the 2006 Torino Olympics held a captive audience with 84 medal events, and 1026 medals were awarded to a contingency of 2508 athletes representing 80 international Olympic Committees. Around 130 countries broadcast the Olympics live, totaling almost 1000 hours representing 50 different languages. In terms of website usage, a record was set reaching 72 million pages visited, 9.4 percent more than the 2004 Athens Summer Olympics.[1]

The Olympics inspire a unique environment not only for athletes and coaches participating in the event, but for a diverse audience of media consumers across the world as well. Because of the diversity and number of events and countries participating in the Olympics, viewers and readers learn about incredible feats accomplished by their particular country of interest. Zaharopoulos (2007: 235) states, "because billions of people watch the Olympics on television, it is one of a few events that can become part of the shared experience for people worldwide". Additionally, Dolles and Söderman (2008) assert that mega-sporting events such as the Olympic Games truly encompass the entire globe and are nearly certain to attract a great deal of worldwide media coverage. Fans are able to follow their favorite athletes participating in a wide array of sports not only via television, but also through other mediums such as newspapers, magazines and websites.

Agenda-setting theory, on which this study is based, asserts that people are told what to think about and how to think about these things based on the information they receive from the mass media (McCombs and Shaw, 1993). Along with this notion, sport sociologists have argued that mass media help create and perpetuate many ideological beliefs, and dominant (for example, traditional) beliefs often override marginalized beliefs, particularly in mainstream media outlets (Kane and Lenskyj, 1998). Billings and Eastman (2002: 352) asserted that "the audience's understandings about their own and others' gender, ethnicity, and nationality can be altered through television's manipulations, especially when similar practices are repeated over long periods of time". Therefore, it is important for media outlets to provide equitable coverage especially in the areas of gender, race and nationality to embody the essence of the Olympic Movement. In the case of the Olympics, however, the extent of the coverage must be limited due to a lack of time or space, so editors and media officials choose the most important topics that play an essential role in shaping what and how people think about the sport or topic covered (McCombs and Shaw, 1972).

Because the Olympic Games include more participating countries and athletes than any other sporting event in the world, and the Torino Games were considered the "most diverse Winter Olympics ever" (Lewis, 2006: 1), the researchers felt it would be valuable to examine media coverage of this mega-event. The purpose of this study, therefore, was to examine US newspaper and magazine coverage of the 2006 Winter Olympic Games in order to determine whether differences existed in the amount of coverage given to athletes of differing gender, race and nationality.

2. Literature review

Several scholars have studied media coverage of the Olympic Games and have focused on a single medium. While many of these studies have examined media portrayals on television or in newspapers, there are no known studies that have examined two print media concurrently during the same Olympics to determine if differences exist in the coverage granted to athletes from these different media. Scholars have, however, studied various aspects related to gender, race and nationality by analysing a single medium. Much of this analysis has historically revealed biased coverage.

2.1. Gender portrayals

Just as type and content of coverage is important, so is the amount of coverage dedicated to male and female sports. In terms of female sport coverage, various studies have noted the lack of coverage of female athletes in a wide range of media. The lack of coverage of sport and female athletes might suggest to a reader or viewer that the particular sport or athlete is insignificant. Wensing and Bruce (2003: 387) noted that "analyses of the western media conducted over the past 20 years have discovered consistent patterns of low coverage and inconsistent quality in women's sport, particularly in everyday sports reporting". Adams and Tuggle (2004) suggest that because women's sports go underrepresented in ESPN's coverage, it is assumed that women's sport is marginal.

Several studies have focused on media portrayals of Olympic competition. Higgs and Weiller (1994) studied the 1992 Barcelona Summer Olympics and noted that more clock time was devoted to male athletes than female athletes. Similar results were noted in a study by Eastman and Billings (1999) of the 1994 Lillehammer Winter Olympic Games. In addition, Billings and Eastman (2003) examined coverage of the 2002 Salt Lake City Winter Olympics and found more clock time coverage afforded to male athletes, thus supporting past research.

The association of gendered traits has not gone unnoticed in the research. In Sartore and Cunningham's (2007) work on gender stereotypes and women in leadership positions, findings suggest that women are characterized as warm, kind and gentle while men are confident, strong, assertive and independent. When female sports are marketed, they are represented in a sexual and trivial way, while male athletes are portrayed as strong and assertive (Lynn, Hardin and Walsdorf, 2004). This portrayal of strength and assertiveness carries over into various media such as radio, television and newspaper, which reinforce and reproduce White and heterogenic, heterosexual femininity (Krane et al., 2004). Hardin, Lynn and Walsdorf (2005: 106) state that "sexual difference, that is, culturally constructed differences between men and women framed as 'natural', is a media construction that supports a hegemonic hierarchy in which (White) men are placed at the top of the social order in the United States". Hardin (2005: 63) notes the "sports/media complex is a hegemonic institution because it perpetuates ideology about the biology of women; what is socialized in U.S. culture is framed as natural". Media practices are a prime contributor to this masculinity hegemony (Birrell, 2000).

This gendered language is also found in Olympic coverage. Billings and Eastman (2002) revealed that coverage of the 2000 Sydney Summer Olympic Games portrayed men as being more athletic and committed compared to females while also receiving greater airtime during television coverage. Moreover, examination of coverage of the 2004 Summer Olympics in Athens suggests that male athletes were portrayed as courageous, lucky and introverted and received a majority of the clock time (Billings and Angelini, 2007). Attaching traits to athletes whether they are male or female and using gendered language must be continually explored to provide fair coverage to all athletes.

While much of the research supports the fact that women are underrepresented in the media, Capranica (2005) notes that the International Olympic Committee (IOC) supports female athletes' achievements and is attempting to increase female participation as well as afford more coverage to the achievement of these athletes. However, the authors recognize that coverage, especially in non-Olympic sport settings, needs to be expanded.

2.2. Race portrayals

The mass media have also shown bias in terms of an athlete's race, with White athletes covered most often and portrayed more positively than athletes of other races. Eastman and Billings (2001) examined sports commentary in college basketball and the application of racial and gender stereotypes to coverage of athletics. They found that commentary reinforces the notion that Black athletes are natural athletes while White athletes rely on mental abilities and leadership skills that Black athletes lack. Furthermore, Billings and Eastman (2002) examined NBC's Olympic coverage and found that White athletes were portrayed as succeeding because of commitment, whereas Black athletes relied on pure athletic skills. Expanding their research in this area, Billings and Eastman's (2003) analysis of the 2002 Salt Lake City Olympics indicated that four-fifths of report commentary was devoted to White athletes. Billings and Angelini's (2007) examination of the 2004 Athens Summer Olympic Games revealed that more than two-thirds of report commentary focused on White athletes with a majority of the top 20 athletes mentioned being White. The topic of race portrayal in sport is one that should be thoroughly examined to include all race and ethnicities to aid in equitable coverage of all athletes.

2.3. Nationality portrayals

The portrayals of varying nationalities of athletes remain a topic of interest, especially with the focus on universal values in each Olympic competition. As Sabo et al. (1995: 6) noted, "Nationalism is likely to remain a feature of televised international sports for some time to come. The 'we-them' mindset, which is such a pronounced dimension of nationalism, is also a common denominator of athletic competition and sport culture. The very fact that individuals compete as representatives of their countries opens the door to nationalistic sentiment and bias."

Several studies have shown that the media do not provide equitable coverage to athletes of differing nationalities. Coverage of the 1988 Seoul Olympics Opening Ceremony in Australia, Great Britain and the USA indicated that most athletic coverage was biased, focusing on home country athletes, and the US broadcast excluded 74 of the participating countries (Larson and Rivenburgh, 1991). Additionally, Sabo et al. (1996) showed several instances of nationalistic biases in an analysis of seven international sporting events. Eastman and Billings (1999) found that out of the top ten most mentioned athletes at the 1994 Olympics, 63 percent were American, indicating a nationalistic bias. Billings and Eastman (2002) found selective representation of athletes from varying countries, with mostly mentions of American athletes at the 2000 Olympic Games. However, in Billings and Eastman's (2003) examination of the 2002 Salt Lake City Olympics, non-American athletes were mentioned more but characteristics such as composure and courage were associated with Americans compared to non-American athletes, who were depicted as successful because of their experience. Alternatively, Billings and Angelini (2007) found that in the 2004 Summer Olympics, the most mentioned athletes were American and again, there were notable differences in descriptors of American athletes compared to non-American athletes.

3. Purpose of study and research questions

Past research has shown inequitable coverage of athletic competition during the Olympic Games in terms of gender, race and nationality. However, most of these studies chose to focus on the medium of television, making it critical to study multiple media, particularly print media. The purpose of this study was to examine multiple mass media (newspaper and magazine coverage) to determine if differences exist in the amount of coverage given to athletes of differing gender, race and nationality. Examining the two mediums provides a comprehensive analysis of these popular mediums to further understand coverage. While focusing on one medium is important, analysing the two simultaneously provides insight and a viewpoint that may inspire practitioners and researchers to apply additional holistic research methodologies. To understand the breadth of the topic explored, a series of research questions were developed to aid in focusing and understanding the research:

RQ1 What percentage of coverage was devoted to female and male athletes in newspaper and magazine coverage of the 2006 Winter Olympics?

RQ2 What percentage of coverage was devoted to athletes of differing race in newspaper and magazine coverage of the 2006 Winter Olympics?

RQ3 What percentage of coverage was devoted to athletes from the USA and international athletes in newspaper and magazine coverage of the 2006 Winter Olympics?

RQ4 Do statistically significant differences exist between the percentage of coverage devoted to athletes of a certain gender and the independent standard of participation by gender in the 2006 Winter Olympics?

RQ5 Do statistically significant differences exist between the percentage of coverage devoted to athletes of a certain race and the independent standard of participation by race in the 2006 Winter Olympics?

RQ6 Do statistically significant differences exist between the percentage of coverage devoted to athletes from a certain country and the independent standard of participation from that country in the 2006 Winter Olympics?

RQ7 What differences in coverage of the 2006 Winter Olympics existed between the two mass mediums studied?

4. Methodology

This study employed a content analysis methodology. A total of 83 newspapers published during a two-week time period were examined, as well as a total of 14 magazines during a four-week time period.

The newspaper issues examined started on the date of the Olympic Opening Ceremonies (start date: 10 February 2006) and ended one day after the Olympic Closing Ceremonies (end date: 27 February 2006). The unit of analysis was the article. A total of five newspapers were examined, including *USA Today, New York Times, Boston Globe, Dallas Morning-News* and *Chicago Tribune*. These newspapers were selected for the following reason: *USA Today* is a national newspaper, and the other four are all major daily newspapers in the USA, as all four rank in the top 15 US dailies in terms of circulation.[2] A total of three magazines were examined in this study, including *Sports Illustrated, ESPN The Magazine* and *The Sporting News*, which are the top three general-interest sport magazines in the USA.[3]

A coding protocol was developed specifically for this study. For each article, the following variables were coded: coder identification, publication name, publication date, title of article, name of author, gender of author, story prominence, number of photos accompanying article, gender focus of article, sport content of article, focus of article, country of sport/athlete/team focused on by the article, article size, section of publication article appeared in and names of athletes featured in the article. The criteria for the coding protocol were unique to this study and the newspapers and magazines studied, and were therefore selected and developed by the researcher.

Two independently trained coders coded a total of 83 newspapers, which resulted in a total of 958 newspaper articles, and a total of 14 magazines, which resulted in a total of 25 magazine articles. First, the coders each coded the same 17 newspapers and the same three magazines, which accounted for 20 percent of the total newspapers and magazines, to establish inter-coder reliability. In order to test for the impact of chance agreement, Cohen's (1960) Kappa was used to test inter-coder reliability. These figures ranged from 0.806 (the lowest) for the focus of the article, to 1.0 (the highest) for all but two variables. According to Wimmer and Dominick (2006), reliability measures of 0.75 or above are acceptable when using Kappa. Therefore, the observations of the two coders were decidedly consistent and confirmed that the coders had reasonably applied the definitions and procedures set forth in the coding protocol.

5. Results

The first research question of this study sought to determine the percentage of coverage devoted to female and male athletes in newspaper and magazine coverage of the 2006 Winter Olympics. Consistent with previous findings, the percentage of coverage devoted to males was higher than females in newspapers, as males garnered 42.3 percent of the coverage, females were afforded 25.4 percent of coverage, 18.2 percent of the coverage was focused on both males and females and 14.1 percent had no gender focus. Magazine coverage, however, showed a much different trend than previous findings, as females received more coverage than males, with 29.2 percent compared to 25 percent. Additionally, 29.2 percent of magazine coverage focused on both male and female athletes, and 16.7 percent of the articles were not focused on a gender (Table 5.1).

The second research question dealt with the percentage of coverage devoted to athletes of differing race in newspapers and magazines. Newspapers provided the widest variety of coverage in this category, with stories focusing on athletes of White, Black, Asian and Latino races, while magazine coverage was limited to only White and Black athletes. See Table 5.2 for the full results.

In terms of nationality, the third research question, newspapers seemed to provide the greatest variety of coverage of athletes from different countries, although the results still revealed that coverage was biased toward US athletes, who garnered 51.1 percent of the coverage, and only 20.3 percent of the coverage was devoted to non-US athletes. Magazines focused 62.5 percent of their coverage on US athletes and just 12.5 percent on non-US athletes, as shown in Table 5.3.

Table 5.1 2006 Olympic games coverage by gender

Gender	Newspaper (%)	Magazine (%)
Male	42.3	25.0
Female	25.4	29.2
Combined	18.2	29.2
No gender focus	14.1	16.7

Table 5.2 2006 Olympic games coverage by race

Race	Newspaper (%)	Magazine (%)
White	82.0	92.9
Black	5.8	7.1
Asian	10.0	0.0
Latino	2.2	0.0

Table 5.3 2006 Olympic games coverage by nationality

Gender	Newspaper (%)	Magazine (%)
USA only	51.1	62.5
Non-USA only	20.3	12.5
Combined	19.9	20.8
No country focus	8.7	4.2

The fourth research question asks if statistically significant differences exist between the percentage of coverage devoted to athletes of a certain gender and the independent standard of participation by gender in the 2006 Olympics (61.7% male athletes, 38.3% female athletes). Chi-square analysis revealed that newspapers did not provide a statistically significant difference ($\chi^2 = 0.447$, $df = 1$, $p < 0.05$), but magazines did provide a statistically significant difference in terms of gender, as more coverage was devoted to female athletes than expected ($\chi^2 = 8.06$, $df = 1$, $p < 0.05$). In both mediums, the majority of female-focused stories were about figure skaters or alpine skiers, and the majority of male-focused stories were on ice hockey players or speed skaters. One positive finding about newspaper coverage of females was that on average, stories about females were longer in column inches than male-focused stories.

In terms of race, a statistically significant difference was found in newspaper coverage of athletes of a certain race when compared to the independent standard of participation by race in the 2006 Winter Olympics, which was 89 percent White and 11 percent minority athletes ($\chi^2 = 5.34$, $df = 1$, $p < 0.05$), meaning that newspapers actually provided more coverage to athletes of differing race than expected. Additionally, minorities received more prominent story placement than White athletes in newspapers when they were covered, and Asian and Black athletes averaged more photos per story than White and Latino athletes. Magazines, however, did not provide a statistically significant difference in its coverage of athletes of a certain race ($\chi^2 = 1.49$, $df = 1$, $p < 0.05$). In both mediums, the majority of minority athletes covered were from the USA.

Both newspapers and magazines provided statistically significant differences in the coverage of athletes from certain countries and the independent standard of participation from each country in the 2006 Winter Olympics. Both newspapers ($\chi^2 = 447.66$, $df = 1$, $p < 0.05$) and magazines ($\chi^2 = 609.92$, $df = 1$, $p < 0.05$) provided the majority of coverage to US athletes, while in actuality these athletes made up only 8 percent of the total participants in the 2006 Winter Olympics (Women's Sports Foundation, 2006).

The seventh and final research question, regarding the differences between magazine and newspaper coverage of the 2006 Winter Olympics, is best answered by examining all of the previous research questions. Magazines surprisingly provided greater coverage to female athletes than male athletes, while newspapers continued the previous trend of focusing more coverage on men. In terms of race, newspapers provided more coverage of athletes of differing race than magazines, which left two races (Asian and Latino) out of its coverage entirely, and in terms of nationality, both mediums exhibited bias in their coverage of US athletes and greatly lacked in their coverage of international athletes. Both magazines were also similar in the sports that received the most coverage, as ice hockey, alpine skiing and figure skating were the top three sports reported on in both mediums. Additionally, both newspapers and magazines focused the majority of their coverage on stories about individual athletes as opposed to groups of athletes or teams.

6. Discussion

This study reveals that, similar to previous research findings, the US media exhibited disparate reporting practices in terms of race, nationality and gender in coverage of the 2006 Winter Olympic Games.

In terms of gender, it is very interesting to find that general-interest sport magazines published in the USA actually afforded more coverage to females than males. Because more male athletes took part in the 2006 Games, this is an example of biased reporting in favor of women. No other known studies on the Olympic Games have found unequal reporting in favor of women. It is an especially remarkable finding considering that previous research on *Sports Illustrated* and *ESPN The Magazine*, which were two of the magazines examined in this study, has shown that both of these magazines have historically provided the vast majority of their coverage to male athletes, virtually excluding females from coverage (Eagleman, Pedersen and Wharton, 2009; Fink and Kensicki, 2002; Salwen and Wood, 1994). While we do not know why this surplus of coverage for females occurred in magazines during the 2006 Olympic Games, it would be interesting to study this in future Olympics to determine whether or not the trend continues.

The findings dealing with race are consistent with those of previous studies in which White athletes have traditionally received much more coverage than their Black, Asian or Latino counterparts. It was encouraging to find that newspapers provided more coverage to athletes from these minority groups than expected, showing a positive trend toward fair and equal reporting practices. It was disappointing, however, to find that magazines only focused coverage on White and Black athletes, leaving out athletes of other races entirely. While the Winter Olympics traditionally have more White athletes competing than any other racial group, it was especially disappointing to see the lack of minority coverage for the 2006 Games considering that several popular and successful athletes of these backgrounds were competing. For example, US athlete and five-time Olympic medalist Apolo Anton Ohno, a short track speedskater, is Asian, and 2006 ice dancing gold medalist Benjamin Agosto is of Latino heritage. These are just two examples of athletes who would theoretically be expected to receive coverage because of their performances, yet they were left out of magazine coverage. While the majority of magazine stories about female athletes focused on the sport of figure skating, all three magazines clearly excluded the women's figure skating gold medalist, Shizuka Arakawa, from their coverage, as she is an Asian athlete from Japan.

In terms of nationality, it is not surprising that the publications in this study devoted the majority of their coverage to US athletes, as all publications that were studied are published in the USA and distributed primarily to a US audience. The lack of coverage for athletes from other countries is concerning, however, as only 8 percent of the total athletes competing in the 2006 Games were representing the USA, yet 51.1 percent of newspaper coverage and 62.5 percent of magazine coverage were devoted solely to US athletes. If the media provided its readers with an accurate account of all that happened in Torino during the Games, these numbers would be expected to be much lower, and the amount of coverage given to international athletes much higher. While it is understandable that many US readers want to know how their fellow countrymen and women fared in Olympic competitions, focusing so much of the coverage on these athletes alone does not accurately report on all that took place in Torino. For those fans who could not travel to Italy to watch the Games in person, this skewed coverage left out a great deal of information about everything that happened in Torino not involving US athletes.

6.1. Limitations

This study includes some limitations. The magazine sample size was very small, as two of the magazines are published weekly, and the other biweekly. The three magazines selected for this study seemed to be the best available choices because, as general-interest sport magazines, they all cover a variety of sports and athletes, as opposed to specialty sport magazines, which focus the majority of their attention on one sport. Additionally, by only examining US-based newspapers and magazines, the results only reveal the trends in coverage from one country.

A second limitation of the study was the fact that only articles were examined, and no photographic coverage was examined. Additionally, the study viewed articles from a quantitative perspective in terms of the amount of coverage devoted to each gender, race and nationality, but did not examine the articles from a qualitative standpoint. Future researchers should consider performing in-depth analyses of the article content in order to determine the ways in which journalists describe athletes, sports and events.

Finally, it should be noted that the findings of this study should not be generalized to all US newspapers or sport magazines, but are representative of the reporting practices of only those mediums studied.

6.2. Future research

While this study adds to the body of research on media coverage of race, nationality and gender in the Olympic Games, it also provides ideas for future research. Television, newspaper and magazine coverage of the Olympic Games have all been studied in the past, but it is also necessary to study web coverage of this event to determine if its coverage is more or less equitable than other media, especially since the web is a fairly new medium that has not received a great deal of attention in the academic literature of the sport management field. Another idea would be to broaden this study and examine newspapers and magazines from countries outside of the USA to compare the coverage of international mass media and determine whether or not it is similar to that of the US media. As previously mentioned, researchers could also perform a qualitative analysis of the articles from this study to determine what differences exist in the language portrayals used to describe athletes of differing race, nationality and gender. Additionally, media coverage of both the Winter Olympics and the Summer Olympics could be studied to determine if differences in the coverage and portrayals of athletes of differing gender, race and nationality occur between the two different Olympics.

While this study has revealed both encouraging and discouraging trends in terms of the media coverage of athletes of differing gender, race and nationality, it will be interesting to study US media coverage of future Olympic Games to determine whether or not such trends continue to occur, and whether the agendas set by the media in this study continue to be perpetuated in future years.

7. Conclusions

This study has praised magazines for their inclusion of more articles about females, and newspapers were praised for their inclusion of more minority athletes from the 2006 Olympic Games. Some of these trends, however, might be attributed to the newspapers' and magazines' readership demographics. In order to sell more newspapers and/or magazines, news outlets often attempt to match their coverage closely to the demographics of their readers. Table 5.4 illustrates the male and female readership of each outlet examined for this study. Information on the race and nationality of readers was not available for any of the outlets examined. It is interesting to note that while magazines provided a higher percentage of coverage to female athletes than male athletes, these publications actually have much higher male readership demographics than newspapers. The male/female readership demographics of the newspapers examined in this study were much more equal than magazines.

Table 5.4 Readership demographics of news outlets examined

	Male (%)	Female (%)
USA Today	67	33
New York Times	51.1	48.8
Boston Globe	49	51
Dallas Morning-News	56.1	43.9
Chicago Tribune	N/A	N/A
Sports Illustrated	N/A	N/A
ESPN The Magazine	82.5	17.5
The Sporting News	87.9	12.1

Source: 'Weekly Boston Globe Coverage 2009', http://bostonglobe.com/advertiser/newspapers/audience/default.aspx?id=12758, retrieved 23.02.2010; 'ESPN Customer Marketing and Sales, MRI Spring 2009', http://www.espncms.com/index.aspx?id=70, retrieved 23.02.2010; 'The Dallas Morning News', http://adsource.dallasnews.com/portal/page?_pageid=34,899277,34_953915&_dad=portal&_schema=PORTAL, retrieved 23.02.2010; 'New York Times: Adult demographic profile 2009', http://www.nytimes.whsites.net/mediakit/quick_links/audience.php, retrieved 23.02.2010; 'Magazine research 2008', http://www.sportingnews.com/mediakit/mag_circulation.php, retrieved 23.02.2010; 'USA Today Advertise Combined audience reach, 2009', http://www.usatoday.com/marketing/media_kit/usat/audience_reach.html, retrieved 23.02.2010.

Overall, it is encouraging to see that both newspapers and magazines showed positive trends in some areas of their reporting on the 2006 Olympic Games, such as the increase in coverage of female athletes in magazines and the amount of coverage afforded to minority athletes in newspapers. In terms of agenda-setting theory, this shows that the media examined in this study are moving in the direction of an agenda of inclusion for all athletes regardless of gender or race. However, both mediums still exhibit inequitable reporting practices in other areas, such as the amount of coverage given to international athletes. This reveals an agenda in which the USA is seen as the most important nation, and might contribute to a feeling of nationalistic superiority among American media consumers.

The mass media serve an important role in bringing every aspect of an event to their readers and subscribers. In providing biased or inequitable coverage of certain genders, sports and/or nations, it seems that an accurate picture of the Olympic Games is not being presented to the consumers of the eight news outlets examined in this study. Equitable coverage in all of these areas can lead to a greater understanding of not only what is taking place at the Olympic Games, but can also have great sociological consequences in the form of a greater understanding of the world as a whole.

Notes

1. 'Torino 2006 in Figures', http://www.torino2006.it/ITA/OlympicGames/home/index.html, retrieved 21.01.2011.
2. 'Top 100 Newspapers in the United States (31.03.2006)', http://www.infoplease.com/ipea/A0004420.html, retrieved 01.05.2009.
3. 'Advertising and PIB – PIB Revenue and Pages: January–March 2007 vs 2006 (22.12.2007)', http://www.magazine.org/Advertising_and_PIB/PIB_Revenue_and_Pages/Revenue____Pages_by_Magazine_Titles__YTD_/21952.cfm, retrieved 01.05.2009.

References

Adams, T. and Tuggle, C.A. (2004) 'ESPN's Sports Center and Coverage of Women's Athletics: "It's a Boys Club"', *Mass Communication and Society*, 7(2): 237–248.
Billings, A.C. and Angelini, J.R. (2007) 'Packaging the Games for Viewer Consumption: Gender, Ethnicity, and Nationality in NBC's Coverage of the 2004 Summer Olympics', *Communication Quarterly*, 55(1): 95–111.
Billings, A.C. and Eastman, S.T. (2002) 'Selective Representation of Gender, Ethnicity, and Nationality in American Television Coverage of the 2000

Summer Olympics', *International Review for the Sociology of Sport*, 37(3/4): 351–370.

Billings, A.C. and Eastman, S.T. (2003) 'Framing Identities: Gender, Ethnic, and National Parity in Network Announcing of the 2002 Winter Olympics', *Journal of Communication*, 53(4): 569–586.

Birrell, S. (2000) 'Feminist Theories for Sport', in J. Coakley and E. Dunning (eds), *Handbook of Sports Studies* (London: Sage): 61–76.

Capranica, L. (2005) 'Newspaper Coverage of Women's Sports During the 2000 Sydney Olympic Games: Belgium, Denmark, France, and Italy', *Research Quarterly for Exercise and Sport*, 76(2): 212–223.

Cohen, J. (1960) 'A Coefficient of Agreement for Nominal Scales', *Educational and Psychological Measurement*, 20(1): 37–46.

Dolles, H. and Söderman, S. (2008) 'Mega-sporting Events in Asia: Impacts on Society, Business and Management – An Introduction', *Asian Business and Management*, 7(1): 1–16.

Eagleman, A.N., Pedersen, P.M. and Wharton, R. (2009) 'Coverage by Gender in ESPN The Magazine: An Examination of Articles and Photographs', *International Journal of Sport Management*, 10(2): 226–242.

Eastman, S.T. and Billings, A.C. (1999) 'Gender Parity in the Olympics: Hyping Women Athletes, Favoring Men Athletes', *Journal of Sport and Social Issues*, 23(2): 140–170.

Eastman, S.T. and Billings, A.C. (2001) 'Biased Voices of Sports: Racial and Gender Stereotyping in College Basketball Announcing', *Howard Journal of Communication*, 12(4): 183–204.

Fink, J.S. and Kensicki, L.J. (2002) 'An Imperceptible Difference: Visual and Textual Constructions of Femininity in Sports Illustrated and Sports Illustrated for Women', *Mass Communication and Society*, 5(3): 317–339.

Hardin, M. (2005) 'Stopped at the Gate: Women's Sports, "Reader Interest," and Decision Making by Editors', *Journal and Mass Communication Quarterly*, 82(1): 62–77.

Hardin, M., Lynn S. and Walsdorf, K. (2005) 'Challenge and Conformity on "Contested Terrain": Images of Women in Four Women's Sport/Fitness Magazines', *Sex Roles*, 53(1/2): 105–117.

Higgs, C.T. and Weiller, K.H. (1994) 'Gender Bias and the 1992 Summer Olympic Games: An Analysis of Television Coverage', *Journal of Sport and Social Issues*, 18(3): 234–246.

Kane, M.J. and Lenskyj, H.J. (1998) 'Media Treatment of Female Athletes: Issues of Gender and Sexualities', in L.A. Wenner (ed.), *Mediasport* (London: Routledge): 186–201.

Krane, V., Choi, P., Baird, S.M., Aimar, C.M. and Kauer, K.J. (2004) 'Living the Paradox: Female Athletes Negotiate Femininity and Muscularity', *Sex Roles*, 50(5/6): 315–329.

Larson, J.F. and Rivenburgh, N.K. (1991) 'A Comparative Analysis of Australian, U.S., and British Telecasts of the Seoul Olympic Ceremony', *Journal of Broadcasting and Electronic Media*, 35(1): 75–94.

Lewis, M. (2006) 'Black Athletes Set to Compete in Most Diverse Winter Olympics Ever', *Black America Web* (11.02.2006), http://news.newamericamedia.org/news/view_article.html?article_id=a0e6e2b02cb051efaf0001a470140f00, retrieved 22.02.2010.

Lynn, S., Hardin, M. and Walsdorf, K. (2004) 'Selling (Out) the Sporting Woman: Advertising Images in Four Athletic Magazines', *Journal of Sport Management*, 18(4): 335–349.

McCombs, M.E. and Shaw, D.L. (1972) 'The Agenda-setting Function of Mass Media', *Public Opinion Quarterly*, 36(2): 176–187.

McCombs, M.E. and Shaw, D.L. (1993) 'The Evolution of Agenda-setting Research: Twenty-five Years in the Marketplace of Ideas', *Journal of Communication*, 43(2): 58–67.

Sabo, D., Jansen, S.C., Tate, D., Duncan, M.C. and Leggett, S. (1995) *The Portrayal of Race, Ethnicity and Nationality in Televised International Athletic Events* (Los Angeles, CA: Amateur Athletic Foundation of Los Angeles).

Sabo, D., Jansen, S.C., Tate, D., Duncan, M.C. and Leggett, S. (1996) 'Televising International Sport: Race, Ethnicity, and Nationalistic Bias', *Journal of Sport and Social Issues*, 20(1): 7–21.

Salwen, M.B. and Wood, N. (1994) 'Depictions of Female Athletes on *Sports Illustrated* Covers, 1957–89', *Journal of Sport Behavior*, 17(2): 98–107.

Sartore, M. and Cunningham, G. (2007) 'Explaining the Under-representation of Women in Leadership Positions of Sport Organizations: A Symbolic Interactionist Perspective', *Quest*, 59: 244–265.

Wensing, E.H. and Bruce, T. (2003) 'Bending the Rules: Media Representations of Gender During an International Sporting Event', *International Review for the Sociology of Sport*, 38(4): 387–396.

Wimmer, R.D. and Dominick, J.R. (2006) *Mass Media Research: An Introduction* (Belmont, CA: Thomson Wadsworth).

Women's Sports Foundation (eds) (2006) *Women in the 2006 Olympic and Paralympic Winter Games: A Women's Sports Foundation Research Report*, http://www.womenssportsfoundation.org/cgi-bin/iowa/issues/disc/article.html?record=1164, retrieved 03.01.2008.

Zaharopoulos, T. (2007) 'The News Framing of the 2004 Olympic Games', *Mass Communication and Society*, 10(2): 235–249.

6
Enhancing Public Sports Facilities: A Representation of the Global Value

Bernard Augé, Arnaud Pedenon and Alexandre Vernhet

1. Introduction

Sports activities, which have long been restricted to specific areas, are today leaving those equipped areas for new zones in town centres or deep in the country, where new activities are being developed. This phenomenon of 'sportivization' of society is the result of the joint effects of the increase of leisure time, the development of hygiene concerns and recreational activities and of the mediatization of physical and sporting activities. However, sports amenities and, more particularly, public facilities are slow to adapt to these evolutions.

In view of the strategic stakes involved in the modernization of public sports facilities and the developments affecting sports activities, local authorities are turning more and more to managerial and marketing techniques "to determine better the needs of the different users, to analyse the local context, and the political stakes related to them, in order to make the right decisions as regards equipping amenities" (Bessy and Hilairet, 2002: 31). Henceforth, the changes in the field of sports activities lead public managers to consider sports facilities as the context of production of a sports service. This change reflects the switch from a mass building policy to satisfy the sports users quantitatively to a qualitative policy of adaptation of the public offer of sports equipment answering the expectations of users. Indeed, in an economy dominated by the users' demand, the performance of the public organizations no longer exclusively depends on the management of production. With the user's satisfaction *a priori* unguaranteed, the latter has a wide choice of products and services at his disposal offering diverse combinations of functionalities enabling to meet his needs. Since then, the user becomes the last place to value the production or the 'servuction' (the contraction of services and production) of the organization (Pociello and Baslé, 1993). The value, at the interface of offer/supply and demand, asserts itself as a centre of development of tools as well as managerial practices. That is why our study aims at grounding an assessment of the performance of the public sports amenities and of their management on this notion of value. This value of public sports amenities appears within an interactionist perspective as an arbitration between the functions of the object and the needs of the user. This share attributed to the subject in the definition of the value of sports amenities makes us wonder about the representation of this value. Therefore this requires us to have access to the mental representations that individuals have of the value of a sports facility.

Our chapter first proposes to reflect on the shaping of the global value as perceived by individuals. It is a matter of identifying the dimensions which affect the global value of a public sports facility. The integration of the two marketing approaches of the value, namely the transactional approach and the relational approach within an integrating model, as developed by Aurier, Evrard and N'Goala (2000), will throw a theoretical light on the components of the global value. From this model it will then be possible to deduct the nature and the components of the value of a sports facility. Secondly, we will explore the mental representations of the main sports actors (the elected town councillors in charge of sport and the town sports service directors) concerning the global value of public sports facilities. To this end, we will organize our study around two average-size local councils. Thus the use of the cognitive approach will allow us to approach the mental representations of the main actors, that is, the structure shaped by beliefs, values and opinions concerning the value of public sports facilities.

2. The global value of sports facilities

2.1. From the consumption value to global value

Studies in marketing research and consumer behaviour concerning value have given rise to two conceptualizations, depending if one adopts the perspective of a sudden purchase (transactional approach) or a lasting relationship (relational approach).

In the beginning, marketing was mainly interested in the study of transactions, in other words, the sudden exchange of values between parties. Drawing on the economic theory of the usage value which suggests that the value of an object comes from its usefulness, the behaviour of the consumer is thus represented as a process of production of usefulness by the allocation of monetary and time resources and as the consequence of perceptions of the different attributes of the object. In a similar way, in marketing, the value perceived is presented as being the result of an arbitration between all the benefits and the costs involved in the transaction, "between the desirable and the attributes of sacrifice" (Gardial et al., 1994: 552). Hence, in this perspective, as shown by Zeitham et al. (1990), the value is seen by consumers as the overall evaluation of the usefulness of the product based on a perception of what is given and received. This approach develops the idea according to which an object would be judged on the basis of its attributes, depending on its capacity to satisfy the aims of the individual. Hence, in this perspective, the user values a sports facility on its ability to satisfy his expectations as regards sports activities. The value is therefore mainly approached as in the transactional perspective as a variable explaining the purchasing behaviour and the choice of a product or service among a choice of alternatives, that is to say, before consuming. However, the works by Gardial et al. (1994) challenge this transactional approach by asking the following question: Does the value remain the same after the experience of consumption or possession? This question also applies to the consumption sports areas where one can wonder if the value of a facility will be the same after several experiences of use.

The relational approach considers the value as the consequence of cumulative experiences of consumption or rather as "a relative preference (comparative, personal, situational) characterising the experience of a subject in interaction with an object" (Holbrook and Corfman, 1985: 45). In this context, the value does not precede but, on the contrary, results from the experience of consumption and/or possession of a product or a service. This no longer simply constitutes the basis of the purchasing decision, but rather represents the consequence of the cumulative experiences of consumption, the sum of the interactions between a person (the demand), the product or service (the offer) and a consumption situation. This approach therefore offers an interactionist vision in so far as the value is seen as neither totally dependent on the subjects, nor totally dependent on the objects. Besides, in this perspective, the context of the consumption experience acts as a determining variable in the process of production of the value. This perspective seems particularly adapted to the study of the value perceived by the users of public sports equipment for several reasons.

First of all, this approach distinguishes three fundamental elements in every consumption experience: the context which in our study of public sports equipment is the product/service, a sports association being considered as a service provider and the user, for example, a practising sportsperson, member of an association. This distinction between these three elements takes on a new and considerable importance in the case of public sports facilities to the extent that it enables us to discern the three actors taking part in the process of co-production of a sports service in such areas. Indeed, the context of practice is very often made available for sports associations by the council, which then takes on the responsibility of the activity in providing a service to the users.

Secondly, the value in this so-called 'transactional approach' comes from the experience of use or of consumption of an object or service. The highly 'experiential' character of the sports activity therefore also justifies the relevance of this approach in the study of the value of sports facilities.

From a literature review, Aurier, Evrard and N'Goala (2000) propose to articulate the two approaches within an integrating model of the global value. The integration of these two approaches in such a model throws a new light on the nature and the components of the value.

According to Aurier, Evrard and N'Goala (2000: 7), "the components of the value of consumption... contribute to form a global value perceived by the individual, this being defined as a ratio of costs to benefits". Generally speaking, one can associate the idea of gain, of general usefulness, of satisfaction of desire or more generally of positive consequences for the individual with the notion of benefit. The concept of cost refers to the sacrifice perceived by the individual or, more generally, to the negative consequences induced by the act of purchasing or consuming. The first approaches of the value tended to reduce the benefits to the practical and functional elements, and the costs to the simple expression of a price. The only elements of benefits and of costs also prevailed in the construction of sports facilities in the 1960s and 1970s. Today, other forms of benefits are to be integrated (notably hedonistic and symbolical) and other types of costs (notably effort and psychological costs) which are linked to the experience of consumption. In every sense, Sheth, Newman and Gross (1991) identify five main types of benefits: functional, social, emotional, epistemological and conditional. For his part, Lai (1995) completes these typologies in suggesting three additional categories: hedonistic, aesthetic and holistic benefits. In return for these different benefits, the costs refer mainly to monetary or temporal resources, to risks and/or to the human energy engaged during the process of evaluation, purchasing and consuming of the product or service.

This literature review leads Aurier, Evrard and N'Goala (2000) to propose a typology of the components of the consumption value based on two criteria:

- On the one hand, the *extrinsic/intrinsic dimension* mainly characterizes the object of the value. Indeed, "the consumer does not only value the product in that it appears to him as a means, an instrument or a mediation in the realisation of his ends which are external to him (for example, quenching his thirst, becoming rich, moving about, showing oneself to advantage, etc.). Intrinsically, the experience of consumption or possession directly produces emotions, pleasure, feelings and contributes, as such, to the formation of the consumer's preference" (ibid.: 5). One also finds this dimension in sports activities to the extent that the sportspeople do not only seek to attain extrinsic ends such as the need for peer esteem. At present, as Bessy and Hilairet (2002) underline, new more personal needs are also expressed by sportspeople for physical and sports activities such as hedonistic needs or even the needs for intra-personal and aesthetic esteem.
- On the other hand, the *orientation towards self/orientation towards others dimension* characterizes above all the individual who cares for increasing his standing. Indeed the value does not proceed exclusively from the quest for benefits as regards oneself; the client or the user as a socialized being also judges experiences and objects of consumption according to others. In the sports field too, sportspeople not only express needs for personal well-being or health. Bessy and Hilairet (2002) also note the expression of needs turned towards integration or social distinction or again towards family and social communication among practising sportspeople.

In crossing the two criteria which are the extrinsic/intrinsic dimension and the orientation towards self/orientation towards others/dimension, Aurier, Evrard and N'Goala (2000) bring to light four families of consumption value (Table 6.1) "This classification is situated... in an interactionist perspective where the value comes from the encounter between the individual and the object, the value being neither a characteristic of the object, nor a characteristic of the individual, but the result of their interaction" (ibid.: 5).

Table 6.1 Global typology of the components of the value

	Extrinsic		Intrinsic	
Oriented towards self	Instrumental value (functional value and knowledge value)	(1)	Hedonistic value	(2)
Oriented towards others	Social value (social link and self-expression)	(3)	Spiritual value	(4)

Source: Aurier, Evrard and N'Goala (2000).

The authors link the four large families of value to the functional theory of attitudes with the aim of linking value judgements to the motivations of the individual. According to this functional approach to attitudes, the individual enhances the products or services whose functions answer one or several needs efficiently. Hence, Aurier, Evrard and N'Goala (2000) reveal four main functions in linking the components of the value of the consumption (see Table 6.1) with the functions of attitude described by Katz and Shapiro (1985).

2.2. The dimensions of the global value of a sports facility

The integration of the two marketing approaches to the value which are the so-called transactional and relational approaches in an integrating model, developed by Aurier, Evrard and N'Goala (2000), will shed a theoretical light. It would thus be possible to deduce the nature of the components of the value of a sports facility.

The *instrumental value* is made up of two dimensions: the functional value and the knowledge value.

The *functional value* of a sports facility rests on the aptitude of the functions offered by it to answer what Bessy and Hilairet (2002) refer to as the 'technological need' of the sportspeople. Indeed, according to the authors, this technological need "is particularly asserted with sportspeople as regards the modern aspect of different facilities and concerned with comfort, safety and efficiency" (ibid.: 55). From a literature review on sports facilities, five dimensions of the functional value of a sports facility were identified: its practical aspect, its comfort, how many can use it, its compliance with standards and its cleanliness. This identification of the value dimensions of a sports facility will enable us to implement the notion required by the methodology followed in this study.

The knowledge value corresponds to the aptitude of a product or service to answer the needs for knowledge and for structuring the environment. This function assigned to sport is founded according to Pociello and Baslé (1993: 127) "on the aim to integrate into schools, sports reputed to be fundamental (generally olympic), which receive a specific pedagogical or didactic treatment, so as to democratise its beneficial effects (health, locomotion, fulfilment of the personality, sociability...)." This is why two dimensions have been identified in the knowledge value of a sports facility: the educational potential and the provision for competitive sports activities.

The *'hedonistic value* or experiential stimulation' (Aurier, Evrard and N'Goala, 2000) was developed in marketing by Holbrook and Hirschman (1982). The hedonistic value of a sports facility rests on its ability to satisfy the hedonistic needs of the sportspeople. According to Pociello and Baslé (1993: 127), "these numerous, hedonistic, informal aspects, are satisfied freely outside the assigned areas, in the country (off-piste or off-limit), and develop according to low constraint organisation modes (that the private sector besides endeavours to produce) on the basis of pleasure and personal achievement". The current distinction process between, on the one hand, public sports facilities available to all but not adapted to each and, on the other hand, business-oriented sports establishments privileging the so-called 'hedonists' but not accessible to all, places local communities in front of the risk of economic and social segmentation of sportspeople. To avoid the creation of 'sociosportive ghettos' (Vigneau, 1998), local authorities must take the new aspirations of sportspeople into account and particularly their hedonistic needs. We have chosen to operate this dimension of the value via three constructs: the play and recreational character, the shaping up and well-being of the population aspect and the relaxation area (relaxation and/getting away from everyday life).

The *social value* is made up of two dimensions: the self-expression function and the social link function. These two components have, according to Aurier, Evrard and N'Goala (2000: 6), an instrumental character since "the product is not consumed here for itself but as an agent promoting communication and social integration".

The self-expression function measures the capacity of the product to project the expression of the self, to play a role as the personality reflection in social communication. Sports practices and consumption also fulfil this function in forming 'real societal' carriers, which are as many distinguishing and valorizing signs as regards 'the other' (Bessy and Hilairet, 2002: 52). Sports facilities supply equipped areas for self-expression via physical and sports activities. Indeed, the sports and practice areas allow "to put yourself forward in front of others and show them your social status" (Desbordes, Ohl and Tribou, 2004: 230). This is why this dimension has been implemented to meet the needs of the methodology by the following item: staging and spectacularization of the practice.

The function of social link corresponds to the product role as an aid to social interaction and to inter-individual exchange. This function commonly attributed to sport is currently characterized by "multiple, flexible and fluctuating social aggregations" (Bessy and Hilairet, 2002: 54). Sports facilities also contribute to this social link function in allowing users to meet and making the confrontation and establishment of human relations possible. However, the purely functional concept of most public sports facilities in France has largely ignored this social dimension of sports facilities. At the moment, modernization projects for public sports facilities are integrating this dimension in envisaging them as real living and meeting areas. This phenomenon is illustrated notably in the public swimming pool renovation projects dating from the 1960s and 1970s, when there was a change from strictly competitive design dominated by the federation standards and the 'Olympic' dimensions, to a 'leisure' design where the friendliness of the site was put forward. For these reasons, we chose to operate this 'social link' dimension of the global value of a sports facility by two items: the pleasure aspect of the facility itself and availability to the largest number of people.

The *symbolic value* is an important dimension of the 'global value of sports facilities' that Vigneau (1998: 56) qualifies as 'sport representation areas'. Although we have left out of our study the facilities used exclusively by high-level performing teams, these facilities are places where sports are presented and more particularly of local teams of all levels, and thus become real showcase areas for the town in question. This "emblematic function of sporting architecture" (Callède, 1984, 2007: 79) confers a symbolic value to certain sports facilities. This has been operated in this study by the following construct: identification factor and symbol of the local authority.

The agreed/granted sacrifice refers to the cost incurred for the individual or, more generally, to the negative consequences incurred by the purchasing and/or consuming act. Beyond the simple economic cost, these days we include the temporal cost, the psychological cost and the physical cost in this notion of agreed sacrifice. This dimension which contributes to the global value of a sports facility has been operated by two items: the fee and the ease of access (space and time). It may appear surprising to have the fee appear as a determining factor for a public sports facility to the extent that access to them is often free (or almost free in that the price never covers the total cost by the user). The fact that access to public sports facilities is free reveals a real pricing policy established by the owning local authorities and is motivated by sporting policies to help the sports movement and to be available to a maximum of people. Thus this policy has a cost for the local community which sets it up and, on the other hand, has consequences on the perception by the users of the value of the facility. As Desbordes, Ohl and Tribou (2004: 340) point out, "it seems that in our consumer society where everything has a price which gives it its value, a free service runs the risk of appearing valueless". In addition, we have chosen to include the ease of access (space and time) in this agreed sacrifice dimension because the location of the facility, parking possibilities or opening times represent constraints for the users; these can generate temporal and/or physical costs.

The perceived global value of a sports facility as an arbitration between the elements of cost (agreed/granted sacrifice) and of benefits (functional, social, hedonistic, symbolic, knowledge) can be represented by Figure 6.1.

The global value of a public sports facility having been explained, it is now time to deal with the mental representation of this perceived value by the main sports facilities management actors: the elected town councillor in charge of sports and the director of the council sports facilities.

3. Towards a cognitive mapping as a tool for the analysis of the global value of a sports facility

The second aim of our research is to deal with the mental representation of the global value of sports facilities of the main sports facilities managers. To do this we have used the method of cognitive mapping to analyse the representations of the referees, that is to say, the structure formed by the beliefs and opinions concerning the value of the sports facilities in establishing causal maps and individual cognitive maps.

3.1. The construction of the cognitive maps

With reference to a number of works (Axelrod, 1976; Eden, 1988; Eden, Ackerman and Trait, 1993; Jenkins, 1994; Langfield-Smith and Wirth, 1992; Laukkanen, 1994; Markoczy, 1994; Markoczy and Goldberg, 1993,

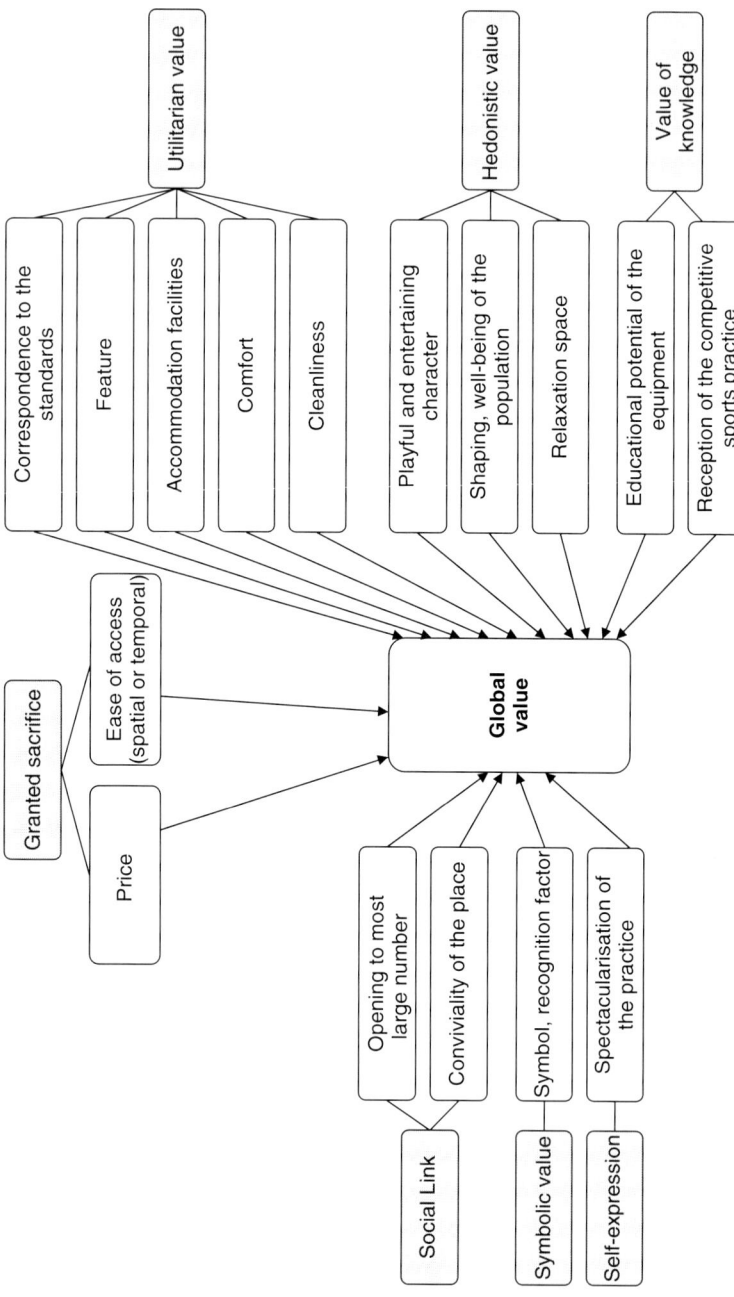

Figure 6.1 The functional model of the value – an application of the value of a public sports facility
Source: Adapted from Aurier, Evrard and N'Goala (2000).

1995; Verstraete, 1996; Weick and Bougon, 1986) we will retain the definition of cognitive maps proposed by Cossette and Audet (1994: 15): "A cognitive map is a graphic representation that the researcher makes of the set of discursive representations stated by a subject from his own cognitive representations, on a particular subject." These authors consider cognitive mapping as the concrete result of a series of operations calling on the representations of the actors concerned; that is, the researcher and the referee. The graphic representation of the cognitive map provides a model at a given time. Once constructed, the map is static whereas the representation is likely to evolve. The cognitive map should be seen, as is the case with photography, as the witness of a past instant. This problematic brings us back to the question of the stability of cognitive maps.

Even though we can assume that the schemas of an individual are likely to change with time and space, Cossette (1994: 122) supports the hypothesis according to which "schemas represented by a cognitive map would be sufficiently stable to constitute a research object which is not 'sliding/elusive' to the point of escaping from the researcher and the subject". Several studies (Argyris and Schön, 1974; Weick and Bougon, 1986) support this hypothesis of the relative stability of personal schemas.

To make up the cognitive maps, we followed the methodological instructions of Markoczy and Goldberg (1993, 1995) which beforehand require the following steps:

- The drafting of a list of pre-established variables of the value of a public sports facility.

    To put this methodology into practice a certain number of variables which have an influential relationship with the value of a public sports facility have to be operated. We have been able to show that the value of a sports facility is made up of numerous components among which we can single out the sources of cost and the sources of benefit. These components of the value of a sports facility have been operated in 16 constructs in all. The distribution of these constructs between the different components of the value is given in Table 6.2.

    The choice of these variables was made from a literature review regarding the management and modernization of public sports facilities. The variables chosen represent the main items quoted in the literature and that we have identified as being potentially a source of value for public sports facilities. These variables were then reallocated to the different components of the global value. For this

Table 6.2 Distribution of the variables between the components of the global value of a sports facility

Granted sacrifice	Utilitarian value	Value of knowledge	Hedonistic value	Social link	Self-expression	Symbolic value	
(n_1) Price	(n_3) Correspondence to the standards	(n_8) Educational potential of the equipment	(n_{10}) Playful and entertaining character	(n_{13}) Conviviality of the place	(n_{15}) Staging, spectacularisation of the practice	(n_{16}) Symbol of the municipality, the recognition factor	V
(n_2) Ease or constraint of access (spatial and temporal)	(n_4) Feature	(n_9) Reception of the competitive sports practice	(n_{11}) Shaping, well-being of the population	(n_{14}) Opening to largest number			A R
	(n_5) Accommodation facilities		(n_{12}) Relaxation space				I A
	(n_6) Comfort						B L
	(n_7) Cleanliness						E S

Constituents of the global value of a sports equipment

reason we can note some heterogeneity in the distribution of the variables between the components of the global value of a public sports facility.
- The selection of a given number of variables by the referees.

  The interviews began by the choice of six or seven variables in the pre-established list. During this phase, the referees were asked to choose from the list of variables those which they considered had the greatest influence on the value of a sports facility.
- The drafting of an association matrix.

  The referees were then asked to assess the influence of each of the variables chosen on the value of a sports facility.

3.2. Sports management actors with a representation of the global value

The method of comparison used in this study to compare cognitive individual or collective maps has been developed by Markoczy and Goldberg (1993, 1995) from the works by Langfield-Smith and Wirth (1992). This technique of comparison measures the distance between two maps. It produces a result comprised between 0 and 1, where 0 means a perfect similarity between two individual cognitive maps and 1 indicates a total difference between the maps.

3.2.1. Comparison between the cognitive maps of the sports service director and an elected town councillor in charge of sports in Town A

The comparison between the association matrixes of the sports service director and that of the elected town councillor presents a relative proximity (distance index 0.36). The analysis of the variables enables us to observe the convergence and divergence points between the two mental representations of the global value of a public sports facility. We thus observe a consensus between these two people to consider tariffs (n_1), accepting competition sportspeople (n_9), the well-being of the population (n_{11}) and availability to the largest possible number of people (n_{14}) as variables having moderate or strong importance on the value of a sports facility.

Both consider that the tariff fixing policy which amounts to free access to most municipal sports facilities constitutes a strong central theme in the sports policy of a town. They also stress the strong link between the tariff fixing policy (n_1) and the local authority desire to democratise access to sports activities (n_{14}), as the comment from one elected town councillor in charge of sports put it: "it's the local council team's wish".

Thus these two variables, and the relation they have with each other, seem to translate a strong central theme in the sports policy of Town A.

Besides, both point to a strong positive influence between the availability to the largest possible number (n_{14}) and the well-being of the population (n_{11}). This is confirmed by the analysis of the central aspect of the cognitive maps. This indicator measures the number of variables exercising an influence on a given variable. Thus we note that the well-being of the population represents the second central variable behind the global value in the two maps envisaged. This signifies that for these two referees, the well-being and shaping up the population constitute an objective of the policy of availability of municipal sports facilities. The calculation of the 'in-degree' of the variable 'well-being of the population' (n_{11}) confirms this since both the cognitive maps of this variable obtain the highest 'in-degree' just after the global value. This indicates that the variable 'the well-being of the population' is the one most strongly influenced by the other variables in both these cognitive maps. Yet we have seen that according to Weick and Bougon (1986), the variables having the highest 'in-degree' in a map are considered as objectives to reach or as consequences. Thus, the calculation of the two indicators which are its central position and the 'in-degree' enables us to note that the well-being of the population constitutes an objective to reach for the availability of sports facilities in Town A.

The elected town councillor generally includes competition sports (n_9) as a factor in the well-being of the population whereas the Director A takes a slightly different stance regarding the virtues of this form of practice which, according to him, "is not necessarily a good thing when it is pushed to the highest level" (interview). Beyond this reserve, he acknowledges the virtues of sensible sporting practice on the health and well-being of the population.

These elements highlight a potential strong central theme in the sports policy of Town A made up of the tracks formed by the maps of Director A, that formed by the maps and by the elected Town Councillor A, by the price-fixing variables (n_1), the availability to the largest possible number (n_{14}), the well-being of the population (n_{11}) and the availability to competition and federation level sports (n_9). The elements of convergence between the cognitive maps of Director A and elected Town Councillor A can be put together as follows (Figure 6.2).

According to Weick and Bougon (1986), the variables having the highest 'out-degree' in a map are considered as explanations of phenomena described in the cognitive map or the means of action on them. Thus the calculation of the 'out-degree' in the two association

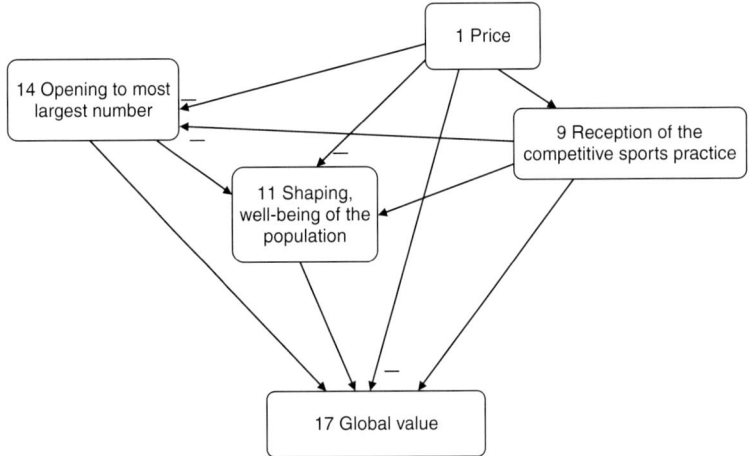

Figure 6.2 Representation of the convergences, Town A

matrices underlines certain differences in the means of action envisaged to reach the objective of the policy of Town A to make sports facilities. Indeed, the variables 'conformity to standards' (n_3) and 'functionality' (n_4) have a higher 'out-degree' in Director A's association matrix than elected Town Councillor A's. These are the 'price, tariff' variables (n_1) and 'availability to competition level sports' (n_9) as well as 'availability to the highest number of people' (n_{14}) which have the highest 'out-degree'.

We note that Director A resorts to functional variables whereas for elected Town Councillor A the value of a facility is essentially influenced by its free availability to the highest number of people. This divergence over the means of action envisaged by the two parties translates quite well the influence that the post they occupy has on their representation of the global value of a public sports facility. Thus it is not surprising to note the importance given by Director A to the functional variables which are the functionality and the conformity to standards when one knows who is in charge of the technical application of the sports policy of Town A. On the other hand, the elected Town Councillor A does not consider the functional variables and maintains a political perspective to explain what influences the value of a sports facility. In fact, she considers that the democratization and the diffusion of practices goes via them being free and all the expectations of the users be satisfied as the quote from her interview reveals: "when you build a facility, your biggest wish is that it be used by a maximum number of people" (interview). To achieve this, the elected Town Councillor A does not envisage the same means of action as Director A. According to her, "for them [the sports facilities of Town A] to be used by a maximum number of people, users have to feel comfortable there, and feel they really want to keep fit in the facility and meet new and different people" (interview).

Thus, if they seem to agree on the objective of a town sports facility, the divergences appear notably in the means envisaged to put this policy into effect. The divergences clearly translate a difference between the representations of the value components of a public sports facility. Moreover, it appears that these representations are strongly influenced by the logics of the actors.

3.2.2. *Comparison between the cognitive maps of the director of the town sports service and the elected town councillor in charge of sport in Town B*

In the same way, the comparison between the association matrices of these two referees enables us to observe a certain distance (distance index: 0.73) between their mental representations of the global value of a sports facility. This difference can be seen most of all in the choice of the explanatory variables: whereas the director of the town sports service (Figure 6.3) retains knowledge value (n_8, n_9) and the value of social link (n_{13}, n_{14}) to explain the value of a sports facility, the elected town councillor seems to give more importance to the functional value (n_3, n_4, n_6) as being of most importance in the value of a sports facility.

The general causality flow of the two maps confirms the difference in the choice of variables. For the director, the variable which explains most strongly the value of a sports facility is it being available to the greatest number of people (n_{14}) with an 'out-degree' of 18, the other explicative variables being in decreasing order: cleanliness (n_7) with an 'out-degree' of 11, competition sports (n_9) with an 'out-degree' of 11 and the pleasantness/friendliness of the premises (n_{13}) with an 'out-degree' of 10. Thus the two variables making up the value of the social link have a greater influence for this referee on the value of a sports facility. For the elected councillor in charge of sports (Figure 6.4), the variables which explain the most strongly the value of a facility are conformity to standards (n_3) with an 'out-degree' of 11, and functionality (n_4) with an 'out-degree' of 10. Thus the two variables having the highest 'out-degrees' belong to the functional value for this referee.

The difference in mental representation of the value of a sports facility by the director of the town sports service and the elected councillor in charge of sports is surprising for two reasons.

Bernard Augé et al. 131

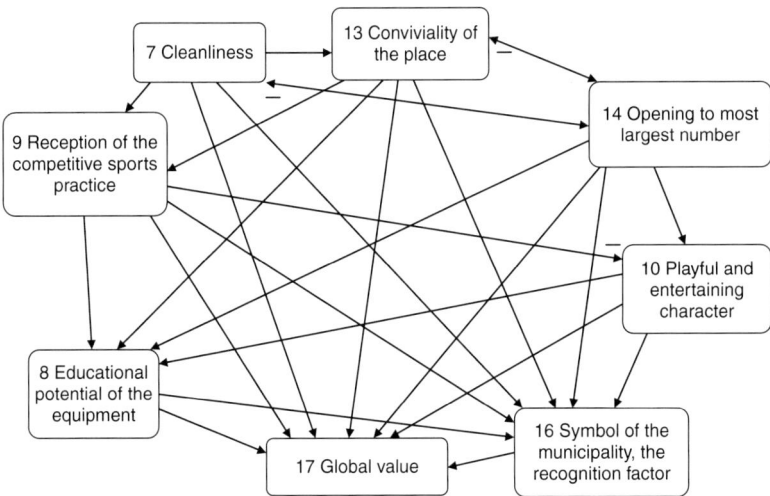

Figure 6.3 Representation of the association matrix of the director of the town sports service in Town B

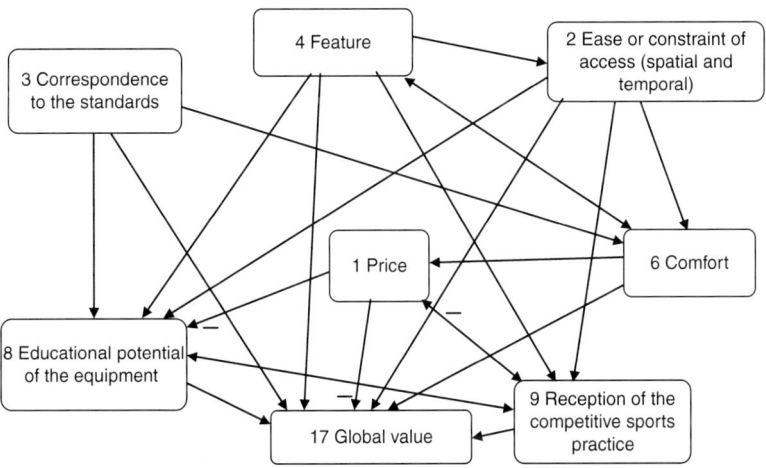

Figure 6.4 Representation of the association matrix of the elected town councillor in charge of sports in Town B

Firstly, it is the large difference between the mental representations which is striking. The distance index between the two maps is as high as 0.73 on a scale of 0–1. Yet the works of Markoczy and Goldberg (1993, 1995) show that the mental representations between the actors of a same organization were most often close with weak distance indexes.

This can be explained by the reaching of a consensus within the same organization, which implies a bringing together of opinions and of the mental representations of the actors of the same organization. Secondly, we expected director to give more importance to the functional value and, on the contrary, the elected councillor to be more sensitive to the social link value. In fact, we observe conflicting results within the same town council.

4. Conclusion

The current evolutions in the field of sporting activities have widened the gap between the public facility offer and the expectations of the end-users. For this reason, we should consider the elements of the dimensions which make up the value that those actors in sporting life are privileging. We have been able to point out in the field of this research a number of significant divergences between the representations of the value of a public sports facility. In addition, we note that the divergences between the mental representations seem to be strongly influenced by the position of the actors in the local sports organization. These locally observed results suggest we can anticipate certain practical stakes as regards the equipping and modernization of public sports facilities. In fact, the adequacy of the functions offered by the equipment to the value dimensions is that players on the local sports depends on the overall value of a sports facility. Also, in a context of scarce public resources, the development of sports facilities is a rich axis of development. Thus, we provide a framework of the modernization of public sports facilities based on the dimensions valued by the actors of the local sport life.

However, from a practical standpoint, this study was part of a process of modernization and rationalization of public service management of sports. This study proposes to develop performance indicators for the management of public sports facilities based on the notion of the overall value. Theoretically, our research aims to contribute to reflection on the concept of value as a principle for evaluating government performance. This approach does not only take into account financial criteria of profitability but also non-financial ones as the value perceived by users (through the level of customer satisfaction) or the various dimensions of the value (that is, the educational value, the social value, the hedonic value and the commercial value as well). Finally, from a methodological point of view, the use of cognitive mapping has helped to understand the representations of the respondents, that is, the structure formed beliefs, values and opinions about the value of public sports facilities. The objective of this research has validated the relevance of this methodology in the organizational framework including the development of individual cognitive maps which are easily comparable. In the future we also need to examine the impact of sustainable development in assessing the global value of sports facilities.

References

Argyris, C. and Schön, D. (1974) *Theory in Practice: Increasing Professional Effectiveness* (San Francisco, CA: Jossey-Bass).
Aurier, P., Evrard, Y. and N'Gola, G. (2000) *Valeur de consommation et valeur globale: une application au cas de la consommation cinématographique*, communication présentée (Montréal: Congrès de l'Association Française du Marketing), 18–20 May.
Axelrod, R. (1976) *Structure of Decision: The Cognitive Maps of Political Elites* (Princeton, NJ: Princeton University Press).
Bessy, O. and Hilairet, D. (2002) *Les espaces sportifs innovants – Tome 1: L'innovation dans les équipements* (Voiron: PUS, Presses universitaires du sport).
Callède, J.P. (1984) *Dynamique spatiale et politiques d'équipement: le cas des équipements culturels et sportifs*, communication présentée (Grenoble: IIe Congrès national de l'Association Française de Sociologie Politique), 25–28 January.
Callède, J.P. (2007) 'Réseaux d'équipements sportifs, innovation culturelle et fonctionnalité urbaine', *Histoire, économie et société*, 26(2): 75–85.
Cossette, P. (1994) *La carte cognitive idiosyncrasique. Etude exploratoire des schèmes personnels de propriétaires-dirigeants de PME*, extrait de *Cartes cognitives et organisations* (Québec: Les presses de l'Université de Laval, éditions Eska).
Cossette, P. and Audet, M. (1994) *Cartes cognitives et organisations* (Québec: Les presses de l'Université de Laval, éditions Eska).
Desbordes, M., Ohl, F. and Tribou, G. (2004) *Marketing du sport*, 3rd edn (Paris: Economica).
Eden, C. (1988) 'Cognitive Mapping: A Review', *European Journal of Operational Research*, 36(1): 1–13.
Eden, C., Ackerman, F. and Trait, A. (1993) 'Comparing Cognitive Maps – Methodological Issues', *communication présentée* (Bruxelles: l'International Workshop on Managerial and Organizational Cognition), 13–14 May.
Gardial, S.F., Clemons, D.S., Woodruff, R.B., Scuman, D.W. and Burns, M.J. (1994) 'Comparing Consumers Recall of Prepurchase and Postpurchase Evaluation Experiences', *Journal of Consumer Research*, 20(4): 548–560.
Holbrook, M.B. and Corfman, K.P. (1985) 'Quality and Value in the Consumption Experience: Phaedrus Rides Again', in J. Jacoby and J.C. Olson (eds), *Perceived Quality: How Consumers View Stores and Merchandise* (Lexington, MA: Lexington Books): 31–57.
Holbrook, M.B. and Hirschman, E.C. (1982) 'The Experiential Aspects of Consumption: Consumer Fantasies, Feelings and Fun', *Journal of Consumer Research*, 9(3): 132–140.

Jenkins, M. (1994) 'Creating and Comparing Strategic Causal Maps: Issues in Mapping Across Multiple Organizations', *communication présentée* (Bruxelles: l'International Workshop on Managerial and Organizational Cognition), 26–27 May.

Katz, M. and Shapiro, C. (1985) 'Networks Externalities, Competition and Compatibility', *American Economic Review*, 75(3): 424–440.

Lai, A.W. (1995) 'Consumer Values, Product Benefits and Customer Value: A Consumption Behavior Approach', in F.R. Kardes and M. Sujan (eds), *Advances in Consumer Research* (Provo, UT: Association for Consumer Research): 381–388.

Langfield-Smith, K. and Wirth, A. (1992) 'Measuring Differences Between Cognitive Maps', *Journal of the Operational Research Society*, 43(12): 1135–1150.

Laukkanen, M. (1994) 'Comparative Cause Mapping of Organizational Cognitions', *Organization Science*, 5(3): 322–343.

Markoczy, L.A. (1994) 'Barriers to Shared Belief: The Role of Strategic Interest, Managerial Characteristics and Organisational Factors', *Dissertation*, Cambridge, University of Cambridge, December.

Markoczy, L.A. and Goldberg, J. (1993) 'A Method for Eliciting and Comparing Causal Maps', *Communication présentée* (Bruxelles: l'International Workshop on Managerial and Organizational Cognition), 13–14 May.

Markoczy, L.A. and Goldberg, J. (1995) 'A Method for Eliciting and Comparing Causal Maps', *Journal of Management*, 21(2): 305–333.

Pociello, C. and Baslé, G. (1993) 'Espaces et équipements sportifs: innovation, prospective et management', in A. Loret (ed.), *Sport et Management – de l'éthique à la pratique* (Paris: Éditions Revue EPS, Dunod): 121–149.

Sheth, J., Newman, B. and Gross, B. (1991) *Consumption Values and Market Choice: Theory and Applications* (Fort Knox, TX: South-Western Publishing).

Verstraete, T. (1996) 'La cartographie cognitive: outil pour une démarche d'essence heuristique d'identification des Facteurs Clés de Succès', *Communication* (Lille: 5ème Conférence Internationale de Management Stratégique), 13–15 May.

Vigneau, F. (1998) *Les espaces du sport* (Paris: Presses Universitaires de France, coll. «Que sais-je»).

Weick, K.E. and Bougon, M.G. (1986) 'Organisations as Cognitive Maps: Charting Ways to Success and Failure', in H.P. Sims, Jr and D.A. Gioia (eds), *The Thinking Organization: Dynamics of Organisational Social Cognition* (San Francisco, CA: Jossey-Bass): 102–135.

Zeitham, L., Valarie, A., Parasuraman, A. and Berry, L.L. (1990) *Delivering Quality Service, Balancing Customer Perceptions and Expectations* (New York: The Free Press).

Part III

Sports Organizations and Governance

7
Sports Organizations, Professionalization and Organizational Conflict: A Review of the Literature

John Schulz

1. Introduction

One of the most common issues facing managers these days is the management of conflict. Managers can spend up to 25 percent of their time dealing with conflict (Burke and Collins, 2000) and whether it is conflict between people, conflict between processes or conflict between people and processes, conflict if ignored can seriously affect an organization's performance. The sporting world and in particular sports organizations are not immune to conflict. Altercations involving high profile players and coaches are commonplace and while less newsworthy, conflict and power plays in local and community sports clubs are common. Sport is a highly emotive area, involving strong-willed, focused individuals with a passion for sport who are usually unwilling to compromise or tolerate alternate perspectives and therefore an inherently conflict-filled environment. The focus of this chapter is to provide an overview of the research examining conflict in sports organizations. The first section provides some background discussion on the changes currently occurring in sports organizations and how these changes have created an environment for conflict. The second section reviews the theoretical and empirical research on conflict in sports organizations.

The delivery of sport in most Western countries relies heavily on local community clubs and associations. There are more than 150,000 local sports clubs in England, Canada and Australia; involving over 8 million coaches, administrators and officials (Cuskelly, Hoye and Auld, 2006).

The majority of these clubs is non-profit and administered by volunteers who are elected from the membership (ibid.). Unlike profit-making organizations, most community sports organizations are established to benefit their members and people closely connected to them (players, participants, coaches, parents and friends) and not to generate an income. These sports organizations operate on a federation system where local clubs send delegates to regional boards, which in turn send representatives to form the national governing body (see Bourke, 2011; Hoye et al., 2006).

In the past few decades these organizations have been subjected to significant changes in their operating environments; such as the professionalization of management and players, increased pressure from commercialization of sport products and services and the internationalization of sport through the media. In most Western countries there has been increased pressure by government and various stakeholder groups to modernize the management (see Cuskelly, Hoye and Auld, 2006; Nichols et al., 2005) and consequently these organizations are changing from simple informal 'kitchen table' type arrangements to formal 'boardroom' and 'executive office' type structures (Kikulis, Slack and Hinings, 1992). In practice, this has meant a rise in the number of formalized policies and procedures covering important aspects of the sports' operation. This also has an effect on recruitment and selection processes, which are now far more formal. Volunteers that were once selected for their commitment are now more likely to be elected because of their business knowledge (Thiabult, Slack and Hinings, 1993).

Hand in hand with these changes has been the increased use and employment of professional staff. "[Volunteers] were so swamped in the day-to-day details of low-level administrative correspondence, with periods of frantic activity for fighting sudden fires or unraveling snarls, that they had no time to think about the direction their sport was heading" (ibid.: 27). Professional staff have been employed to handle the tedious, time-consuming operational tasks. However, in addition to this assistance, professionals have been able to provide new skills, knowledge and expertise to aid the organization. All of these changes have been positively associated with various indicators of effectiveness, such as athlete success and resource acquisition (Kikulis, Slack and Hinings, 1992; Whitson and MacIntosh, 1988) and have therefore been seen as successful.

However, these changes have also had negative effects on sport. In the UK, intervention by the government following various health and active lifestyle concerns and the performance issues associated with the approaching Olympics have placed significant pressures on the volunteers who deliver sport. Clubs now face an array of administrative and legislative procedures, health and safety obligations, goal and target setting and financial reporting mechanisms to receive funding from government and development authorities. This phenomenon is not limited to the UK, for example, Cuskelly, Hoye and Auld (2006: 47) notes that national sports organizations in Australia are required "to achieve greater rates of active participation and increased membership as a condition of funding". Despite the support offered by various governments and sports governing bodies, volunteers have found the processes and procedures overly complex; at times inappropriate for their organization; and in some cases beyond the skill and knowledge level of members (see Harvey et al., 2005; Nichols and Taylor, 2010; Nichols et al., 2005).

Auld (1994, 1997) also noted a tension has sometimes developed between the volunteer management and paid staff in these new structures and in some cases this tension has led to pushing the volunteer sideways or out of the system. The introduction of paid staff also changed the social structure in many organizations. Some volunteers have become unable to determine their new role, where they have expertise, and are uncertain about the division of responsibilities (Auld, 1994). The increased size and complexity of organizations, with greater differentiation and specialization of labor, has sometimes exceeded individuals' comprehension. What all these changes mean is that the interaction between those people who administer sports organizations is fraught with conflict.

2. What is conflict?

Conflict refers to the conditions that arise when individuals or groups feel negatively affected by other people or groups (De Dreu, 1997). It can result from a clash of cultures or personalities, a disagreement over the distribution of funds or resources, imperfect relationships between individuals or emerge because of ineffective communication between groups. Conflict can refer to the situations and processes that give rise to competition or struggles; or the affective responses of individuals caught in these struggles, such as stress and hostility. Conflict can also describe 'cognitive states' – the perception that some other person is acting against their interests or it can refer to the verbal and non-verbal behaviors that emerge.

Traditionally conflict in organizations has been considered harmful and to be avoided; and is often associated with workplace violence. King and King (1990) suggested that one of the negative consequences of conflict was that it interfered with goal accomplishment. Conflict leads to poor communication, a lack of openness and trust between individuals. Conflict can cause tension between individuals and therefore leads to situations when individuals cannot perform together. Although there are individual differences in the ability to tolerate conflict, most people find conflict stressful (Kahn et al., 1964). The need to reduce conflict is a primary determinant of human behavior (Sorrentino and Short, 1986).

However, others view conflict as a natural condition and inevitable within any group. Proponents of this view accept that it cannot be eliminated and can sometimes bring benefits to an organization. Conflict can provide the basis for individual achievement and social progress. Furthermore, conflict can lead to creativity and the development of new ideas and values, as individuals strive to resolve their differences and can facilitate adoption to changing circumstances (Kramer, 1985). For example, in Yoshioka's (1990) study of leisure service providers the amount of uncertainty and ambiguity in a role contributed to administrative flexibility, which paradoxically also served to reduce the conflict.

3. Conflict in sports organizations

As mentioned earlier sports organizations are not immune to conflict but while it has been studied exhaustively within the public and private sectors, when it comes to sport there has been limited research. This creates problems for managers in sport. Firstly, there is an underdeveloped understanding of how the various types of conflict within sports organizations manifest and secondly, there is little knowledge of how conflict is related to other organizational processes. The remainder of this chapter focuses on studies that address these concerns.

The literature on conflict in sports organizations can be grouped into two approaches. The first approach discussed here examines conflict at the organizational level (organizational conflict), the second approach looks at how individuals are affected (role conflict and role ambiguity).

3.1. Organizational conflict in sports organizations

The study of organizational conflict is confusing, because it is characterized by a diversity of definitions and models. In the popular press (see Falconer, 2004) up to six types of organizational conflict are identified. However, in the research literature there is general acceptance of two or three types of organizational conflict. Jehn (1995) suggests there are two types of conflict – relationship and task conflict. Relationship conflict concerns interpersonal animosities and tensions between individuals, and occurs because members of organizations come with a diverse range of backgrounds, perceptions, beliefs, cultures, expectations and behaviors. Task conflict concerns disagreements over the way tasks are carried out or arranged, and revolves around the division of work among individuals in an organization and the coordination of the activities towards the organization's goals and objectives.

Robbins' (2003) model suggests that there are three types of organizational conflict, namely, personal conflict, structural conflict and communication conflict. Personal and structural conflict correspond approximately with Jehn's (1995) relationship and task conflict. However, Robbins believed communication was an additional element. Communication conflict occurs when there are misunderstandings, and 'noise' in communication channels. These problems usually result from differences in competence, which arise from training and experience, and inadequate information dissemination within the organizations.

Numerous studies have investigated the relationship between the different types of organizational conflict and various organizational outcomes (see Medina et al., 2002). Relationship conflict appears to be associated with negative emotional reactions such as anxiety, fear, mistrust and resentment (Jehn, 1995). Furthermore, high levels of relationship conflict can lead to dysfunctions in the organization and raise levels of stress (Friedman et al., 2000). Conversely, task conflict is often perceived as being beneficial as it is related to better quality ideas, increased debate over issues and that it facilitates a more effective use of resources (Jehn, Northcraft and Neale, 1999). The underlying thought appears to be that organizational conflict is beneficial, so long as it functions to encourage the airing of ideas, the examination of different solutions or involvement in decision-making. When conflict escalates to the point where it prevents these processes from occurring, it becomes dysfunctional and reduces performance within the organization (Wall and Nolan, 1986).

Two outcomes that have become particularly important in the study of organizational conflict are job satisfaction and organizational commitment. These are important because they, in turn, have been associated with other positive organizational outcomes. For example, individuals who are more satisfied with their jobs are less likely to leave and less likely to be absent; similarly, individuals who are more committed are more likely to perform well, behave prosocially and less likely to leave (Kirkman and Shapiro, 2001). To date, the mixed results of research have been usually attributed to the type of organization studied and most authors agree that the context and industry of the organization play an important part in the impact of conflict.

One of the first studies into organizational conflict in sports organizations was that by Slack, Berrett and Mistry (1994). Slack and his colleagues studied, through a case study, the impact that the introduction of a rational planning process had on a large national sports organization in Canada. The aim of the planning process was to enhance the effectiveness and efficiency of the organization and improve the organization's future direction. The organization at the beginning of the study was of a simple kitchen table design (see Thiabult, Slack and Hinings, 1993). Power was concentrated with a small group of volunteers who were all located in close proximity. Although the organization had experienced conflict in the past, the concentration of power had allowed the management committee to control the situation. Sport Canada used their funding mechanisms to encourage the organization to undertake a formal planning process. The final outcome of the process led to a relocation of the offices, a formalization of the structure, turnover of staff and a more democratic management with the breakdown of the original volunteer power-base. However, this did not occur without substantial resistance and conflict. Slack, Berrett and Mistry (1994: 324) suggested that most of the "conflict arose structurally out of the task differentiation and resulting interdependence that was initiated through the organizations plan", rather than just interpersonal differences. The changes challenged the ways things had been done in the past, the long-standing values and beliefs. For example, hiring of paid staff "meant pressure to move towards professional not volunteer control of decision making" (ibid.). Although they also noted that it was difficult to disentangle the extent to which the conflict was the result of the new structures, values or beliefs about methods of operation. One of their final comments was about the conflict in the planning process. While the planning attempted to remain a technical process that focused on impersonal aspects of the organization such as the structure or decision-making processes, it was also a relational or interpersonal process that challenged existing patterns of authority and cultural norms.

Following on from the previous study, Amis, Slack and Berrett (1995) provided a more extensive discussion of the structural antecedents of conflict in voluntary sports organizations. Conflict had become for them, a paradox. "On the one hand, [managers] have to design structures and systems to effectively accomplish the work of the organization; on the other hand, these same structures and systems give rise to conflict which can hinder the attainment of organizational goals" (ibid.: 3).

They based their analysis on interviews of members of Canadian sports organizations that had been involved in significant conflict, and from these interviews, four case studies were formed. The first case centered on the relocation of the national office of a Canadian Winter Olympic sport. The change created a variety of problems for the organization. For instance, there was a perceived loss of ownership from those who lived in the previous location. The second case was associated with the firing of a technical director in a Summer Olympic sport. The director had begun a series of changes aimed at increasing grassroots provision, however this put him at odds with local and regional offices who felt he was intruding on their domains. This lead to conflicts regarding roles, authority and decision-making. The third study concerned a small sports organization and its executive director. The director had been in place since the organization was small and the director had not managed to change his management style as the organization grew. He "insisted on making every decision, and proofreading every document" (ibid.: 10). The fourth case concerned the firing/rehiring of the national coach and the interactions of the various parties involved in the incident. The overall findings of the case studies suggested that, similar to the previous article, conflict was not just interpersonal but arose due to the organizational design or structural arrangements. In all of their case studies, structural conflict was directly related to the degree that sub-units within the organizations were differentiated and reliant on each other for success. These differences included spatial differences, technical and administrative differences and volunteer/professional disparities. The researchers also noted two additional issues – resource scarcity and the ambiguity associated with various administrative procedures had the potential to escalate organizational conflict. However, these issues were often problematic as these two processes were frequently out of the control of the organization. Finally, similar to Robbins' (2003) model, Amis, Slack and Berrett (1995) suggested that communication problems contributed to the conflict. Even though communication is often associated with conflict resolution, communication was also used as a tool to escalate the issue.

Verhoeven et al. (1999) are one of the few to study organizational conflict in sports organizations in Europe. Unlike the previous two studies that examined actual conflict situations, they focused on potential sources of conflict. It is argued that conflict is not an isolated event but rather it is a chain of events that slowly escalates and therefore they believed it was important to study potential sources of conflict. They carried out in-depth interviews with 25 volunteers from Flemish sports federations and sports clubs, with the aim to help managers in sport to understand the underlying sources of conflict. Similar to Amis, Slack and Berrett (1995) findings, they reported that sports organizations in Belgium competed for a share of limited resources. Because of the small geographic area, clubs competed for sponsors, members, grants and even players. Additionally they noted that some sports clubs were now competing with leisure activities and other obligations in life. Changes in societal attitudes have also caused problems. They argued that as sport has become more commercialized and formalized people have become less willing to offer their services as volunteers; and furthermore consumers (members and players) have become more demanding and critical of the commercialized service. Verhoeven et al. (1999) also argued that sports organizations because of their resource dependency were caught between the conflicting values and demands of players, sponsors, government and the media. Overall, their findings suggested that the increasing levels of formalization and changes from simple to more formal organizational structures of sport, coupled with the increasing lack of fit between the skills and tasks needed to run a sports organization and the profile of the volunteer, make them unable to operate effectively. They believed the long-term presence of conflict would have a negative effect on the retention of volunteers, without which the current sports infrastructure would collapse. Therefore, they suggested that it was important to develop strategies to manage conflict effectively.

Schulz (2005) studied perceptions of organizational conflict in sports organizations in Australia. He interviewed paid staff and senior volunteers in state level sports organizations. In particular, he explored the differences in opinion between paid and voluntary staff; and whether these differences helped or hindered the management of their organizations. The main outcome of the research was that volunteers and paid staff held quite different and potentially conflicting opinions of three key management concepts. The first difference was in the perception of the mission of the organization. The volunteers in his study suggested that there was a set of ideals that underpinned sports organizations, which were inseparable from the membership. This view was contrasted with the business/service perspective of paid staff. Schulz argued that it was possible that the values of paid staff aligned closer to that of sponsors and government and are likely to lead or direct sports organizations in unfamiliar and maybe undesired directions. The second issue was difference in the volunteers and paid staff members' motivation for involvement in the organization. Volunteers were involved in their spare time and often worked for the organization after hours and on the weekend. In contrast, paid staff preferred to work in conventional times. This lead to various workflow issues – the timelines and scheduling of the different parties were at odds with each other. Thirdly, there were issues over structure, decision-making and expertise of volunteers. Schulz (2005: 51) suggested the differences stemmed from a lack of understanding of "the nature of volunteers and VSOs [Voluntary Sport Organizations] and consequently the adoption of inadequately developed management models and practices".

The previous studies adopted qualitative approaches. A study by Mills and Schulz (2009) of organizational conflict in basketball clubs in the UK adopted the more quantitative approach favored by organizational psychologists. Their study was undertaken in two stages. The first stage used a questionnaire to examine the relationship between organizational conflict (task and relationship) to organizational commitment and job satisfaction. The second stage involved semi-structured interviews following up aspects of the statistical analysis. The results of the study demonstrated that relationship conflict was related negatively to both organizational commitment and satisfaction and task conflict was related to job satisfaction; this was similar to most mainstream management studies. However, what was more surprising to the authors was the absence of a relationship between task conflict and organizational commitment. They argued that individuals in sports organizations saw their commitment to something greater than the club or association (that is, the sport or some idealist notion of sport) and were therefore likely to 'put up' with high levels of dissatisfaction associated with poor management processes, since they where imposed on the club by external or higher authorities such as national governing bodies or government funding agencies.

The last article to be discussed in this section is by Auld, Nichols and Schulz (2010). Similar to the issues raised by the paper by Slack, Berrett and Mistry (1994) earlier, Auld, Nichols and Schulz (2010) suggest that the dominant approach to management in sport is to draw on classical management theory and to adopt a rational systems perspective. This means that decisions about the organization's structure and operating procedures are reached from the rational assessment of the organization's needs, goals and external influences. However, they argue that the use of a rational systems perspective is questionable. Firstly, it is difficult for a sports organization to identify its aims and objectives. Sports organizations comprise a variety of internal (players, relatives, coaches, officials, paid staff and board members) and external (government and other third sector organizations) constituencies who function together to achieve a variety of often-disparate goals. Secondly, rational approaches encourage a clear separation between governance and delivery within the organization. However, in sport this is not the case, a person can be on the management committee, and can also be a player and a coach (Auld and Godbey, 1998; Hoye and Cuskelly, 2003). Thirdly, they argue that rational management structures are designed to function independent of the current role incumbents. Auld, Nichols and Schulz (2010) believe that this is unrealistic in an organization that relies on a core base of committed volunteers. Finally, in rational management the cost of production is passed onto clients who then evaluate the price. However, they argue that this is problematic in organizations that are funded or subsidized by grants and where the price of the service is determined by what clients can afford. The overriding issue for them, however, is that there are few alternative models or frameworks available for sports organizations to follow.

What this collection of studies suggests is that the organizational design, processes and procedures combined with political and economic pressures provide the environment for conflict. However, they also seem to say that the interpersonal relations and interactions between individuals or groups of individuals have a significant effect on the conflict experience as well. It is possible that regardless of the choice of the design of the organization or decision-making processes, interpersonal/relational conflict still occurs.

3.2. Role conflict and role ambiguity in sports organizations

As mentioned earlier, the second approach to conflict in sports organizations focuses on the stress associated with an individual's role within their organizations. There are two aspects to role stress – role conflict and role ambiguity (Kahn et al., 1964). Role conflict occurs when people with different role expectations impose pressures towards different kinds of behavior (Van Sell, Brief and Schuler, 1981). Role ambiguity occurs when individuals have inadequate information available for them to perform their job adequately. Most role conflict and ambiguity can be thought of as an inadequate communication or a lack of agreement or coordination among individuals in an organization. This produces a set of expectations which is incompatible with, or which takes inadequate account of, the needs and abilities of each person. Kahn et al. (1964) stated that the presence of role conflict and ambiguity in an individual's role tends to undermine their relations with others and produces weaker bonds of trust, respect and attraction. Like organizational conflict, role stress has received attention in the literature because of its effect on other organizational processes and it has been demonstrated to be related to satisfaction, decision-making and communication processes (see Jackson, 1983; Schuler, 1979).

Schulz and Auld (2006), using a survey design, examined the perception of role ambiguity by chairpersons and executive directors of state level sports organizations in Queensland, Australia. They were specifically interested in the relationship between role ambiguity, organizational design, communication and tenure. Their first finding was that there was very little difference between chairpersons (who are volunteers) and executive directors in their experiences of role ambiguity and their perception of the organization. Furthermore, they suggested that the real differences might lie between this group and other volunteers in the organization. Secondly, similar to the studies mentioned earlier in Canada and Belgium, they found the organizations to be relatively informal in design. However, contrary to expectations the organic design was associated with low levels of role ambiguity. It is possible that the simple organizational designs allowed the flexibility to respond to new situations, which would be constrained within a more formalized structure (see also Yoshioka, 1990). Their third finding was the relationship between role ambiguity and tenure. The longer a person had been involved in the organization, the lower the level of role ambiguity. This may have occurred because the knowledge to manage the organization was developed over time. However, it can become a problem for organizations. It is possible that strategies used to encourage initial involvement (such as job descriptions) will conflict with strategies adopted for encouraging long-term participation (such as encouraging autonomy and creativity).

Agarwal (1999) found similar results. He argued that formalization may support initial introduction to the organizational operations by reducing role ambiguity. However, it may also prevent individuals from drawing on their expertise and experience thereby creating dilemmas and stress for more experienced staff or volunteers. An earlier report (Schulz, 1998) examined the perception of role conflict in Queensland sports organizations. His study suggested, again contrary to expectations, that the organic design was associated with low levels of conflict. It is possible that the informal communication networks and open blurred boundaries between roles facilitated the clarification of tasks and processes and consequently served to reduce conflict rather than create it.

Sakires, Doherty and Misener (2009) also studied role ambiguity. They were interested in how role ambiguity was related to job satisfaction and organizational commitment. Their sample consisted of 222 volunteer board members and paid staff of provincial sports organizations in Canada. Their results, similar to Schulz and Auld (2006), indicated that sports administrators experienced low levels of role ambiguity and they suggested that role ambiguity was negatively associated with satisfaction. They argue that it was possible that the narrow and simple roles (rather than multiple roles) of volunteers served to reduce ambiguity. Furthermore, their findings suggested that when volunteers and staff have a clear understanding of their role they have a greater sense of attachment and therefore greater commitment. This is particularly important, as commitment is a good predictor of intent to leave and turnover. However, they suggested it might be possible that those people who have a low tolerance for ambiguity leave the organization before they are promoted to more senior roles. One issue that they considered was of particular importance was "that different dimensions of role ambiguity appear to have varying impacts on important individual variables" (Sakires, Doherty and Misener, 2009: 637). For instance, they suggested that formal job descriptions may be useful to reduce ambiguity related to responsibilities but not effective in managing ambiguity associated with performance outcomes. Like Schulz and Auld (2006), they suggested it was important to manage role ambiguity for those who are less experienced but how this may change as they gain experience in the organization is still unclear.

What these three studies suggest is that the effect of role conflict and role ambiguity in sports organizations varies with type of role, the experience and knowledge of the volunteer or staff member and the length involvement. Therefore, similar to the conclusions about organizational conflict, the management of role conflict and role ambiguity is very person and context-specific.

4. What can we conclude from these studies?

The sports organizations described in most of these studies began as simple 'kitchen table' designs with low levels of formalization and relatively centralized decision-making. This design was associated with low levels of role conflict and role ambiguity (see Sakires, Doherty and Misener, 2009; Schulz and Auld, 2006) and high levels of satisfaction and commitment amongst administrators (Sakires, Doherty and Misener, 2009). However, the informal design was also associated with structures that encouraged narrow power-bases controlling the sport (Amis, Slack and Berrett, 1995; Slack, Berrett and Mistry, 1994) and that filtered entry of new personnel into senior roles in the organization (Sakires, Doherty and Misener, 2009; Schulz and Auld, 2006). Both of these conditions led to the emergence of conflict.

As mentioned earlier there have been significant changes in the sport environment due to professionalization of management and players, commercialization of sport and internationalization. These forces have been the impetus for change in sport and the movement towards more modern management practices and formalized bureaucratic structures. However, Amis, Slack and Berrett (1995) noted that in many cases the change itself brought about new conflicts, as the organizations sought to establish new operating procedures and processes. Furthermore, Auld, Nichols and Schulz (2010) (see also Thiel and Mayer, 2009) argue that the new formal structures being adopted by sports organizations may not be appropriate for sports organizations and will lead to future conflict. What has transpired is a (conflict-laden) movement away from one conflict-filled environment to a new environment that is likely to be equally conflictual.

Perhaps the most important lesson to be learnt from the review is that although it is possible to modify the structures and operating procedures to reduce certain forms of conflict, new conflicts emerge. The real issue is how to manage the interactions of individuals within these processes. In the sport literature, only Burke and Collins (2000) approach this topic and while they provide a theoretical discussion of conflict management processes, they only touch the surface of a complex issue. They conclude that "we still know very little about the process of conflict management in sports organizations. How it is dealt with? What kinds of training and development exist... and to what extent does current training provision cater for industry-specific [sport] problems?" (ibid.: 60). What is needed, in the future, is research that explores how sports administrators successfully manage conflict in their organizations.

References

Agarwal, S. (1999) 'Impact of Job Formalization and Administrative Controls on Attitudes of Industrial Salespersons', *Industrial Marketing Management*, 28(4): 359–368.

Amis, J., Slack, T. and Berrett, T. (1995) 'The Structural Antecedents of Conflict in Voluntary Sport Organizations', *Leisure Studies*, 14(1): 1–16.

Auld, C. (1994) 'Changes in Professional and Volunteer Relationships: Implications for Managers in the Leisure Industry', *Australian Journal of Leisure and Recreation*, 4(1): 14–21.

Auld, C. (1997) 'Professionalization of Australian Sport Administration: The Effects on Organizational Decision-making', *European Journal of Sport Management*, 4(2): 17–39.

Auld, C. and Godbey, G. (1998) 'Influence in Canadian National Sport Organizations: Perceptions of Professionals and Volunteers', *Journal of Sport Management*, 12(1): 20–38.

Auld, C., Nichols, G. and Schulz, J. (2010) 'Issues in the Management of Volunteers', in B. Houlihan and M. Green (eds), *Handbook of Sport Development* (London: Routledge): 432–445.

Bourke, A. (2011) 'International and Professional Dimensions of National Governing Bodies: Insights from the Gaelic Athletic Association', in H. Dolles and S. Söderman (eds), *Sport as Business: International, Professional and Commercial Aspects* (Houndsmills, Basingstoke: Palgrave Macmillan): 153–169.

Burke, V. and Collins, D. (2000) 'Dealing with Work Conflict: Issues, Approaches, and Implications for Sport Managers', *European Journal for Sport Management*, 7(1): 44–64.

Cuskelly, G., Hoye, R. and Auld, C. (2006) *Working with Volunteers in Sport: Theory and Practice* (London: Routledge).

De Dreu, C. (1997) 'Productive Conflict: The Importance of Conflict Management and Conflict Issue', in C. De Dreu and E. Van De Vliert (eds), *Using Conflict in Organizations* (London: Sage): 9–22.

Falconer, H. (2004) *IRS Managing Conflict in the Workplace* (London: LexisNexis).

Friedman, R., Tidd, S., Currall, S. and Tsai, J. (2000) 'What Goes Around Comes Around: The Impact of Personal Conflict Style on Work Conflict and Stress', *International Journal of Conflict Management*, 11(1): 32–55.

Harvey, J., Lévesque, M., Donnelly, P., Safai, P., Rose, M. and Pitre, S. (2005) 'Volunteerism: Researching the Capacity of Canadian Sport' *Soumis à Sport Canada*, http://www.crssc.uottawa.ca/final_report_on_volunteerism.pdf, retrieved 16.05.2007.

Hoye, R. and Cuskelly, G. (2003) 'Board-executive Relationships Within Voluntary Sport Organizations', *Sport Management Review*, 6(1): 53–74.

Hoye, R., Smith, A., Westerbeek, H., Stewart, B. and Nicholson, M. (2006) *Sport Management: Principles and Applications* (Oxford: Elsevier).

Jackson, S. (1983) 'Participation in Decision-making as a Strategy for Reducing Job-related Strain', *Journal of Applied Psychology*, 68(1): 3–19.

Jehn, K. (1995) 'A Multimethod Examination of the Benefits and Detriments on Intragroup Conflict', *Administrative Science Quarterly*, 40(2): 256–282.

Jehn, K., Northcraft, G. and Neale, M. (1999) 'Why Differences Make a Difference: A Field Study of Diversity, Conflict and Performance in Workgroups', *Administrative Science Quarterly*, 44(4): 741–763.

Kahn, R., Wolfe, D., Quinn, R., Snoek, J. and Rosenthal, R. (1964) *Organizational Stress: Studies in Role Conflict and Role Ambiguity* (New York: John Wiley).

Kikulis, L., Slack, T. and Hinings, B. (1992)'Institutionally Specific Design Archetypes: A Framework for Understanding Changes in NSOs', *International Review for the Sociology of Sport*, 27(4): 343–367.

King, L. and King, D. (1990) 'Role Conflict and Role Ambiguity: A Critical Assessment of Construct Validity', *Psychological Bulletin*, 107(1): 48–64.

Kirkman, B. and Shapiro, D. (2001) 'The Impact of Cultural Values on Job Satisfaction and Organizational Commitment in Self-managing Work Teams: The Mediating Role of Employee Resistance', *Academy of Management Journal*, 44(3): 557–569.

Kramer, R. (1985) 'Toward a Contingency Model of Board-executive Relations', *Administration in Social Work*, 9(3): 15–33.

Medina, F., Munduate, L., Dorado, M., Martinez, I. and Ciseros, I. (2002) 'Types of Conflict and Personal and Organizational Consequences', Paper and Presentation (Salt Lake City, Park City, UT: Association for Conflict Management Conference), 9–12 June.

Mills, H. and Schulz, J. (2009) 'Exploring the Relationship Between Task Conflict, Relationship Conflict, Organizational Commitment, and Job Satisfaction in Voluntary Sport Organizations in the UK', *Choregia Sport Management International Journal*, 5(1): 5–18.

Nichols, G. and Taylor, P. (2010) 'The Balance of Benefit and Burden? The Impact of Child Protection Legislation on Volunteers in Scottish Sports Clubs', *European Sports Management Quarterly*, 10(1): 31–47.

Nichols, G., Taylor, P., James, M., Garrett, R., Holmes, K., King, L., Gratton, C. and Kokolakakis, T. (2005) 'Pressures on the UK Voluntary Sport Sector', *Voluntas: International Journal of Voluntary and Nonprofit Organizations*, 16(1): 33–50.

Robbins, S. (2003) *Organizational Behavior: International Edition*, 10th edn (Upper Saddle River, NJ: Pearson Prentice Hall).

Sakires, J., Doherty, A. and Misener, K. (2009) 'Role Ambiguity in Voluntary Sport Organizations', *Journal of Sport Management*, 23(3): 615–643.

Schuler, R. (1979) 'A Personal Perception Transactional Model for Organizational Communication-Outcome Relationships', *Organizational Behavior and Human Performance*, 23(3): 268–291.

Schulz, J. (1998) *Perceptions of Role Conflict Amongst Chairpersons and Executive Officers in Queensland State Sporting Organizations*, Paper and Presentation (Griffith University, Gold Coast: Annual Conference of the Sport Management Association of Australia and New Zealand), 26–29 November.

Schulz, J. (2005) 'Paid Staff in Voluntary Sporting Organizations. Do they Help or Hinder?', in G. Nichols and M. Collins (eds), *Volunteers in Sports Clubs* (Eastbourne: Leisure Studies Association): 35–56.

Schulz, J. and Auld, C. (2006) 'Perceptions of Role Ambiguity by Chairpersons and Executive Directors in Queensland Sporting Organizations', *Sport Management Review*, 9(2): 183–202.

Slack, T., Berrett, T. and Mistry, K. (1994) 'Rational Planning Systems as a Source of Organizational Conflict', *International Review for Sociology of Sport*, 29(3): 317–328.

Sorrentino, R. and Short, J. (1986) 'Uncertainty Orientation, Motivation, and Cognition', in R. Sorrentino and E. Higgins (eds), *Handbook of Motivation and Cognition* (New York, NY: Guilford Press): 379–403.

Thiabult, L., Slack, T. and Hinings, B. (1993) 'A Framework for the Analysis of Strategy in Non-profit Sport Organizations', *Journal of Sport Management*, 7(1): 25–43.

Thiel, A. and Mayer, J. (2009) 'Characteristics of Voluntary Sports Clubs Management: A Sociological Perspective', *European Sport Management Quarterly*, 9(1): 81–98.

Van Sell, M., Brief, A. and Schuler, R. (1981) 'Role Conflict and Role Ambiguity: Integration of the Literature and Directions for Future Research', *Human Relations*, 34(1): 43–71.

Verhoeven, M., Laporte, W., De Knop, P., Bollaert, L., Taks, M. and Vincke, J. (1999) 'In Search of Macro-, Meso-, and Micro Sociological Antecedents of Conflict in Voluntary Sports Federations and Clubs with the Flemish Situation as Case Study', *European Journal for Sport Management*, 6(1): 62–77.

Wall, V. and Nolan, L. (1986) 'Perception of Inequality, Satisfaction, and Conflict in Task-oriented Groups', *Human Relations*, 39(11): 1033–1052.

Whitson, D. and MacIntosh, D. (1988) 'The Professionalization of Canadian Amateur Sport Questions of Power and Purpose', *Arena Review*, 12(1): 81–96.

Yoshioka, C. (1990) 'Organizational Motives of Public, Non-profit, and Commercial Leisure Service Agencies', *Journal of Applied Recreation Research*, 15(1): 59–70.

8
International and Professional Dimensions of National Governing Bodies: Insights from the Gaelic Athletic Association

Anne Bourke

1. Introduction

Sport in Ireland is popular and widespread with levels of participation and attendance high. In common with other Western European regions, participation has been dropping due to increased popularity of other activities such as watching television and playing computer games. The more popular team sports in Ireland in terms of participation are soccer, Gaelic football, hurling, rugby union and field hockey, but in terms of attendances, Gaelic football and hurling are by far the more popular. For many sports national governing bodies (NGBs), international activities refer to hosting events and organizing competitions, while professional dimensions refer to overseeing and monitoring player/athlete salaries, contracts and conditions.

This chapter considers the characteristics of sports NGBs and describes their organizational structure and governance arrangements. Using the Gaelic Athletic Association (GAA) as a case study, insights are provided on its mission, vision and organizational structure. Two key policy changes are used to illustrate the international and 'professional' dimensions of the association. The GAA is an All-Ireland body (includes Northern Ireland, part of the United Kingdom) and has an increasing number of units (clubs and county boards) in many parts of the world. The GAA is of interest given its long history, roots, cultural and social dimensions and the extent to which it is, in Houlihan's (1997) view, woven into the fabric of Irish society. Initially, the GAA was established in 1884 to nurture a sense of Irish national identity with the parish club at the heart of the community. Its activities are not confined to sport as the GAA promotes Irish culture – the Irish language, traditional music and dance.

The chapter draws primarily on secondary source materials – official publications, web pages, journal articles and reports and consists of six sections. Following this brief introduction, Section 2 describes the key characteristics of (NGBs), making the distinction between NGBs and global sports organizations. In Section 3, the essence of competitive advantage for sports bodies is considered along with the factors which facilitate or inhibit strategic change. A brief profile of the GAA is provided in Section 4, detailing its origin, history, organizational structure and infrastructure. In Section 5, reference is made to GAA's strategic plans and how they indirectly contributed to policy development and change in two areas: (1) use of Croke Park for other sports and (2) the extension of its international activities. These examples illustrate the factors driving change (internal, external or a combination), and also the complexities within an association with cultural and political roots. The final section provides concluding comments and pointers for further research.

2. Sports organizations and sports governing bodies – key characteristics

Wilson (2000) and Chelladurai (2001) identify the main features of organizations some of which are common to sports bodies. Slack (1997) asserts that sports bodies are not unitary entities but complex processes and sets of socially and historically constituted relationships. He defines a sport organization as "a social entity involved in the sport industry: it is goal directed, with a consciously structured activity system and a relatively identifiable boundary" (ibid.: 5). Depending on their ownership and type (for-profit, not-for-profit) sports organizations aim to achieve strategic objectives such as to increase the number of participants in their sport raise the profile of the game and/or make efficient use of their key resources and capabilities. The attainment of such goals is influenced by political, social, economic and competitive developments both within and outside the organization.

Hoye et al. (2006) group sports organizations according to sector: public, non-profit and professional, noting that these sectors overlap and are interlinked. While many sports organizations now operate in a manner which is similar to that of business firms and enterprises, it is important to recognize the unique features of sport – not-for-profit, performance measures, competitive balance, sports product (game) quality and so on – as they contribute to the challenges and complexities of organizational structure, management and governance. One common feature of many sports organizations and NGBs is their reliance on input by volunteers for both service delivery (stewarding, paramedical support at major venues) and governance (membership of committees, strategic reviews, audits and so on) roles, which in certain cases may hinder change. Some sports organizations (GAA included) were created and maintained on the basis of a set of values or beliefs about the service or opportunities the organization provides, consequently, variation in the interpretation of these values can make governance a difficult issue.

In the business literature, governance definitions emphasize relationships between the board, shareholders and stakeholders (OECD, 1999), while Mallin (2004) highlights governance as the exercise of power and responsibility for corporate entities. Business definitions are used to explain governance in sport, with the interrelated nature of the sporting world and diverse stakeholder groups being noted. Hums and MacLean (2009) mention power and authority, the hierarchical nature of sports bodies and refer to the tiers of governance – local, national and international. Hoye and Cuskelly (2007) summarize the essence of governance in sport as follows: (a) establishing a *direction or overall strategy* to guide the organization and ensuring the organization members have some say in how that strategy is developed and articulated; (b) *controlling the activities* of the organization, its members and staff so that all are acting in the best interest of the organization and working towards an agreed strategic direction; and (c) *regulating behaviour* which entails setting guidelines or policies for individual members or member organizations to follow.

Sports governing bodies come in a variety of different forms (Amis and Slack, 2003) ranging from small, community-based voluntary organizations (soccer, Gaelic football or hockey club that play in local and/or regional leagues) to very large professionally operated organizations (International Olympic Committee (IOC) or the Fédération Internationale de Football Association (FIFA)) which organize and stage large international events. Such bodies are complex and diverse which have an economic aspect, and are mission related with particular operational forms and activities as shown in Table 8.1.

In some sports, separate bodies may exist, based on organizational status (amateur/professional) or gender. In Ireland, the Golfing Union of Ireland and the Irish Ladies Union oversee men's and ladies' golf respectively. Sports governing bodies are normally not-for-profit enterprises, but that is not to suggest that particular ones (professional sports leagues) do not earn profit on their activities. As NGBs have sole

Table 8.1 Sport governing bodies – forms and activities

Forms	Activities
• International Federation	Responsible for one sport or group of sports
• National federation	Similar to international federation but operates within one country
• National olympic committees	Responsible for a country's participation in the Olympic Games
• Multi-sports event organizers	Responsible for organization of a certain event – IOC Olympic Games
• General sports organizations	Responsible for sports-related topics – university sport
• Professional leagues	May be local or international – National Basketball Association (NBA)
• Trusts	Organizations that have control of money to be used to help someone else

Source: Forester (2006).

responsibility for overseeing a specific sport in a country (in conjunction with a regional/world body), they are to all intents and purposes monopolies, which is frequently evident in their behaviour.

There are 60 plus NGBs in Ireland which mainly operate on a part-time, semi-professional basis. While the GAA is referred to as a NGB, it might also be labelled as global sports organization. Forester (2006: 72) defines a global sports organization as a "supreme organ of governance in sport whose authority is global". He details the roles of a global sports organization as usually being a subset of the following: (a) make laws; (b) monitor and coordinate global/national development within a sport; (c) develop and govern athletes within a sport; (d) engage in arbitration and resolution of disputes; (e) organize events and competitions; and (f) maintain relationships with affiliated bodies, governments, regulatory authorities and commercial entities (ibid.). Essentially, NGBs are subsidiaries of global sports organizations as reflected in their roles and functions but little attention has been given to the parenting role and how the 'subsidiary' could/should be developed.

3. Competitive advantage and strategic change in sports bodies/organizations

According to Porter (1985), competitive advantage can only be understood by looking at the many discrete activities (value chain) a firm/organization performs. He asserts that an organization's strategy is to be different from competitors, and that the match between it and the environment should result in a competitive advantage which no other firm can copy. Grant (2010) maintains that an organization's competitive advantage stems from its ability to respond to external environmental changes and the extent to which it prevents imitation of its products/processes using isolating mechanisms (Rumult, 1984).

Two schools of thought exist as to how firms can gain and sustain competitive advantage (Peteraf, 1993; Verdin and Williamson, 1994). One school views competitive advantage primarily as a function of industry attractiveness and the market position of individual firms (Porter, 1980, 1985). This view extols the benefits of the firm looking outwards. The alternative view emphasizes the bundle of resources in the form of tangible and intangible assets on which the firm can draw. This framework (resource-based view) notes that the differences in firm resources will lead to differences in sustainable competitive advantage (Black and Boal, 1994; Connor, 1991; Grant, 1991). To be a source of sustainable competitive advantage, resources must be valuable, rare among the firm's current and potential competitors, imperfectly imitable and there must not be any strategically equivalent substitutes for this resource/skill (Barney, 1991). NGBs like business enterprises decide what they can do better than others (their competitive advantage) drawing on their unique bundle of resources (financial, physical, human) and capabilities. Amis, Slack and Hinnings (2004) note that within the sport industry, increasing commercialization, alterations to geopolitical boundaries, technological advancements and greater competition in the market place have resulted in pronounced changes to many organizations, often over very short periods of time.

Hums and MacLean (2009) note that changes in sport organizations often stem from three sources: (a) events occurring within the organization; (b) factors arising outside the organization; and (c) an interaction of external and internal factors. Strategic change has been defined in different ways – change in a single, specific strategic dimension (product, geographic, diversification or R&D investment intensity) to overall change in a firm's pattern in multiple key strategic dimensions. Zhang and Rajagopalan (2010: 335) conceptualize strategic change "as the variation over time in a firm's pattern of resource allocation in key strategic dimensions that goes beyond industry-wide changes in these dimensions". While change impacts on organization performance, 'high level' change can be disruptive rather than adaptive, and a response often demands new capabilities and new resources. Chapman (2002), drawing on Watzlawick, Weakland and Fisch (1974), considers levels of change: 'first order' and 'second order' while Ford and Backoff (1988) equate 'second order' change to transformational change which reflects a movement to a different plane of understanding. Transformational change requires a basic shift in attitudes, beliefs and cultural values or "a redefinition of the relevant psychological space" (Golembiewski, 1979: 413). Chelladurai (2001) notes the impact of the external environment on organizational change and maintains that individuals in sports organizations must be aware of what is happening in the external environment and adapt accordingly.

There are many barriers to organizational change such as location, tradition, success, failure, technology, vested interests and management systems and bureaucracy. According to Pettinger (2004), behavioural barriers to change include – 'it cannot be done', 'there is no alternative', lack of clarity, fear and anxiety and perfection. Resistance to change frequently emerges in the form of power struggles and political contests at the top of an organization, as managers strive to influence decision-making to protect and enhance their positions (Hill and Jones, 1995). Amis, Slack and Hinnings (2004) aver that leadership can enable or constrain change, while Gill (2003) advocates that developing a culture of sustainable shared values that supports the vision and strategy for change, and motivates and inspires those affected or involved, is needed to implement successful change. In many cases organizational communication strategies are crucial in managing or reducing resistance to change. There is no shortage of prescriptions for organizational change processes and management in the literature, nevertheless the forces and factors driving change in every situation/context is different and this needs to be considered.

4. Profile of the Gaelic Athletic Association

The Gaelic Athletic Association (GAA) was established in 1884 to promote athletics and to revive the game of hurling (Garnham, 1999). Bairner and Walker (2001) maintain that the express aim of the GAA was to divert Irish nationalists from British pastimes. When Gaelic football was codified in 1886, it was played on Sundays and was accompanied by cultural activities – Irish dancing and poetry recitals.[1] An important GAA principle is the Parish Rule, that is, one club per parish, which is located in a particular geographic area with its playing personnel from that area.[2] This club arrangement tends to foster local community spirit and over the years the All-Ireland Club Championship has deepened that spirit – each year the final is played in Croke Park on St Patrick's Day (17th March).

The GAA has a well-developed playing infrastructure throughout the country with each club owning its own playing pitch, training, changing and social facilities. It is estimated that the value of GAA assets (grounds and clubs) is approximately €2.4 billion. At provincial level, several stadia (capacity in brackets) have been redeveloped – Semple Stadium, Thurles (55,000); Gaelic Grounds, Limerick (50,000); Pairc Ui Chaoimh, Cork (43,000) and the Association's major redevelopment project (Croke Park, Dublin – capacity 82,300) was completed in 2002, largely with its own funding. Plans are in place to upgrade facilities and develop Centers of Excellence (15) throughout the country. These Centers are designed to serve the needs of County teams, Development Squads, Clubs, Schools and Colleges. The GAA football and hurling figuration (Dunning, 1999) consists of many individuals (especially in the local parish and club) and groups who perform the unglamorous tasks (marking the pitches, opening dressing rooms, making tea at half time etc.), players managers, coaches and administrators (schools, club, county, provincial levels), Gaelic players Association, referees, supporters/fans, sponsors, media, suppliers and government.

The GAA *Official Guide* contains the Constitution and Rules of the Association as approved by the most recent Annual Congress. The GAA jealously guards its 'amateur status' (Rule 1.10; GAA, *Official Guide*, 2010b: 7) among players, managers and coaching personnel (De Burca, 1999). While this excludes 'pay for play', in recent times it no longer holds as the demands of players' fitness and skills levels along with supporters' expectations have led to the emergence of 'career managers' and players and coaching personnel are given travel, insurance and equipment expenses. Devine and Devine (2005) describe Gaelic football as fast-paced, skilled, high scoring games that any sports fan will respond to. Moran (2004) refers to hurling as a type of aerial hockey played in Ireland which is regarded as one of the fastest games in the world. Both hurling and Gaelic football fans are passionate about their sport at club and elite level (county) which makes the atmosphere very intense during games. The GAA's main competitions are played on a county (includes Northern Ireland) and club basis. During 2009, 1.9 million people attended inter-county and All-Ireland club games, an increase of 2 per cent on 2008 (GAA, *Annual Report*, 2010a).

Cronin (1999) notes that what is fascinating about the GAA as a sporting body is the use of the lessons it learned from British sport to become an effective medium. According to Devine and Devine (2005), the GAA is not just a form of recreation but an expression of the people and their culture. These authors observe that while the sport is still 'amateur', it is the most professionally organized in Ireland. O'Thuathaigh (2009) reviewed the GAA's contribution to Irish society, highlighting its impressive record of adaptation to change – social, economic, financial and cultural. He maintains that the legendary 'purists' have not inhibited GAA leaders from engaging fully with the world of business and finance, in ground development (Croke Park and other stadia), corporate sponsorship, media relations and broadcasting rights, team sponsorship and flexible scheduling, all of which have provided testing issues for a voluntary, community-centred organization.

According to Rule 1.9 (GAA, *Official Guide*, 2010b: 7), the GAA is a democratic organization comprising the following units: clubs, county committees, provincial councils, the Central Council and the Annual Congress. There are a number of full-time professional employees including the director general (Árd Stiurheoir), the president (voluntary position for three-year term), finance officer, games development officer and regional development personnel. To facilitate the attainment of its aims and objectives, the GAA has 32 subunits – committees, sub-committees, work groups and task forces[3] which report to the Central Council. The management committee equates to the board of directors and in recent years, external non-executive directors have been appointed for a three-year term of office. The Annual Congress (GAA Annual General Meeting) takes place before 1st May and its role is (i) to consider the reports and audited accounts of the Central Council and subsidiary councils; (ii) to consider motions and to enact rules or amend or rescind rules; (iii) to elect a president (by secret ballot) and two representatives of Congress to the Central Council; (iv) to appoint the secretary of the Disputes Resolution Authority on the nomination of the Central Council; and (v) to formulate association policy in broad outline (Rule 3.46, GAA, *Official Guide*, 2010b: 42). The Congress is the only forum at which changes can be made to the *Official Guide*.

The GAA has 800,000 members attached to clubs in Ireland and overseas (detailed later in this chapter). Over the years, the GAA has maintained its strong links with Ireland's schools (primary and secondary) and higher education institutions. The Games Development Unit oversees the provision of learning support for teachers and there is now a separate unit which coordinates matters for the higher education sector. During 2009, just over €10.1 million was invested in games development (coaching, coach education, summer camps, player development squads) in schools, clubs and counties in 2009 (GAA, *Annual Report*, 2010a).

5. The Gaelic Athletic Association – managing and organizing change

The GAA is Ireland's largest sporting organization and in seeking to preserve Irish games it was consistently 'exclusivist' in its policies collectively known as the 'ban' (Fulton and Bairner, 2007). Its collective identity was always evident and while the organization was well run, there was always a suspicion among many members in relation to 'professionalism' and 'things British'. During the 1970s and onwards, much attention focused on the divided community in Northern Ireland, with many debates (media, written) in relation to grounds for this division, that is, religious, social, political and economic. Ultimately, following much discussion and reflection by various parties (social commentators, politicians, members of county committees and provincial councils), and with the approval (vigorously contested at times) of the Annual Congress the GAA ban on 'foreign' games[4] was rescinded in 1971, while the ban (Rule 21) on the admission of members of the British security forces (Police Service of Northern Ireland) was removed in 2005.

Over the years, presidents of the Association have strived to reform the operations and activities of the GAA. Two reviews are worth noting: (a) the McNamee Review which was set up in 1969 and reported in 1971 and (b) the Strategic Review set up in 2000 and reported in 2002. The McNamee Review provided a 'blueprint' that guided the GAA through the latter part of the last century, while the Strategic Review was more in-depth, with very detailed terms of reference. Members of the Strategic Review Committee (SRC) were internal and external to the Association and were given a remit to review the role and function of the GAA and recommend strategic direction, policies and functions appropriate for the twenty-first century.[5] Governance and management practice were reviewed along with operating and administrative structures. The main drivers of the SRC included the changing profile of sport in Ireland (and elsewhere), the opportunities for and expectations of players and spectators, the increasing economic prosperity in Ireland, changes in technology and the changing political situation in Northern Ireland. The SRC identified the GAA's unique features (*competitive advantage*) as the continued (a) voluntary efforts and commitment of thousands of people in the games administration, playing and management and (b) its amateur status. While all SRC recommendations were not implemented, changes were introduced in relation to the operation and management of various units, subunits and personnel.

The outcomes of the SRC 2002 provided the basis of the recently published GAA, *Strategic Vision and Action Plan* (*2009–2015*). This document sets out the GAA response to key changes in Ireland (economic, demographic, education, health and well-being, community and volunteering) and its plans for future development. In formulating its Strategic Vision and Action Plan, input from more than 8,000 members (volunteer administrators, players, non-traditional GAA communities, club; county and college coaches, team managers, referees; GAA staff, schools and the media) was gathered (GAA, 2009). The GAA values, that is, community identity, amateur status, inclusiveness, respect, player welfare and teamwork are restated and its mission rearticulated as follows: "the GAA is a community based volunteer organization promoting Gaelic Games, culture and lifelong participation."[6] In addition, 11 key issues to be addressed are identified with milestones and targets agreed for the next five-year period. As noted previously, change in sports organizations can stem from various sources (Hums and MacLean, 2009) and the change of use of Croke Park clearly illustrates this, and the potential for major division within the organization. The second policy change refers to the overseas units and their impact on the organization – resources and coordination capabilities.

5.1. Use of Croke Park

Croke Park is not just a sporting venue; it is the single most important asset of the GAA. It has been redeveloped into a modern stadium between 1992 and 2005 at a cost of €260 million mainly funded by internal sources apart from government funding of €63.8 million. Over the years, Croke Park has emerged, as it has in the past, as a space in and through which Irish national identities are reproduced. Since its formation, the GAA has always presented itself as a sporting and cultural organization dedicated to the promotion of a distinctively Irish national identity (Fulton and Bairner, 2007). On 21st November 1920 (later known as 'Bloody Sunday'), 12 spectators and a player were killed and 50 spectators injured by British forces during a football match in Croke Park. This incident bore testimony in the minds of many people of the GAA's history and nationalist credentials. Rule 42 (now Rule 5.1, GAA, *Official Guide*, 2010b) governed the use of GAA assets and stated that playing rugby and soccer was banned on GAA grounds and more particularly in Croke Park. As Rule 42 (now Rule 5.1, ibid.: 27) stipulated that "all property (including grounds, clubhouses, halls, dressing rooms, handball alleys) owned or controlled by units of the association shall be used for the purpose of or in connection with the playing of games controlled by the association",[7] this posed a dilemma both internally and externally. With the planned redevelopment of Lansdowne Road (home to Irish rugby and soccer internationals), the merits of the GAA Rule 42 (now Rule 5.1) were seriously questioned in and outside the Association. The Annual Congress is the main policy-making body, and to amend this rule, a motion needed to be approved by Congress.

What might seem to be a simple decision for another sports organization regarding the use of its facilities turned out to be a highly contentious and contested matter. Certain GAA members took the view that the Association had invested much in its infrastructure, and this should not be handed over to competing sports bodies for their international activities. Similarly, former presidents of the Association were criticized for their role in reviewing the particular motion. Much of the resistance to change came from delegates representing the counties in Northern Ireland, which is hardly surprising in light of political developments over the years. One former player (J.J. Barrett) withdrew his father's All-Ireland medals from the GAA Museum in protest – he promised to return them when the arrangement ends! Barrett's main objection stemmed from the possible playing and singing of the English Anthem ('God Save the Queen') at Croke Park. Many politicians, media commentators and members of the Irish public engaged in the debate and the motion to open Croke Park to rugby and soccer was ultimately voted on (secret ballot) and approved by Annual Congress in 2005. Rule 42 (now Rule 5.1) was amended, but not abolished. Opposition to the change stemmed as much from 'group think' and the fact that the stadium is owned by an association which is rooted in a traditional nationalist past. The role of the then President of the GAA (Sean Kelly) was crucial as he set out to seek this rule change and considered its approval an important milestone of his reign.

The Croke Park 'arrangement' for soccer and rugby ended in March 2010 and from the GAA perspective yielded a massive income during the three-year period (February 2007 to March 2010) returning a clear profit of €36 million (Breheny, 2010). The loss in extra rent will pose a major challenge for the GAA in the future, as detailed by the current president when releasing the annual accounts for 2009 – the GAA posted an operating surplus of €24.7 million.

5.2. GAA international activities

In Ireland, elite players in other sports – soccer, rugby union, golf, tennis – have many opportunities to play and compete at international level, but for GAA players this is confined to participating in Exhibition games overseas, and in the International Rules Competition. Healy (1998) describes the international dimension of Gaelic Games as International Rules and shinty. The experiment with Australian Rules dates back to 1967 and amounted to a compromise game (new game) based on the similarities between the two codes – Gaelic football and Australian football. During the 1980s, international games were organized by the two bodies (GAA and AFL) and the first series was played in 1984 (GAA centenary year). At that stage, these games were sometimes violent affairs and in 2006 were temporarily suspended due to player indiscipline. Dunne (2009: 186) describes the 2008 version which was played in Australia as "exciting and enjoyed by the 42,823 spectators". An unintended consequence of the establishment of the International Rules Competition is the recruitment of Irish Gaelic football players by a number of Australian national football league clubs. Due to the scarcity of international opportunities for Irish players, there is little resentment at their turning to the professional game in Australia, but there has been much criticism of the recruitment strategies used by the Australian clubs and the timing of their recruitment drive – the beginning of the All-Ireland Championships. The Scottish game of shinty is several hundred years old (Healy, 1998). It is a form of hurling and the Irish version (*camanacht*) played in Ireland in the past died out and gave way to the current form of hurling. Shinty is ground hurling and the compromise game used for international purposes is called hurling-shinty. In this arrangement, only the goal keeper can handle the ball – this fact greatly restricts the ability of the Irish players.

The SRC recommended that GAA overseas units be brought more into the Association's mainstream activities and be given more support for games development and promotion in schools. From a playing perspective, the extent of assimilation which has occurred is evidenced by the inclusion of London and New York teams in the early rounds of major competitions – the All-Ireland Championships and the National League. Increased support for games development has been allocated to overseas units, but representation on the Central Council for the newer units (Asian County Board) has yet to be resolved. The GAA *Official Guide* (Rule 3.46, GAA, *Official Guide*, 2010b: 42) specifies that the

Central Council shall consist of particular representation (voting and non-voting) which includes four representatives from outside Ireland. Currently, these are from Britain, the London County Committee, the North American Board, the New York Board.

Until relatively recently, documentary evidence in relation to GAA clubs overseas were scarce. Many clubs had web pages but information pertaining to club personnel, club structure and organizational arrangements was fragmented. The recently published GAA *Overseas Guide* provides details of county boards in seven regions – Britain, Europe, Asia, Australasia, New York, North America and Canada, along with key information related to overseas clubs – location, key personnel, teams, competitions and so on. There is now an overseas portal on the official GAA web page. Dunne (2009) outlines recent developments in GAA clubs overseas and reports on various competitions such as the All China Games and Australasian Games. He is intrigued that something so intrinsically Irish as the GAA could prosper overseas. It is interesting to note that the number of GAA clubs overseas which are located in 41 countries has increased from 250 in 2002 to 398 in 2009.[8]

The Asian County Board actively promotes GAA activities through various events and competitions. Its Asian Gaelic Games (regional championships) commenced in Manila in 1995 and the most recent one took place in Bangkok (16–18 October 2009). These championships are not just a sporting event (they attracted 500 players and 40 teams from 16 countries) they are a celebration of Irish sport, business and culture success. The event commenced with an Asia Pacific Ireland Business Forum (a network event) with keynote speakers from the region and Ireland. The competitive games were played on Saturday and Sunday and were sponsored by various firms including the Tourism Authority of Thailand, Guinness, Enterprise Ireland, Etihad and the Kerry Group. With the financial support provided for these games, the Asian County Board was able to donate funds to three local designated charities.

The GAA has appointed regional development officers to promote and develop the game in overseas locations. In addition, for players who opt to go to the United States, Canada or Australia, Rule 6.13 (GAA, *Official Guide*, 2010b: 67) details the arrangements and requirements for weekend authorization to play with an overseas club. It is widely known that overseas club personnel pay particular attention to newly arrived emigrants and facilitate them in settling in by continuing their participation in GAA games and events.

6. Concluding comments and pointers for further research

This chapter focuses on Ireland's leading sports NGB, identifies its key characteristics and the basis of its competitive advantage – availability and access to resources (personnel, financial), the volunteer input into games administration and its 'amateur status' as players are not paid to play in competitions. It is usual for NGBs to operate within national boundaries but the GAA is different in that it has internationalized with almost 400 units established in 41 countries. The Irish Diaspora drives the GAA's international dimension to a certain extent, and in recent years is getting increased financial, management and personnel support. Participation in international competition is limited to the Australian International Rules Competition for GAA players, and the unintended consequences of this (player recruitment to the Australian professional game) require more effective communication between representatives from both organizations.

Unlike other sports NGBs in Ireland, the GAA engaged in strategic planning many years ago (late 1960s), and while changes occurred on an incremental basis, the Association managed to retain its core values, and yet embrace aspects of the world of business and other agencies, to ensure that its infrastructure was redeveped and enhanced, and that the status and popularity of its games and cultural activities were increased. The Croke Park dilemma was driven partially by external political and sporting forces, that is, the redevelopment of Lansdowne Road for rugby and soccer, and provides examples of behavioural barriers to change (Pettinger, 2004). The issue forced many GAA members to engage in some soul searching, taking into consideration the changed sports environment given recent commercial and professional developments. Many commentators contend that the then GAA president provided the strategic leadership required, but as with some democratic organizations the mechanism for getting approval demanded patience, informed debate and took time and energy. Opening up Croke Park to rugby and soccer internationals was financially beneficial for the GAA, and it has jolted certain members from their 'exclusivist' position to recognize that all sports have a role in Irish life which need to be accommodated. It could be concluded that GAA policy change (re. Croke Park) is more of a 'first order' change rather than being 'transformational', that is, a redefinition of the relevant psychological space (Golembiewski, 1979).

Sports bodies contribute to economic, social and political development within an area/region. To maintain a leading position, the focus must be on the sports market, its players, its future development, bearing in mind the roles and responsibilities of key stakeholders. In addition, special attention needs to be paid to the interests of the different organizational subunits (cultural and sporting, local and overseas), the distribution of power within the organization (particularly the role of the clubs) and the capacity for change. The GAA is a complex entity with international and professional dimensions, but the latter emerges more at the organizational level rather than on the playing fields. Unusually for an Irish entity (cultural, political, sporting) there has never been a 'real split' within the GAA, and the organization's capability to manage the Rule 42 question (now Rule 5.1, GAA, *Official Guide*, 2010b) suggests that it possessed strategic leadership traits in 2005. These traits will be needed to progress the organization's mission, vision and values for the next decade. Further research is needed on the strategic role of the GAA's overseas units (clubs), and their reliance (or otherwise) on the Irish Diaspora for future development and growth.

Notes

1. Sunday soccer continues to be difficult for certain sections of the Northern Ireland population.
2. In certain cases, for example, universities, the club will represent an organization/institution and will draw its players from members of the organization.
3. A complete list of committees and so on, their membership and terms of reference covering the three-year period is provided on the official web page http://www.gaa.ie, retrieved 20.09.2010.
4. 'Foreign' in this context refers to games emanating from England and include soccer, rugby, cricket and hockey.
5. http://www.gaa.ie, retrieved 20.09.2010.
6. http://www.gaa.ie/content/documents/publications/strategic_plans/GAA_Strategic_Vision_and_Action_Plan_2009_2015_100110235634.pdf, retrieved 22.09.2010.
7. http://www.gaa.ie/content/documents/publications/official_guides/Official_Guide_2010_Part1.pdf, retrieved 22.09.2010.
8. http://www.gaa.ie, retrieved 20.09.2010.

References

Amis, J. and Slack, T. (2003) 'Analyzing Sports Organizations: Theory and Practice', in B. Houlihan (ed.), *Sport and Society: A Student Introduction* (London: Sage): 201–217.
Amis, J., Slack, T. and Hinnings, C.R. (2004) 'Strategic Change and the Role of Interests, Power and Organizational Capacity', *Journal of Sport Management*, 18(1): 158–198.

Bairner, A. and Walker, G. (2001) 'Football and Society in Northern Ireland: Linfield Football Club and the Case of Gerry Morgan', *Soccer and Society*, 2(1): 81–98.

Barney, J. (1991) 'Firm Resources and Sustainable Competitive Advantage', *Journal of Management*, 17(1): 99–120.

Black, J.A. and Boal, K.B. (1994) 'Strategic Resources: Traits, Configurations and Paths to Sustainable Competitive Advantage', *Strategic Management Journal*, 15(1): 131–148.

Breheny, M. (2010) 'Its Been Emotional', *Irish Independent* (01.02.2010), http://www.irishindependent.ie, retrieved 15.02.2010.

Chapman, J. (2002) 'A Framework for Transformational Change in Organizations', *Leadership and Organizational Development Journal*, 23(1/2): 16–25.

Chelladurai, P. (2001) *Managing Organizations for Sport and Physical Activity: A Systems Perspective* (Scottsdale, AZ: Holcomb Hathaway).

Connor, K.R. (1991) 'A Historical Comparison of Resource Based Theory and Five Schools of Thought Within Industrial Organization Economics: Do We Have a New Theory of the Firm?', *Journal of Management*, 17(1): 121–154.

Cronin, M. (1999) *Sport and Nationalism in Ireland* (Dublin: Four Courts Press).

De Burca, M. (1999) *The GAA: A History*, 2nd edn (Dublin: Gill and Macmillan).

Devine, A. and Devine, F. (2005) 'Sports Tourism: Marketing Ireland's Best Kept Secret – The Gaelic Athletic Association', *Irish Journal of Management*, 26(2): 7–32.

Dunne, A. (2009) *Around the World in GAA Days* (Edinburgh: Mainstream Publishing).

Dunning, E. (1999) *Sport Matters: Sociological Studies of Sport, Violence and Civilization* (London: Routledge).

Ford, J. and Backoff, R.H. (1988) 'Organizational Change In and Out of the Dualities and Paradox', in R.E. Quinn and K.S. Cameron (eds), *Paradox and Transformation: Towards a Theory of Change in Organization and Management* (Cambridge, MA: Ballinger): 81–121.

Forester, J. (2006) 'Global Sports Organisations and Their Governance', *Corporate Governance*, 6(1): 72–83.

Fulton, G. and Bairner, A. (2007) 'Sport, Space and National Identity in Ireland: The GAA, Croke Park and Rule 42', *Space and Polity*, 11(1): 55–74.

Gaelic Athletic Association (2009) *Strategic Vision and Action Plan 2010–2015* (Dublin: GAA).

Gaelic Athletic Association (2010a) *Annual Report* (Dublin: GAA).

Gaelic Athletic Association (2010b) *Official Guide – Part 1* (Dublin: GAA).

Garnham, N. (1999) *The Origins and Development of Football in Ireland* (Belfast: Ulster Historical Foundation).

Gill, R. (2003) 'Change Management or Change Leadership?', *Journal of Change Management*, 3(4): 307–318.

Golembiewski, R.T. (1979) *Approaches to Planned Change* (New York, NY: Marcel Dekker).

Grant, R.M. (1991) 'The Resource Based Theory of Competitive Advantage – Implications for Strategy Formulation', *California Management Review*, 33(3): 119–135.

Grant, R.M. (2010) *Contemporary Strategy Analysis*, 7th edn (Chichester: John Wiley & Sons).

Healy, P. (1998) *Gaelic Games and the Gaelic Athletic Association* (Dublin: Mercier Press).
Hill, C. and Jones, G. (1995) *Strategic Management Theory: An Integrated Approach*, 3rd edn (Boston, MA: Houghton Mifflin).
Houlihan, B. (1997) *Sport Policy and Politics: A Comparative Analysis* (London: Routledge).
Hoye, R. and Cuskelly, G. (2007) *Sport Governance* (Oxford: Elsevier Butterworth-Heinemann).
Hoye, R., Smith, A., Westerbeek, H., Stewart, B. and Nicholson, M. (2006) *Sport Management: Principles and Applications* (Burlington, MA: Elsevier Butterworth-Heinemann).
Hums, M. and MacLean, J. (2009) *Governance and Policy Development in Sport Organizations*, 2nd edn (Scottsdale, AR: Holcomb Hathaway).
Mallin, C. (2004) *Corporate Governance* (Oxford: Oxford University Press).
Moran, A. (2004) *Sport and Exercise Psychology: A Critical Introduction* (Hove: Routledge).
OECD (1999) *Principles of Corporate Governance* (Paris: OECD).
O'Thuathaigh, G. (2009) 'The GAA as a Force in Irish Society: An Overview', in M. Cronin, W. Murphy and P. Rouse (eds), *The Gaelic Athletic Association 1884–2009* (Dublin: Irish Academic Press): 237–257.
Peteraf, M. (1993) 'The Cornerstones of Competitive Advantage: A Resource Based View', *Strategic Management Journal*, 14(3): 179–191.
Pettinger, R. (2004) *Contemporary Strategic Management* (Houndmills, Basingstoke: Palgrave Macmillan).
Porter, M. (1980) *Competitive Strategy: Techniques for Analyzing Industries and Companies* (New York, NY: The Free Press).
Porter, M. (1985) *Competitive Advantage: Creating and Sustaining Superior Performance* (New York, NY: The Free Press).
Rumult, R. (1984) 'Towards a Strategic Theory of the Firm', in R. Lamb (ed.), *Competitive Strategic Management* (Englewood Cliffs, NJ: Prentice Hall): 556–570.
Slack, T. (1997) *Understanding Sports Organizations* (Champaign, IL: Human Kinetics).
Verdin, P.J. and Williamson, P.J. (1994) 'Core Competencies, Competitive Advantage and Market Analysis: Forging the Links', in G. Hamel and A. Heene (eds), *Competence Based Competition* (New York, NY: John Wiley): 77–110.
Watzlawick, P., Weakland, J.H. and Fisch, R. (1974) *Change: Principles of Problem Formation and Problem Resolution* (New York, NY: W.W. Norton & Co).
Wilson, D. (2000) 'Why Divide Consumer and Organizational Buyer Behaviour?', *European Journal of Marketing*, 34(7): 780–791.
Zhang, Y. and Rajagopalan, N. (2010) 'Once an Outsider, Always an Outsider? CEO Origin, Strategic Change and Firm Performance', *Strategic Management Journal*, 31: 334–346.

9
The Role of Central Brokers and Their Influence on Effectiveness in an Intentionally Created Sports Professionalization Network

Simon G. Martin, Maureen Benson-Rea and Nitha Palakshappa

1. Introduction

This chapter is concerned with understanding how the role of the central broker influences the effectiveness of an intentionally created network in an elite sports context. Intentionally created networks, in contrast to organic or naturally occurring networks, are a conceptually undeveloped area (Benson-Rea and Wilson, 2003; Pihkala, Varamäki and Vesalainen, 1999; Tikkanen and Parvinen, 2006). Few studies have been undertaken into networks in either the sports sector context (Cousens and Slack, 2005; Erickson and Kushner, 1999; Thibault and Harvey, 1997; Wolfe, Meenaghan and O'Sullivan, 2002) or the not-for-profit sector, making this particular study a newer context for network research. Our work also answers calls by Håkansson (2006) and Möller and Rajala (2007) to identify and categorize the different types of network structure and their important features. The study seeks to develop a deeper understanding of causal events for the effectiveness of networks, and to discover conditions under which these events occur and how they are related to network effectiveness.

Many prior network studies have been approached from a static one-point-in-time perspective which does not capture or explain the dynamic and complex nature of networks (Brass et al., 2004; Coviello, 2005; Halinen and Törnroos, 2005; Soda, Usai and Zaheer, 2004). Despite extensive study of networks, many unresolved theoretical issues and empirical questions remain (Parkhe, Wasserman and Ralston, 2006). These include: (1) further understanding of the intentional creation of networks; (2) capturing the complex and dynamic nature of networks, rather than a static examination of them; (3) understanding network context – especially as network theory has not been applied to the sports industry, and few academic studies have focused on high performance sport provision; and (4) examining effectiveness, rather than just the efficiency, of networks. The chapter is structured as follows: first, the key conceptual terms and context of the study are presented. Second, the data collection and analysis methods are described. Third, results and discussion are combined, in which we argue that intentionally created and managed networks can be durable and effective, but that their effectiveness depends on the role of the central broker. We identify and describe a new network type, a *structured* network, and conclude with recommendations for future research.

2. Key network concepts

Networks play a critical role in the acquisition of resources for organisation growth and survival in the global environment (Benson-Rea and Wilson, 2003; Dyer and Singh, 1998; Ford et al., 2000; Gomes-Casseres, 1994; Gulati, 1998; Håkansson, 2006; Hite and Hesterly, 2001; Sadler and Chetty, 2000). Parkhe, Wasserman and Ralston (2006) note that this has given rise to the phenomenal impact of networks in global business. This is because relationships created in the formation of networks (Gummesson, 1997, 1999) are important tools in developing competitive strategy, and so organizations join or use networks to reduce uncertainty, acquire resources, achieve collective goals and enhance the legitimacy of their organization to others (Brass et al., 2004; Hellgren and Stjernberg, 1987; Hoang and Antoncic, 2003). Networks also allow members to generate greater returns than those obtained solely from the individual organization's resources (Coviello and Munro, 1995; Dyer and Singh, 1998).

2.1. Organic and intentionally created networks

Two types of network appear in the literature: organic networks which are informal and naturally occurring, and networks which are intentionally formed with a degree of formalization (Birkinshaw, Bessant and Delbridge, 2007; Blundel, 2002; Chetty and Agndal, 2008; Chetty and Patterson, 2002; Coviello, 2006; Lechner and Dowling, 2003; Pihkala, Varamäki and Vesalainen, 1999). Organic networks emerge slowly and continually evolve. They emerge through a dynamic process which is dependent on an exchange relationship that has value for the parties involved, is underpinned by trust and commitment, and is slowly developed and built over time (Brass et al., 2004; Mattsson, 1997; Powell, 1987; Uzzi, 1997). Håkansson and Johanson (1993: 212) note: "Each actor controls certain activities and resources directly, but as the dependencies to some extent means control, the actor has indirect control over the counterparts' activities and resources".

Intentionally created networks are characterized by the formal management of inter-organizational relationships. Intentionally formed networks are referred to in the network literature as value-creating networks, virtual networks, clusters, joint action groups or business nets (Anderson, Håkansson and Johanson, 1994; Campbell and Wilson, 1996; Chetty and Blankenburg-Holm, 2000; Dyer and Nobeoka, 2000; Galaskiewicz, 1996; Powell, 1990). These networks seek to gain the same advantages as organically forming networks (Achrol and Kotler, 1999; Jarillo, 1988). They depend on a network catalyst or central broker to bring the network together and to facilitate action (Campbell and Wilson, 1996; Chetty and Patterson, 2002; Pihkala, Varamäki and Vesalainen, 1999). Such networks are formed by governments in other industries with the intention of the central broker handing over eventual control to the network members (Chetty and Blankenburg-Holm, 2000; Chetty and Patterson, 2002; Welch et al., 1996, 2000). Within the context for this study, the government agency acting as a central broker had no intention of handing over control to network members. Campbell and Wilson (1996: 127) characterize these networks as purposefully creating strategic intent for the group where: "a series of dyadic and triadic relationships... have been designed to generate greater customer value and build a sustainable competitive advantage to the creator and the manager".

The difference between the two types of network is sufficient to warrant investigation of intentionally created networks that are coordinated by a central broker. Despite the high level of practitioner interest in developing intentionally created networks, there appear to be few studies into them (Dyer and Nobeoka, 2000; Galaskiewicz, 1996; Pihkala, Varamäki and Vesalainen, 1999; Tikkanen and Parvinen, 2006).

2.2. Network effectiveness

Effectiveness is evidenced by the 'business development' of the networks (Mouzas, 2006) through the management of structures and relationships (Tuominen, Rajala and Möller, 2000). However, few studies have investigated whether network partnering has been effective. Instead, researchers have examined cost-efficiencies, critical success factors or failures, rather than effective business development from networks (Campbell and Cooper, 1999; Mouzas, 2006; Parkhe, Wasserman and Ralston, 2006). As business development and growth are outcome of network effectiveness, our study answers calls by Mouzas (2006) and Tuominen, Rajala and Möller (2000) for more research into this area.

2.3. Key network constructs

For this particular study a network comprises many nodes, each representing an actor. Actors in a network may be individuals, work units or organizations (Brass et al., 2004; Emirbayer and Goodwin, 1994; Wasserman and Faust, 1995). The connections or links between the nodes represent relationships (Emirbayer and Goodwin, 1994; Johannisson, 1987; Mitchell, 1969) and shared resources and dependencies (Håkansson and Johanson, 1993). This occurs in a flexible environment with voluntariness and openness (Emirbayer and Goodwin, 1994; Johannisson, 1987) in which actors are informally connected to others in an identifiable structure (Emirbayer and Goodwin, 1994; Grieco and Hosking, 1987; Wasserman and Faust, 1995). The mutual orientation between the actors in a network enables knowledge to be exchanged and trust to be developed based upon a framework of rules observed by those actors (Blankenburg-Holm, Eriksson and Johanson, 1996; Håkansson and Johanson, 1993; Johanson and Mattsson, 1987). There is an expectation of interactions that respect the interests of others (Johanson and Mattsson, 1987). The term 'central broker' is used in this chapter to refer to an actor who coordinates network activities, connects actors to others and is a gatekeeper for information, choosing to which actor(s) this information is passed (Borgatti, Everett and Freeman, 2002; Hanneman, 2001).

Within our study the term 'actor' means the 'organization' and this important distinction is made possible because the literature describes a network as comprising many nodes, with each representing an actor, and does not specify what a node consists of. Geser (1992: 429) argues that "Organizations can be conceptualized as social actors capable of interacting with each other". Our reasoning is that individuals cannot remove their basic actions from the influencing processes of belonging to various organizational levels which are dependent on the external environment for economic survival (ibid.). For the purpose of our study a broad network definition is used: we define a network as a set of nodes and the set of ties representing some relationship, or lack of relationship, between the nodes. We refer to the nodes as actors (organizations).

2.4. Study context

The elite and high performance sports setting context of the study is an appropriate setting for the research as it is similar to other settings in terms of the flow of goods and services with the goal of increasing professionalism (Dong, Droege and Johnson, 2002; Gibson, 2003; Higham and Hinch, 2003).

An intentionally created network approach was adopted by the New Zealand Government to improve its athletes' success at the highest international level, the Olympic Games. It relied on leveraging competitive advantages by bringing together a number of organizations to share resources under a national programme with global objectives. The intentionally created network was contractually formed and relied on three interdependent components working together with their respective community partners. Each interdependent part forms a regional network which is coordinated by a central broker. This is different from approaches adopted by other nations as most elite sport systems encompass specially built training facilities.

3. Research design and method

A single case design with multiple embedded cases was used (Yin, 1994). The embedded cases consisted of three interdependent high performance networks that comprise the New Zealand Academy of Sport (NZAS) system: NZAS-North, NZAS-Central and NZAS-South Island. To provide triangulation, data were also gathered from the New Zealand Olympic Committee (NZOC) and NZAS-National Office which is controlled by and based in the offices of Sport and Recreation New Zealand (SPARC) to which the networks report. Data were also gathered from the client organizations of the embedded networks comprising 20 National Sports Organisations (NSOs). All 20 NSOs were invited to participate in the research, and of the ten that accepted, two effective and one ineffective NSOs were selected for in-depth analysis. Effectiveness was determined by the NSO in a self-selection questionnaire and also by a panel of five experts (Chetty and Campbell-Hunt, 2003, 2004; Hoye and Auld, 2001). The self-selection questionnaire was based on the NZAS' own self-evaluation tool for high performance assessment. In-depth face-to-face interviews were conducted with the High Performance Manager of each NSO because they hold the key position responsible for

Table 9.1 Summary of interviews

Research phase of study	Number of interviews conducted	Number of research participants	Number of organizations represented
National office/NZOC	7	5	2
NZAS networks	45	37	21
NSOs	4	4	4
Total	56	46	27

liaising and working with the NZAS system. Table 9.1 summarizes the interviews conducted.

The unit of analysis was the space between actors in each network and has two components: (1) a social and economic relational component that occurs between actors in the NZAS network; (2) a structural component of each network which is defined by the relational component (Halinen and Törnroos, 2005). Each of the interdependent networks was coordinated by a central broker, NZAS-North Inc., NZAS-Central Inc. and NZAS-South Island Inc. The network boundary was determined by the research participants located in the network actors by identifying: the actors in each network, other research participants and the level of research participants, that is, CEO/Board, work unit and individual, which is discussed in the next section. This emergent 'snowball' approach (Hanneman, 2001; Seidman, 1991) is appropriate for uncovering the full network from the focal-actor viewpoint.

3.1. Retrospective longitudinal aspects

A retrospective approach which relied on the participants' memories was used to address the concern of time (Carson and Coviello, 1996; Medlin, 2004). A cognitive mapping technique was also used to plot the stages of development for each network. This technique also acted as a memory trigger for participants, as recommended by Huff (1994). PAJEK software was used to produce network maps at different stages of development (See Figures 9.1, 9.2, 9.3).

3.2. Data collection and analysis

Selection of multiple levels for data collection offered a way of gauging the extent, understanding and support for both the network and its activities. This approach provided an understanding of cross-level pressures and these were investigated at three levels: (1) the CEO/Board level by interviewing at the CEO/Board level responsible for strategy of

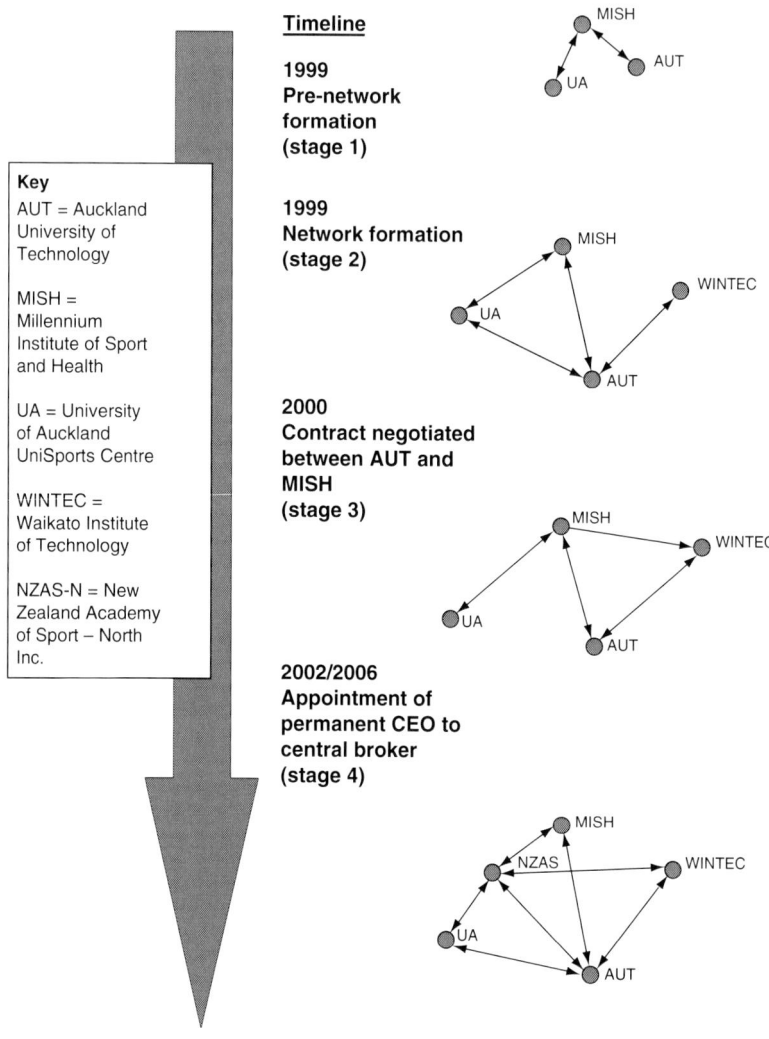

Figure 9.1 NZAS-North network stages of development

each embedded network actor; (2) the work unit level by interviewing at the senior manager level whose operations are directly involved in each network; and (3) the individual level by interviewing staff responsible for the day-to-day operation of the network's business. Some participants were interviewed more than once to clarify our understanding. Background data on each NZAS network was audited for accuracy by

Key

CGT = Cooks Garden Trust
CIT = Central Institute of Technology
EIT = Eastern Institute of Technology
GHWan = Good Health Wanganui
MssyP = Massey University, Palmerston North Campus
MssyW = Massey University, Wellington Campus
NZAS – C = New Zealand Academy of Sport – Central
SpG = Sport Gisborne
SpHB = Sport Hawkes Bay
SpM = Sport Manawatu
SpT = Sport Taranaki
SpWan = Sport and Recreation Wanganui
SpWR = Sport Wellington Region
UCOL–P = Universal College of Learning Palmerston North Campus
UCOL–Wan = Universal College of Learning, Wanganui Campus
UHCC = Upper Hutt City Council
UHEDA = Upper Hutt Economic Development Board
UO = University of Otago
VU = Victoria University
WanInc = Wanganui Incorporated
WCC = Wellington City Council
WDC = Wanganui District Council
WRMTB = Wanganui River Maori Trust Board

Timeline
1999 Network formation (stage 1)

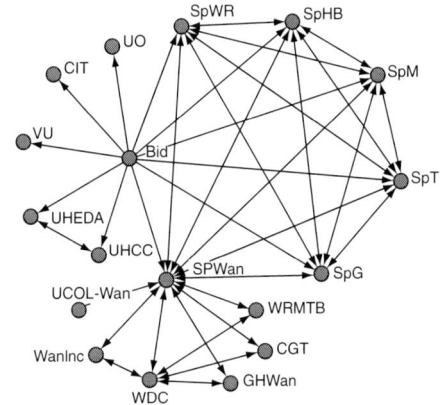

2000–05 Appointment of CEO with no prior sport background to central broker, and University of Otago and CIT exiting network (stage 2)

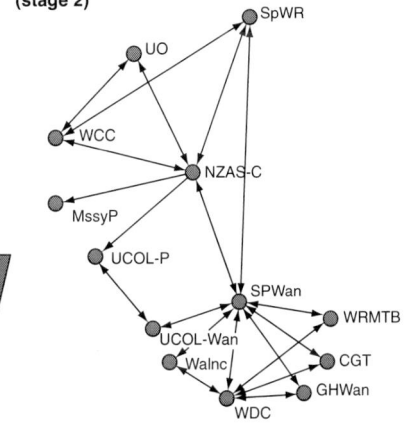

Figure 9.2 NZAS-Central network stages of development

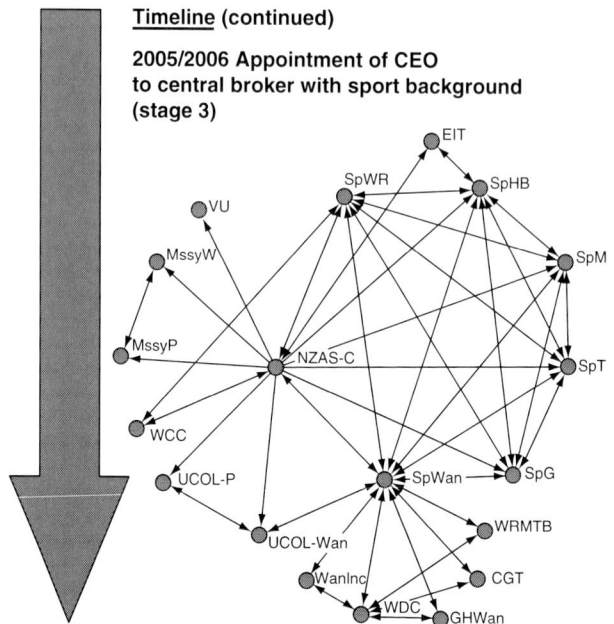

Figure 9.2 (Continued)

feeding back to each of the CEOs of the central brokers to confirm accuracy and clarify understanding (Denzin, 1994; Miles and Huberman, 1994; Patton, 2002; Richards, 2005). For the purpose of qualitative data management, NVIVO software was used. Findings from the qualitative data were used to build a descriptive within-case summary of each network. Each within-case description was conducted separately across multiple levels – CEO/Board, work unit and individual – by the construct areas identified from prior network studies (Brown and Eisenhardt, 1997). These construct areas were *context, formation, structure* and *interaction*.

A cross-case analysis was conducted after the within-case analysis (Eisenhardt, 1989; Miles and Huberman, 1994; Patton, 2002). The cross-case analysis developed a deeper understanding of causal events for the effectiveness of the networks, and identified the conditions under which these events occurred and how they were related to network effectiveness. This process involved comparison of the three embedded cases and data gathered from the three NSOs (Miles, 1979; Miles and Huberman, 1994).

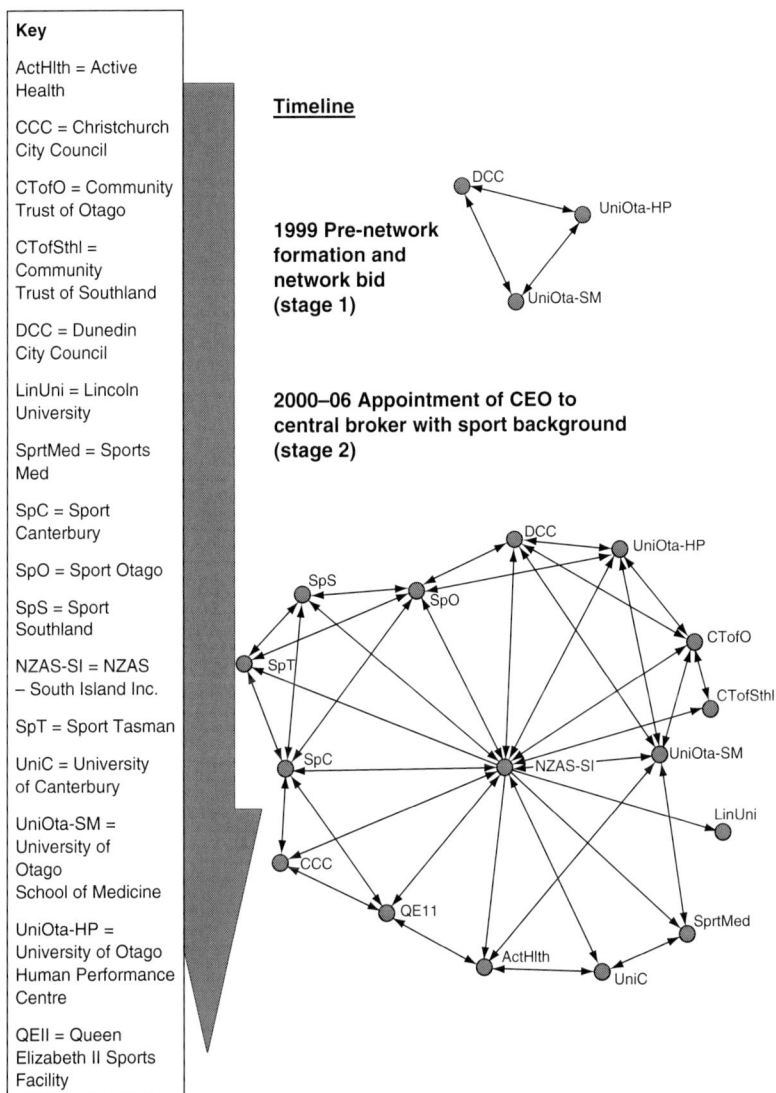

Figure 9.3 NZAS-South Island network stages of development

4. Results and discussion

Effectiveness is defined and operationalized from the perspective of the research participants at multiple levels, and from multiple actor perspectives. Effectiveness is treated as a relative, rather than an absolute measure, depending on the participants' viewpoint. Findings were strengthened as one of the networks – NZAS-Central – was identified by participants as being ineffective, and one of the NSOs was also identified as ineffective. The difference in effectiveness enabled us to use polarized embedded cases which afforded a contrast, allowing the limits of any conclusions drawn from each of these embedded cases to be tested (Eisenhardt, 1989; Miles, 1979; Miles and Huberman, 1994). The results from the study show that network durability depends on the central broker's ability to add value in order to contribute towards network effectiveness. The central broker added value to actors and clients through: (1) strategic focus; (2) coordinating resources for network business development; (3) the coordination mechanism; (4) bridging structural holes; and (5) communication. These findings are presented next.

4.1. Strategic focus

The role of the central broker was to ensure that the vision and strategic direction was inclusive of all actors, and that this drove the development of the network. For NZAS-South Island the move to a strategic focus at the earliest stage was paramount and the central broker identified actors based on resource capability for network purposes. This finding is congruent with research noting the need for a network to determine its resource base to avoid resource scarcity (Baum, Calbreses and Silverman, 2000; Birkinshaw, Bessant and Delbridge, 2007; Chetty and Blankenburg-Holm, 2000; Coviello, 2006; Gomes-Casseres, 1994; Sadler and Chetty, 2000; Witt, 2004). "We needed to make sure that we could provide services for the national sports through their service agreements. It was a case of lining up and finding the service providers... aligning to experts who met the quickly established criteria of the national standards for providers" (interview, CEO/Board level, NZAS-South Island).

For NZAS-North a strategic focus to identify resources for network development was not possible, as although actors were motivated by a strategic purpose at the outset of the network's formation, this was for their own self-interest. Actors were aware of these strategic motivations for network membership. The self-interest motivation of actors limited the network's development by preventing others from joining: "They wanted to keep others out. So there was a protectionism driver which probably was more so led by the tertiaries" (interview, CEO/Board level). "I guess the partners have seen it as an opportunity to have support for their individual organisational ambitions...patch protection" (interview, Individual level).

NZAS-Central had not moved to a strategic focus nor identified resource capabilities necessary for network tasks. Within the network there were different perceptions between the three organizational levels about cooperation at the formation and early initiation stages of the network's development. Perceptions ranged from actors trying to achieve their own objectives through to actors not coming with their own agendas. Generally, actors had little awareness of others' motivations for joining the network. The effective NSOs had strategic plans which were jointly prepared with NZAS staff and had been tailored to meet the specific requirements of the NSOs. The NSO that was ineffective reported struggling to develop a strategic plan. The NSO had also experienced difficulty getting the NZAS system to understand their sport's unique requirements; they also dealt almost exclusively with NZAS-Central. The effective NSOs dealt with NZAS-North and NZAS-South Island, and saw no value in dealing with NZAS-Central.

4.2. Coordinating resources

The central broker added value to the network by understanding network actors and their objectives; this enabled opportunities to be identified and the appropriate actors to become involved. The role of the central broker should be to ensure value and desirability of relational opportunities which entails the recognition of complementary resources (Cowan, Jonard and Zimmerman, 2007; Pihkala, Varamäki and Vesalainen, 1999).

Actors in NZAS-North were motivated by strategic self-interest of protecting their market from competitors and developing their own business by building additional revenue. Actors competed in the same market for the same clients with similar products. Actors did not share information or knowledge concerning their businesses and, as a consequence, did not develop joint projects. The central broker had thus been unable to add value. However, this had created a network that operated efficiently, driven by actors needing to remain competitive with each other and to maximize their return on their involvement: "I think there's quite a lot of people, the various stake holders looking to maximise the return to them rather than us looking at it in terms for the greater good" (interview, CEO/Board level). "I think each member still probably guards itself a little bit about what they do...it's the need to focus on your own particular activities as opposed to the collective activity" (interview, Work unit level).

In NZAS-Central, the central broker had not been able to add value to the network by developing new business initiatives. The reasons for this were attributed to a combination of factors: (1) actors not understanding the objectives or motivations of others for being in the network so being unable to identify joint projects; (2) the exit of one network actor with an associated diversion of resources; and (3) a change in the network structure due to the central broker relocating to different premises. Actors had a general concern over NZAS-Central's poor performance: "What we haven't done is added value outside of the contract" (interview, CEO level). "I think there is a great deal of improvement to be made" (interview, Individual level).

For NZAS-South Island, the central broker *had* been able to add value and develop network business by understanding actor objectives, and matching business opportunities to the appropriate actors. The business opportunities were developed from core competencies of the network. The network had lived up to expectations: "An excellent CEO has been appointed and she's done an outstanding job in my view. And making the ASI, Academy of Sport, feeling like it serves the whole of the South Island" (interview, CEO level). "It's definitely exceeded my expectations in terms of the relationship we have with Southern Academy now" (interview, Work unit level). "I think it's fantastic. These guys here, there's no ego or flexing their own influence… it becomes more successful almost by the month" (interview, Individual level).

At all levels within the network there was a shared understanding of how to take network core competencies into different markets and from this developing the network's business: "bringing the right people together with the right knowledge base, and the right expertise, the right experiences" (interview, CEO/Board level). "[CEO of NZAS-South Island Inc., added by the authors] worked with our marketing and communication department to create something that is known as the X-factor brand. She's all about providing that something, that little bit extra. So yeah the relationship is, in my opinion, quite cleverly, put right up front" (interview, Work unit level).

> The other thing we have down here which we've worked on over the last few years is a motorsport academy and so that's privately funded through MotorSport New Zealand. So there are people contributing to the funding systems from minority sports I guess but on a private basis which we see as a growth area. There's the Human Performance

Centre and Physical Education School. The X-Factor is sort of one of our branding logos.

(Interview, Individual level)

There was a distinct contrast between the findings for the effective and ineffective NSOs. The effective NSOs reported the NZAS system had adapted resources to meet their needs and to understand their sport, although this had taken some time to achieve. In contrast, the ineffective NSO struggled to get its needs met through its dealings with NZAS-Central.

4.3. Coordination mechanism

For a network to increase the potential return on investment to actors the coordination mechanism employed must be self-enforcing, based on norms of behaviour and underpinned by trust and familiarity between actors (Dyer and Singh, 1998; Thorelli, 1986). This needs a collective focus, otherwise there is no incentive for performance (Gomes-Casseres, 1994; Gulati, 1998). The coordination mechanism influences structure because all actors depend on each other for joint planning (Håkansson and Johanson, 1993). The role of the central broker in adding value to the coordination mechanism is achieved at the formation stage by ensuring a formal mechanism is enforced whereby the network and no single actor is disadvantaged. In the later stages it is achieved by monitoring and policing network activities to protect network and actor interests. Once network relationships develop and become established the coordination mechanism moves from a formal to an informal process which may be loosely guided by memorandums of understanding, although these were unlikely to be referred to or used. Employing an informal coordination mechanism contributes to network effectiveness.

NZAS-North actors used a contract and a Memorandum of Understanding to provide direction, illustrating the informality of their coordination mechanism, although initially a formal means of coordination was in place: "it's a heads of agreement or a memorandum agreement... but pretty informal arrangement" (interview, CEO/Board level). "If you have to refer closely to the contract you've probably lost the plot" (interview, Work unit level). "At our level it's pretty informal" (interview, Individual level).

NZAS-South Island was viewed as sensitively coordinated by the central broker, and that ultimately it was the NSOs that were in control. The central broker encouraged informal coordination mechanisms based on norms of behaviour and facilitated by the development of social ties which were inclusive of actors and assisted by the central broker: "So there are a number of partnerships which, in some cases are more formal. But in some cases they're quite informal because of the friendships that they've made with the staff here" (interview, Work unit level). "[The NZAS-South Island network actors, added by the authors] do like to feel like they're contributing. They don't like to feel like they're at the end of the chain and they're, they want to get involved, they don't just want to be told what to do" (interview, Individual level).

In contrast, actors within NZAS-Central commented on the inability to own network processes due to interference by SPARC. Consequently, coordination was through a formal mechanism. "SPARC is still the key player... you just tend to keep questioning, really, what power have we got relative to what the national agency has got when they're providing such a high portion of your funds and also stipulating a lot of things that they want done" (interview, CEO/Board level).

4.4. Bridging structural holes

Coordination of resources for network development is achieved by bridging structural holes which present opportunities for actors to act as a broker by connecting parts of the network (Brass et al., 2004; Burt, 1997; Granovetter, 1973). The central broker adds value to actors through bridging structural holes to connect actors that may not know each other, and consequently appraise actors of opportunities within the network for business development. Bridging structural holes enables the central broker to be the most influential and powerful actor in the network and, as a consequence, maintain their network position.

For an actor to act as a broker, they must have many connections to others (Ahuja, 2000; Burt, 1992). This has certainly been the case for the central broker within NZAS-South Island. All structural holes were effectively bridged by the central broker and there was clear evidence that they had the most power and control within the network. The central broker provided connections to new information and ideas and, consequently, the network was more creative and innovative. By comparison, NZAS-North was a closed dense network – all actors were aware of all other actors, and of who the key individuals were within each actor at the three different organizational levels. The strength of connections between actors was high. In such a network, the ability of the central broker to bridge structural holes was limited. Therefore, there was no requirement for a broker as everyone knew of everyone else

(Brass et al., 2004; Burt, 1997). The finding of the Auckland University of Technology (AUT) and the central broker having an equal number of connections within the network explains why AUT was able to compete for the central broker position, and also explains the exclusion of the central broker in the network maps by actors. However, dense networks in which everyone is connected by strong ties are rigid and provide no creativity or new ideas (Burt, 1992). NZAS-North had not developed new business outside of the SPARC contract. In terms of the position of AUT in the network and the influence of the central broker:

> "I think AUT is clearly dominant just purely by numbers, they've got so many staff in that applied sports area and providing services for AUT. We all take leadership from the Academy [the central broker]... So from [my] point of view I really see the leadership coming from the Academy.
>
> (Interview, Individual level)

However, NZAS-Central had too many structural holes which had the effect of reducing trust and network developments; ties between actors in the network were also weak (Ahuja, 2000). Other actors were able to successfully bridge these structural holes – so much so that there was little difference between the central broker and the Regional Sports Trusts at all stages of the network's development in terms of the power and control that they could exert in the network. Power was based on the ability of actors to bridge structural holes and connect parts of the network together. This indicates a weak level of power held by the central broker, and an imbalance of power in the network, with the outcome that the central broker's power and control within the network were perceived to be low. Density was also much lower for the NZAS-Central network compared to the other two networks; each of the actors at the three organizational levels were not aware of all the other network actors.

4.5. Communication

The central broker needs to facilitate communication between all partners in the network. By doing so, cooperation, knowledge and information sharing, trust and commitment are all cultivated between actors contributing to connectedness between actors and leading to network effectiveness (Powell, 1990).

NZAS-North relied on both informal and formal mechanisms for communication, facilitated by the central broker and involving all actors. Levels of trust and commitment were high. As a consequence, actors cooperated well together – but on NZAS business only because actors were competing in the same market against each other. However, information and knowledge sharing did occur at individual level, with the amount of communication between actors perceived to be high. At all organizational levels (CEO/Board, work unit and individual) there was a shared understanding that regular meetings occurred. There were six-weekly meetings at CEO/Board and work unit level, and a weekly meeting at the individual level. Actors had representation on the board of NZAS-North which allowed them to influence the network business. There was an annual meeting for all levels of NZAS-North actors. The informal and formal communication processes were facilitated by the central broker who had office space in the premises of all actors. Staff within the central broker were described as the glue that bound actors in the network together.

> [The board of NZAS-North Inc.] tend[s] to meet about every couple of months... I would be in... either by email or by telephone, we would be in contact three or four times a week... and the others [work unit level] that's much more irregular... would be about once a month. But I suppose, the other thing is that once we've got something on like we've had just recently with this review, the great advantage is that we bring them all in together and the attitude is to be inclusive rather than exclusive.
>
> (Interview, CEO/Board level)

"We are trying to meet at least quarterly or every other month" (interview, Work unit level). "Management level would be two to three times a year, the providers [individual level] would be pretty much the same; two or three times a year, monthly sometimes" (interview, Individual level).

For the NZAS-South Island network, communication was perceived to be effective and was attributed to the CEO of the central broker involving all actors in the network business and updating them regularly on developments. Informal communication processes also existed in which actors regularly shared information to identify opportunities and keep informed of business developments. At all levels of the network there was a shared understanding about six-weekly meetings and an annual forum organized by the central broker for all the NZAS-South Island network actors to discuss and be informed of developments in the NZAS system and to share good practice. The regularity and effectiveness of communication between actors was important:

> A combination really [of face-to-face meetings and conversations over the telephone], I mean when necessary for me to talk in detail about something, then it's probably a face-to-face meeting...we update by e-mail as well, so we'll pick up the phone and have a chat. Or again, as I said, meeting at the forum [about the annual conference organised by the central broker]. So that's been a very positive and good interaction, you know, between lots of different organisations, but it's also a subtle balance between overloading us with demands.
>
> (Interview, Work unit level)

> [T]he academy forum...tries to facilitate communication, discussion with them and that works really well...So that's particularly one thing that the academy is doing well at the moment as regard to bringing people together and discussing issues and talking and letting people know what direction they are going in and what's happening.
>
> (Interview, Individual level)

In contrast, NZAS-Central had poor levels of communication between actors. There was little communication between actors at work unit and individual levels. Liaison between actors at CEO/Board level was primarily on issues concerning the exit of one actor from the network. As for the constraints that contributed to the lack of communication and understanding between actors:

> I think our great constraints over the last couple of years have been administrative largely [about actor exiting the network]...Also the lease arrangements [about the same actor who is the lease holder of the central broker's premise] and then, it sounds like a nightmare to me. I mean that was what our board papers used to be full of. That's pretty frustrating.
>
> (Interview, CEO/Board level)

The effective NSOs reported having regular communication on both an informal and formal basis with key staff in the central broker of NZAS-North and NZAS-South Island. The communication facilitated informal and flexible working with the NZAS system based on the NSOs' needs. NZAS staff were viewed as easy to deal with and knowledgeable. In contrast, the NSO which was ineffective reported communication between themselves and NZAS-Central had been poor resulting in low levels of trust and no understanding of the NZAS system. The ineffective NSO was unsure who to contact concerning NZAS services, and felt isolated in the system, with limited understanding of it.

5. Conclusion

The findings from our three embedded networks highlight the importance of the role of the central broker in adding value to network actors and clients for network effectiveness. The findings also reveal that the durability of the network depends on the central broker's ability to add value. The central broker adds value to actors and clients through: (1) strategic focus; (2) coordinating resources for network business development; (3) coordination mechanism; (4) bridging structural holes; and (5) communication.

Prior research shows that the central broker's role in networks intentionally created by governments is temporary, with power and control being handed back to network actors; these networks have been found to be not durable (Chetty and Patterson, 2002; Welch et al., 1998). What is *different* about the findings within this study is that the central broker had not handed back power and control to actors and that the networks *were* durable. Dyer and Nobeoka (2000) identified an intentionally formed network in which the central broker retained power in one industry but the points of difference with the NZAS network are that a *government* organization had *retained* power over actors and the actors were from *differing* business sectors to each other – although there were overlapping business objectives which enabled network membership. This is an important finding as it means this is a new form of network in which the central broker remains as the focal actor. The new network type is termed here a 'structured' network. Our finding answers calls for further research (Håkansson, 2006; Liu and Brookfield, 2000; Möller and Rajala, 2007) to identify and categorize the different types of network structure and their important features.

The practical implication for the adoption of a network approach for elite sport provision in New Zealand and other countries to increase overall professionalization is that constructing designated training facilities may not be necessary. Instead a network approach that accesses community partners may provide an alternative means of cost-effective elite sport development, allowing smaller nations to compete at the highest level.

This study was exploratory and a more detailed in-depth study of a single network which combines both qualitative and quantitative methods in which data are gathered from all actors in the network is warranted. Such a study would also allow for rigorous testing of the findings developed in the present study. Future research directions include building a conceptual model for network effectiveness, testing this, examining Olympic Games medal outputs as a direct result of the network approach and, finally, comparisons with other countries' elite sport systems.

References

Achrol, R.S. and Kotler, P. (1999) 'Marketing in the Network Economy', *Journal of Marketing*, 63(Special Issue): 146–163.

Ahuja, G. (2000) 'Collaboration Networks, Structural Holes, and Innovation: A Longitudinal Study', *Administrative Science Quarterly*, 45(3): 425–455.

Anderson, J.C., Håkansson, H. and Johanson, J. (1994) 'Dyadic Business Relationships Within a Business Network Context', *Journal of Marketing*, 58(4): 1–15.

Baum, J.A.C., Calbreses, T. and Silverman, B.S. (2000) 'Don't Go It Alone: Alliance Network Competition and Startups' Performance in Canadian Biotechnology', *Strategic Management Journal*, 21(3): 267–294.

Benson-Rea, M. and Wilson, H. (2003) 'Networks, Learning and Their Lifecycle', *European Management Journal*, 21(5): 599–597.

Birkinshaw, J., Bessant, J. and Delbridge, R. (2007) 'Finding, Forming, and Performing: Creating Networks for Discontinuous Innovation', *California Management Review*, 49(3): 67–84.

Blankenburg-Holm, D., Eriksson, K. and Johanson, J. (1996) 'Business Networks and Cooperation in International Business Relationships', *Journal of International Business Studies*, 27(5): 1033–1053.

Blundel, R. (2002) 'Network Evolution and the Growth of Artisanal Firms: A Tale of Two Regional Cheese Makers', *Entrepreneurship and Regional Development*, 14(1): 1–30.

Borgatti, S.P., Everett, M.G. and Freeman, L.C. (2002) *UCINET for Windows: Software for Social Network Analysis* (Harvard, MA: Analytic Technologies).

Brass, D.J., Galaskiewicz, J., Greve, H.R. and Tsai, W. (2004) 'Taking Stock of Networks and Organisations: A Multilevel Perspective', *Academy of Management Journal*, 47(6): 795–817.

Brown, S.L. and Eisenhardt, K.M. (1997) 'The Art of Continuous Change: Linking Complexity Theory and Time-paced Evolution in Relentlessly Shifting Organizations', *Administrative Science Quarterly*, 42(1): 1–34.

Burt, R.S. (1992) *Structural Holes: The Social Structure of Competition* (Cambridge, MA: Harvard University Press).

Burt, R.S. (1997) 'The Contingent Value of Social Capital', *Administrative Science Quarterly*, 42(2): 339–365.

Campbell, A.J. and Cooper, R.G. (1999) 'Do Customer Partnerships Improve New Product Success Rates?', *Industrial Marketing Management*, 28(5): 507–519.

Campbell, A.J. and Wilson, D.T. (1996) 'Managed Networks: Creating Strategic Advantage', in D. Iacobucci (ed.), *Networking in Marketing* (Thousand Oaks, CA: Sage): 125–143.

Carson, D. and Coviello, N.E. (1996) 'Qualitative Research Issues at the Marketing/Entrepreneurship Interface', *Marketing Intelligence and Planning*, 14(6): 51–58.
Chetty, S.K. and Agndal, H. (2008) 'The Role of Interorganizational Networks and Interpersonal Networks in an Industrial District', *Regional Studies*, 42(2): 175–187.
Chetty, S.K. and Blankenburg-Holm, D. (2000) 'Internationalisation of Small to Medium-sized Manufacturing Firms: A Network Approach', *International Business Review*, 9(1): 77–93.
Chetty, S.K. and Campbell-Hunt, C. (2003) 'Paths to Internationalisation Among Small-to Medium-sized Firms', *European Journal of Marketing*, 37(5/6): 796–820.
Chetty, S.K. and Campbell-Hunt, C. (2004) 'A Strategic Approach to Internationalization: A Traditional Versus "Born-global" Approach', *Journal of International Marketing*, 12(1): 57–81.
Chetty, S.K. and Patterson, A. (2002) 'Developing Internationalization Capability Through Industry Groups: The Experience of a Telecommunications Joint Action Group', *Journal of Strategic Marketing*, 10(1): 69–89.
Cousens, L. and Slack, T. (2005) 'Field-level Change: The Case of North American Major League Professional Sport', *Journal of Sport Marketing*, 19(1): 13–42.
Coviello, N.E. (2005) 'Integrating Qualitative and Quantitative Techniques in Network Analysis', *Qualitative Market Research*, 8(1): 39–60.
Coviello, N.E. (2006) 'Network Dynamics in the International New Venture', *Journal of International Business Studies*, 37(5): 713–731.
Coviello, N.E. and Munro, H.J. (1995) 'Growing the Entrepreneurial Firm: Networking for International Market Development', *European Journal of Marketing*, 29(7): 49–61.
Cowan, R., Jonard, N. and Zimmerman, J.-B. (2007) 'Bilateral Collaboration and the Emergence of Innovation Networks', *Management Science*, 53(7): 1051–1067.
Denzin, N.K. (1994) 'The Art and Principles of Interpretation', in N.K. Denzin and Y.S. Lincoln (eds), *Handbook of Qualitative Research* (Thousand Oaks, CA: Sage): 500–515.
Dong, L.C., Droege, S.B. and Johnson, N.B. (2002) 'Incentives and Self-interest: Balancing Revenue and Rewards in China's Tourism Industry', *Tourism and Hospitality Research*, 4(1): 69–77.
Dyer, J.H. and Nobeoka, K. (2000) 'Creating and Managing a High Performance Knowledge-sharing Network: The Toyota Case', *Strategic Management Journal*, 21(3): 345–367.
Dyer, J.H. and Singh, H. (1998) 'The Relational View: Cooperative Strategy and Sources of Interorganizational Competitive Advantage', *Academy of Management Review*, 23(4): 660–679.
Eisenhardt, K.M. (1989) 'Building Theories from Case Study Research', *Academy of Management Review*, 14(4): 532–550.
Emirbayer, M. and Goodwin, J. (1994) 'Network Analysis, Culture, and the Problem of Agency', *American Journal of Sociology*, 99(6): 1411–1454.
Erickson, G.S. and Kushner, R.J. (1999) 'Public Event Networks: An Application of Marketing Theory to Sporting Events', *European Journal of Marketing*, 33(3/4): 348–364.

Ford, D., Gadde, L.-E., Håkansson, H., Lundgren, A., Snehota, I. and Turnbull, P. (2000) *Managing Business Relationships* (Chichester: John Wiley and Sons).

Galaskiewicz, J. (1996) 'The "New Network Analysis" and Its Application to Organisational Theory and Behavior', in D. Iacobucci (ed.), *Networks in Marketing* (Thousand Oaks, CA: Sage): 19–31.

Geser, H. (1992) 'Towards an Interaction Theory of Organizational Actors', *Organization Studies*, 13(3): 429–451.

Gibson, H.J. (2003) 'Sport Tourism: An Introduction to the Special Issue', *Journal of Sport Management*, 17: 205–213.

Gomes-Casseres, B. (1994) 'Group Versus Group: How Alliance Networks Compete', *Harvard Business Review*, 72(4): 62–74.

Granovetter, M.S. (1973) 'The Strength of Weak Ties', *American Journal of Sociology*, 78(6): 1360–1379.

Grieco, M.S. and Hosking, D.M. (1987) 'Networking, Exchange, and Skill', *International Studies of Management and Organisation*, 17(1): 75–87.

Gulati, R. (1998) 'Alliances and Networks', *Strategic Management Journal*, 19(4): 293–317.

Gummesson, E. (1997) 'Collaborate or Compete', *Marketing Management*, 6(3): 17–20.

Gummesson, E. (1999) *Total Relationship Marketing* (Boston, MA: Butterworth-Heinemann).

Håkansson, H. (2006) 'Business Relationships and Networks: Consequences for Economic Policy', *The Antitrust Bulletin*, 51(1): 143–163.

Håkansson, H. and Johanson, J. (1993) 'The Network as Governance Structure: Interfirm Cooperation Beyond Markets and Hierarchies', in G. Grabher (ed.), *The Embedded Firm: The Socio-economics of Industrial Networks* (London: Routledge): 35–51.

Halinen, A. and Törnroos, J.-Å. (2005) 'Using Case Methods in the Study of Contemporary Business Networks', *Journal of Business Research*, 58(9): 1285–1297.

Hanneman, R.A. (2001) *Introduction to Social Network Methods* (Riverside, CA: University of California Press).

Hellgren, B. and Stjernberg, T. (1987) 'Networks: An Analytical Tool for Understanding Complex Decision Processes', *International Studies of Management and Organisation*, 17(1): 88–102.

Higham, J.E.S. and Hinch, T.D. (2003) 'Sport, Space, and Time: Effects of the Otago Highlanders Franchise on Tourism', *Journal of Sport Management*, 17(3): 235–257.

Hite, J.M. and Hesterly, W.S. (2001) 'The Evolution of Firm Networks: From Emergence to Early Growth of the Firm', *Strategic Management Journal*, 22(3): 275–286.

Hoang, H. and Antoncic, B. (2003) 'Network-based Research in Entrepreneurship: A Critical Review', *Journal of Business Venturing*, 18(2): 165–187.

Hoye, R. and Auld, C. (2001) 'Measuring Board Performance in Nonprofit Sport Organisations', *Australian Journal on Volunteering*, 6(2): 108–116.

Huff, A.S. (1994) *Mapping Strategic Thought* (Chichester: John Wiley and Sons).

Jarillo, C.J. (1988) 'On Strategic Networks', *Strategic Management Journal*, 9(1): 31–41.

Johannisson, B. (1987) 'Anarchists and Organizers: Entrepreneurs in a Network Perspective', *International Studies of Management and Organisation*, 17(1): 49–63.

Johanson, J. and Mattsson, L.-G. (1987) 'Interorganizational Relations in Industrial Systems: A Network Approach Compared with the Transaction-cost Approach', *International Studies of Management and Organisation*, 17(1): 34–48.

Lechner, C. and Dowling, M. (2003) 'Firm Networks: External Relationships as Sources for the Growth and Competitiveness of Entrepreneurial Firms', *Entrepreneurship and Regional Development*, 15(1): 1–26.

Liu, R.-J. and Brookfield, J. (2000) 'Stars, Rings and Tiers: Organisational Networks and their Dynamics in Taiwan's Machine Toll Industry', *Long Range Planning*, 33(3): 322–348.

Mattsson, L.-G. (1997) '"Relationship Marketing" and the "Markets-as-Networks Approach" – A Comparative Analysis of Two Evolving Streams of Research', *Journal of Marketing Management*, 13(5): 447–461.

Medlin, C.J. (2004) 'Interaction in Business Relationships: A Time Perspective', *Industrial Marketing Management*, 33(3): 185–193.

Miles, M.B. (1979) 'Qualitative Data as an Attractive Nuisance: The Problem of Analysis', *Administrative Science Quarterly*, 24(4): 590–601.

Miles, M.B. and Huberman, M.A. (1994) *Qualitative Data Analysis: An Expanded Sourcebook*, 2nd edn (Thousand Oaks, CA: Sage).

Mitchell, J.C. (1969) 'The Concept and Use of Social Networks', in J.C. Mitchell (ed.), *Social Networks in Urban Situations: An Analysis of Personal Relationships in Central African Towns* (Manchester: Manchester University Press): 1–50.

Möller, K. and Rajala, A. (2007) 'Rise of Strategic Nets – New Modes of Value Creation', *Industrial Marketing Management*, 36(7): 895–908.

Mouzas, S. (2006) 'Efficiency Versus Effectiveness in Business Networks', *Journal of Business Research*, 59(10/11): 1124–1132.

Parkhe, A., Wasserman, S. and Ralston, D.A. (2006) 'New Frontiers in Network Theory Development', *Academy of Management Review*, 31(3): 560–568.

Patton, M.Q. (2002) *Qualitative Research and Evaluation Methods*, 3rd edn (Thousand Oaks, CA: Sage).

Pihkala, T., Varamäki, E. and Vesalainen, J. (1999) 'Virtual Organization and the SMEs: A Review and Model Development', *Entrepreneurship and Regional Development*, 11(4): 335–349.

Powell, W.W. (1987) 'Hybrid Organizational Arrangements: New Form or Transitional Development?', *California Management Review*, 30(1): 67–87.

Powell, W.W. (1990) 'Neither Market Nor Hierarchy: Network Forms of Organization', *Research in Organizational Behavior*, 12: 295–336.

Richards, L. (2005) *Handling Qualitative Data: A Practical Guide* (Thousand Oaks, CA: Sage).

Sadler, A. and Chetty, S.K. (2000) 'The Impact of Networks on New Zealand Firms', *Journal of Euromarketing*, 9(2): 37–58.

Seidman, I.E. (1991) *Interviewing as Qualitative Research: A Guide for Researchers in Education and the Social Sciences* (New York, NY: Teachers College Press).

Soda, G., Usai, A. and Zaheer, A. (2004) 'Network Memory: The Influence of Past and Current Networks on Performance', *Academy of Management Journal*, 47(6): 893–906.

Thibault, L. and Harvey, J. (1997) 'Fostering Interorganizational Linkages in the Canadian Sport Delivery System', *Journal of Sport Management*, 11(1): 45–68.
Thorelli, H.B. (1986) 'Networks: Between Markets and Hierarchies', *Strategic Management Journal*, 7(1): 37–51.
Tikkanen, H. and Parvinen, P.M.T. (2006) 'Planned and Spontaneous Orders in the Emerging Network Society', *Journal of Business and Industrial Marketing*, 21(1): 38–49.
Tuominen, M., Rajala, A. and Möller, K. (2000) 'Intraorganizational Relationships and Operational Performance', *Journal of Strategic Marketing*, 8(2): 139–160.
Uzzi, B. (1997) 'Social Structure and Competition in Inter-firm Networks: The Paradox of Embeddedness', *Administrative Science Quarterly*, 42(1): 35–67.
Wasserman, S. and Faust, K. (1995) *Social Network Analysis: Methods and Applications* (Cambridge: Cambridge University Press).
Welch, D., Welch, L., Wilkinson, I. and Young, L. (1996) 'Network Development in International Project Marketing and the Impact of External Facilitation', *International Business Review*, 5(6): 579–602.
Welch, D., Welch, L., Wilkinson, I. and Young, L. (2000) 'An Export Grouping Scheme', *Journal of Euromarketing*, 9(2): 59–84.
Welch, D., Welch, L., Young, L. and Wilkinson, I. (1998) 'The Importance of Networks in Export Promotion: Policy Issues', *Journal of International Marketing*, 6(4): 66–82.
Witt, P. (2004) 'Entrepreneurs' Networks and the Success of Start-ups', *Entrepreneurship and Regional Development*, 16(5): 391–412.
Wolfe, R., Meenaghan, T. and O'Sullivan, P. (2002) 'The Sports Network: Insights into the Shifting Balance of Power', *Journal of Business Research*, 55(7): 611–622.
Yin, R.K. (1994) *Case Study Research: Design and Methods*, 2nd edn (Thousand Oaks, CA: Sage).

10
Business Ecosystem Co-evolution: The Ultimate Fighting Championships

Simon Ford and Clive Kerr

1. Introduction

The first Ultimate Fighting Championships (UFC) event was held in Denver, Colorado on 12 November 1993. In an eight-man elimination tournament, fighters representing the disciplines of boxing, Brazilian jiu-jitsu, catch wrestling, karate, kickboxing, savate, sumo and tae kwon do competed for the title of 'Ultimate Fighting Champion'. This first exposure of the North American public to what was initially marketed as 'no holds barred' combat saw Royce Gracie from the discipline of Brazilian jiu-jitsu prevail as the tournament winner (Gentry, 2004).

Fast forward to 2008: 'no holds barred' fighting has evolved into the sport of 'mixed martial arts' (MMA), and the UFC has established an almost unshakeable competitive advantage over its competitors, with its events generating annual pay-per-view revenues in excess of US$200 million. The most prominent UFC fighters have established mainstream exposure, featuring on the covers of sports magazines, have made appearances in non-sporting TV shows and films and had action figures made in their image.

But this story is not one of continued success from inception to the time of writing, either for the sport of MMA or for its leading promoter the UFC. As in most nascent markets, the story has been a turbulent one, with political pressure and regulation leading to the near eradication of the sport and the collapse of the firm, before new standards and acquisition gave the sport and firm new life, respectively.

New sports that have global appeal and significant commercial returns do not appear often, nor do they grow and generate revenues as rapidly as the UFC has done since 2005. In this chapter, we analyse this growth through the lens of the business ecosystem, seeking insight by studying the actors and co-evolutionary complex dynamics that operate in this ecosystem. Similar perspectives have been employed within the socioeconomic sciences to explain industrial dynamics in technology-based sectors (Garnsey, Heffernan and Ford, 2007; Langlois, 1992; Moore, 1996; Shapiro and Varian, 1999). Accordingly, it can provide us with a conceptual position from which we can understand how the organization has stimulated the growth of mixed martial arts and how it has achieved its current position of dominance within the sport.

2. Conceptual position: co-evolution and business ecosystems

Recent efforts to improve our understanding of socioeconomic change have seen researchers draw from the biological domain and take an evolutionary perspective. Proponents of evolutionary accounts of socioeconomic change emphasize that although such theories are derived from the biological sciences, evolution is a 'generic generative mechanism' that explains processes of change within systems, whether they are biological or otherwise (Metcalfe, 1998). The simplest models of evolutionary change in the social domain provide accounts in which the generation of variety and selection processes are central. More substantive accounts also include further processes of propagation (or retention), along with the conflict for resources.

In the natural world co-evolution operates as a meta-evolutionary process in which the interaction of participants contributes to the collective creation of a habitat that shapes their prospects. Selected forms of mutual accommodation or symbiosis can occur without intentionality when blind accommodating responses are rewarded by survival, as where the form of fitness rewarded by natural selection depends on the capacity to 'fit into' a co-evolving ecosystem (Goodwin, 1994).

Analogous to biological ecosystems, the concept of the 'business ecosystem' has emerged to refer to an ecology of firms that through co-operative actions attempt to realize financial returns (Moore, 1993). From this perspective, industries can be regarded as systems of innovation and production in which firms collaborate to further develop the ecosystem to their mutual benefit. Firms at the centre of the ecosystem become successful by developing an innovation trajectory that is vital to the ecosystem, through ensuring that their contribution is valued by end customers and other members of the ecosystem, and by embedding their products, processes and organization with those of the ecosystem

(Moore, 1996). The direction shared by these central firms ('keystones') and their partners result in institutional and technological co-evolution across the ecosystem, in turn generating sustainable competitive advantages. In this manner, joining a leading or growing ecosystem is more likely to yield returns than joining alternative ecosystems that have smaller market penetration or recognized growth potential (Iansiti and Levein, 2004).

In the economy, consumer demand, competition and the allocation of investments operate as selection forces that shape progress (Nelson and Winter, 1982). Intelligent agents are not blind to the operation of selection forces; on the contrary, they can learn to anticipate the rewards and sanctions exerted, and respond to perceived incentives through entrepreneurial action (Nelson, 1995). Moreover, the frequent creation of partnerships by entrepreneurs may be seen to represent entrepreneurial attempts to shape a new business environment hospitable to their efforts (Gomes-Casseres, 1996). By anticipating gains from innovative goods and services under changing and uncertain conditions entrepreneurial entrants often initiate changes in business ecosystems (Bhidé, 2000).

As the outcomes of co-evolutionary processes impact on further activity, these iterations generate recurrent feedback processes. The role of negative feedback in restoring equilibria has long been promulgated in the economic literature. That positive feedbacks also operate in the economy has been highlighted relatively recently (Arthur, 1989, 1990; David, 1985). In these accounts, positive feedbacks are manifest as increasing returns created by consumption and production externalities. Positive production externalities are apparent around core architectures because these provide an enabling function to which complementary products and services can be contributed by other agents in the ecosystem (Shapiro and Varian, 1999).

Accordingly, the successful selection and propagation of a business ecosystem can be partially attributed to the effective harnessing of positive feedback effects. The addition of complements to these ecosystems has been observed to contribute to the growth of the ecosystem, increasing the value of these externalities to producers and consumers alike. However, potential participants must first be convinced that they should partner in the development of these complements. Providing potential partners with the perception that the future prospects of the ecosystem are attractive is a key element in growing the business ecosystem where further innovative behaviour develops complementary products and services of mutual benefit (Ford and Garnsey, 2007).

3. Methodology

As a recent phenomenon, there has been little academic literature published on the UFC, with those studies that have focused on the subject doing so through different lenses (for example, sociology (Downey, 2007) and marketing (Andrew et al., 2009)). Given the wealth of online information sources available on the subject, we have chosen to draw on these as our primary source of information. To assist the reader in familiarizing themselves with the UFC and the growth of MMA, we provide a brief history of the UFC. As evolutionary and complexity thinking informs us that the history of systems matters to their future development, we use this account as a starting point for further exposition, drawing on further data collected on UFC events and the fighters competing within the organization. This provides us with the necessary perspective to analyse the co-evolutionary dynamics operating in the UFC business ecosystem.

4. A brief history of the growth of the ultimate fighting championships

4.1. The launch of the UFC

The UFC was conceived by Art Davie, Rorion Gracie and Bob Meyrowitz. Together they formed WOW Promotions in 1993, securing funding for a first event from a group of 28 investors and a television partner in pay-per-view operator Semaphore Entertainment Group (SEG). Its first event in November 1993 was an eight-man elimination tournament between fighters representing the disciplines of boxing, Brazilian jiu-jitsu, catch wrestling, karate, kickboxing, savate, sumo and tae kwon do. The event was promoted as 'no holds barred' fighting in the style of Brazilian *vale tudo* (translation: 'anything goes'). However despite these claims, there were some limited rules in place that prohibited biting, eye gouging and groin strikes. An attendance of 2800 people and pay-per-view audience of approximately 86,000 saw the tournament won by the smallest fighter in the competition, Royce Gracie from the discipline of Brazilian jiu-jitsu.

Following the success of this first event, further UFC events were held, with these each continuing in the single-night tournament structure with no weight limits. In addition to these tournaments, the organization's first 'superfight', a fight between the UFC's two biggest stars, Royce Gracie and Ken Shamrock, was held at UFC 5 on 7 April 1995. The event drew a pay-per-view audience of 260,000, an MMA record that would stand for a decade (Meltzer, 2008a). Following UFC 5, Davie and Meyrowitz sold their stake in WOW to SEG, although they continued to work with SEG to organize and promote UFC events.

4.2. The ban on ultimate fighting

While the UFC was attracting significant audiences, by 1996 its violent nature had also attracted the attention of legislators. After seeing video footage of early UFC events and finding the spectacle too brutal, Senator John McCain used his political influence to push for a ban. These attempts were successful, with 36 US states subsequently enacting laws that banned 'no holds barred' events from being held inside their borders.

These bans forced the UFC into holding shows in smaller markets such as Alabama, Iowa and Louisiana, and experimenting outside the USA with events in Japan and Brazil. Of even greater significance than the change of geographical location was the decision of the major cable operators to stop airing UFC events. The move strangled the UFC's addressable audience from 35 million to 7.5 million, with actual sales shrinking to around 15,000 per show in 1999 (Plotz, 1999).

4.3. The unified rules of mixed martial arts

The ban on 'no holds barred' fighting forced the UFC to reconsider the nature of its events. The UFC began to engage and co-operate with the state athletic commissions to develop rules that would eliminate the more brutal elements of fighting while retaining the essential nature of multidiscipline combat. This led the UFC to begin to introduce a number of rules with the aim of protecting the safety of the combatants (Table 10.1) and led to the abandonment of the single-night tournament format.

Engagement with the California and New Jersey State Athletic Commissions led to the development of the 'Mixed Martial Arts Unified Rules of Conduct', a comprehensive set of rules that describe the conditions under which MMA fights can occur.[1] The rules includes specifications over weight classes, the duration of rounds, the combat arena, the equipment and apparel used by fighters, a list of 25 fouls, the scoring process and the types of bout results. The New Jersey State Athletic Commission was the first state to enact these rules into legislation. UFC 28 on 17 November 2000 in Atlantic City, New Jersey was the first UFC event to incorporate these changes.

Table 10.1 Significant rules change introduced to the UFC

Event	Date	Nature of rule change
UFC 12: *Judgement Day*	7 February 1997	Weight classes are introduced for the first time
UFC 14: *Showdown*	27 July 1997	4–6 oz. gloves become mandatory equipment for all fighters
UFC 15: *Collision Course*	17 October 1997	The number of permissible striking areas is reduced: headbutts, groin strikes, strikes to the back of the neck and head, kicks to a downed opponent, small joint manipulation, pressure point strikes and hair-pulling become illegal
UFC 21: *Return of the Champions*	16 October 1998	Five-minute rounds are introduced, with three rounds for non-title bouts and five rounds for title bouts. The 'ten point must' system is also introduced for judging fights
UFC 28: *High Stakes*	17 November 2000	The 'Mixed Martial Arts Unified Rules of Conduct' are adopted for the first time

4.4. Acquisition of the UFC

Despite the reform over the rules and the adoption of the unified rules, the reduced revenue streams from smaller shows and a limited pay-per-view audience pushed SEG to the brink of bankruptcy and prompted the organization to put the UFC up for sale in late 2000. The UFC was then acquired by Lorenzo and Frank Fertitta, owners of the Las Vegas-based Station Casinos in January 2001 for US$2 million. Their first actions were to create Zuffa LLC as the parent company of the UFC and to install Dana White, a close friend and MMA manager, as President of the UFC. The UFC held its first event under the new ownership, UFC 30, on 23 February 2001 in Atlantic City, New Jersey. As a former member of the Nevada State Athletic Commission, Frank Fertitta was well-placed to help push through the sanctioning of the reformed rules in Nevada. This opened up the opportunity to hold events in Las Vegas, 'the fight capital of the world', with the first being UFC 33 on 28 September 2001.

The belief of the UFC management was that success would follow once the UFC returned to pay-per-view broadcasts. However, despite returning to the pay-per-view market, the majority of events only attracted buy rates of 35,000-50,000 per show. The exception to this was UFC 40, which featured a much-hyped grudge match between early UFC star Ken Shamrock and the brash-talking rising star Tito Ortiz. The event, held at the MGM Grand Garden Arena in Las Vegas on 22 November 2002, sold 150,000 on pay-per-view and was the first UFC event to generate a live gate in excess of US$1 million. Despite the success of this event, pay-per-view revenues did not pick up and between 2001 and 2005 the UFC accrued losses of approximately US$33 million (Meltzer, 2008b).

4.5. The Ultimate Fighter

The turning point for the UFC's fortunes was the decision to commission 'The Ultimate Fighter' (TUF), a reality TV show that was broadcast over 12 weekly episodes on the cable network Spike TV. The premise for the show was that eight middleweight and eight light heavyweight fighters would compete in tournaments to determine the best fighter in each weight division. On offer to the winners of each division was a '6-figure, three year contract with the UFC'. The twist was that the show was filmed over a six-week period in which the 16 contestants lived in a shared house and were continually under video surveillance, in a similar style to other reality TV shows such as 'Big Brother' and 'Survivor'. In addition, Randy Couture, the light heavyweight champion, and Chuck Liddell served as coaches on the series, with the aim of the series also being to provide these two fighters with greater public exposure prior to their fight at UFC 52.

The finals of the tournament were broadcast at 'The Ultimate Fighter Finale' on Spike TV on 9 April 2005. The highlight of the event was the final of the light heavyweight category between a former police officer, Forrest Griffin, and a former Golden Gloves boxing champion, Stephan Bonnar. Significantly, the event attracted an audience of 2.6 million.[2] The Griffin versus Bonnar fight has subsequently been described by Dana White as 'the most important fight in UFC history' (Meltzer, 2008b).

4.6. The UFC Enters the Mainstream

'The Ultimate Fighter' served as a catalyst for an explosion of interest in the UFC in the USA. Held one week after 'The Ultimate Fighter Finale',

UFC 52 set new UFC records for gate receipts (US$2.58 million) and pay-per-view sales (280,000). On the back of this surge in popularity, the UFC began to promote a greater number of events than before. In the four years prior to the first season of TUF, the UFC had held 22 events. In comparison, in the four years since the first season of TUF the UFC has held 67 events. Another seven seasons of 'The Ultimate Fighter' have also been produced and aired on Spike TV.

Figures from the Nevada State Athletic Commission give an indication of the rising popularity of the UFC, with gate receipts at Las Vegas shows consistently generating US$2-3 million per event since TUF (Figure 10.1). Up to 2008, the biggest UFC event in terms of revenues has been UFC 66 on 30 December 2006, which generated gate receipts of US$5.4 million and drew a pay-per-view audience of 1,050,000.

The increased revenues generated by the UFC have also allowed Zuffa to acquire a number of other promotions, most notably the Japanese-based 'Pride Fighting Championships' (Pride FC), and US-based organizations, 'World Extreme Cagefighting' (WEC) and 'World Fighting Alliance' (WFA). In the case of Pride FC and the WFA, fighters under contract to those organizations were brought into the UFC, while the WEC operates as a sister organization to the UFC, focusing on lighter

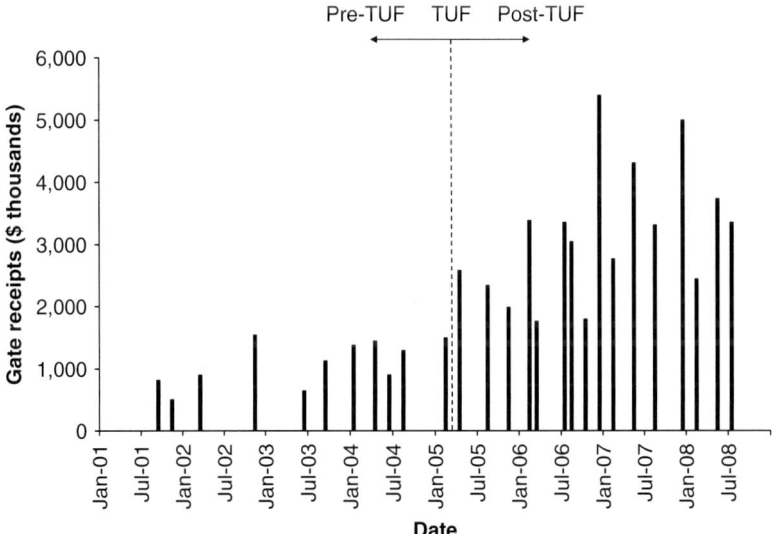

Figure 10.1 Gate receipts for Las Vegas-based UFC events
Source: Nevada State Athletic Commission.

weight categories (featherweight, under 145 lbs, and bantamweight, under 135 lbs).

5. Co-evolution in the ultimate fighting championships business ecosystem

Now that the reader is familiar with the UFC, its origins and activities, we can begin to analyse the actors in the UFC business ecosystem and identify the processes and feedbacks that operate within it.

5.1. Trialability of the UFC's product

As an organization that had faced extinction during the ban on MMA in the USA, the challenge facing the Zuffa-owned UFC was how to grow from its 'hardcore' roots and to bring in new fans from the mainstream. The introduction of the unified rules of MMA provided the UFC with the platform to establish legitimacy. However, as was described in the historical account, the turning point for the UFC didn't come until four years later when the first season of 'The Ultimate Fighter' reality TV series proved a ratings success. As a free-to-air programme on the cable channel Spike TV, TUF provided an avenue by which MMA could be exposed to a new audience and through which this audience could relate to the fighters. That it achieved record figures for its finale and increased pay-per-view figures for the events that followed prompted the UFC to increase its number of free-to-air events in partnership with Spike TV.

By the end of 2008, eight seasons of 'The Ultimate Fighter' had been commissioned by Spike TV and produced by the UFC. At the end of each of these, the UFC held 'The Ultimate Fighter Finale', featuring bouts between the finalists, along with the runners-up, and often headlined by a pair of established fighters the UFC wants to showcase. To expand its free offerings, on 6 August 2005, the UFC produced the first in its 'Ultimate Fight Night' series with Spike TV. Through to the end of 2008, 17 of these shows had been aired.

The UFC has also sought to grow its audience through global expansion and in 2007 and 2008 it held five events in the UK in an attempt to establish a European presence. However, the time difference between the UK and the USA resulted in poor pay-per-view figures for the first event held in the UK and prompted the UFC to also offer future UK-based events for free on Spike TV. This decision appeared to be a wise one as the main event of the first free-to-air UK event that the UFC offered on Spike TV, UFC 75 became the most watched MMA match in US history.

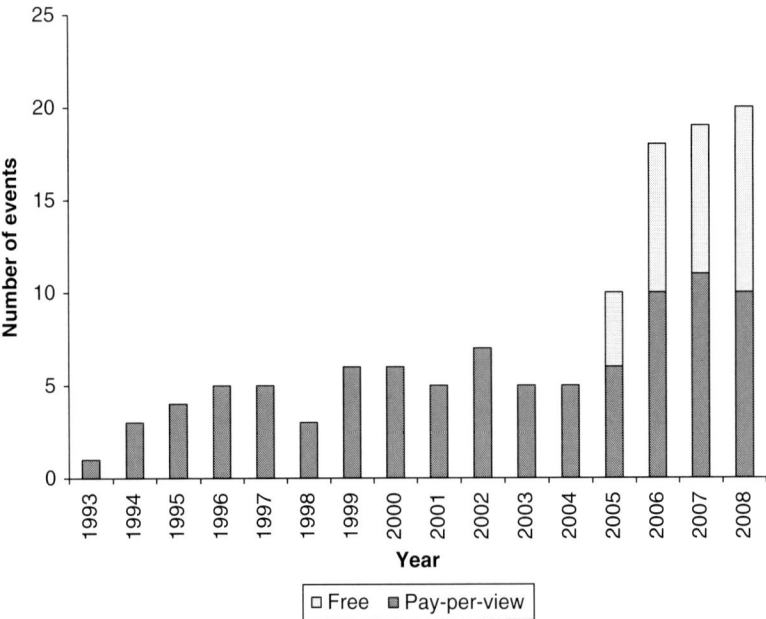

Figure 10.2 Growth in the number of UFC events
Source: http://www.ufc.com.

The incorporation of these free events into the UFC product portfolio has grown to the extent that in 2008 there were as many free UFC events as there were pay-per-view events (Figure 10.2). The ability to attract a new audience that has not previously been exposed to the UFC through these free events has been a critical element to the UFC's growth, representing the 'trialability' aspect relating to the diffusion of an innovation (Rogers, 1995). As a consequence of the growth in the number of events it has held, UFC content has become an integral component of Spike TV's broadcasting schedule.

5.2. Recruitment and retention of successful fighters

With each UFC event featuring a fight card that usually comprises nine or ten bouts, the fighters are a central component of the UFC product. Positioning itself as the premier MMA organization, the UFC has carefully cultivated and acquired a roster of high-level fighting talent. According to the international rankings of the World Alliance of Mixed Martial Arts (WAMMA), at the end of 2008, 60 per cent of the top ten fighters in the five weight classes that the UFC operates fight in the UFC, with the other 40 per cent, divided between six other organizations.

Fighters are recruited to the UFC either through being identified as a prospect in a regional MMA promotion (for example, 'King of the Cage' in the USA, 'Cage Fury' in Brazil or 'Spirit MC' in Korea), from a successful appearance on 'The Ultimate Fighter' reality TV series or through transferring the contracts of fighters following the UFC's acquisition of a competing promotion (for example, 'Pride Fighting Championships', 'World Fighting Alliance'). Fighters entering the UFC through the first two routes are usually lower-level talent that require cultivation and gradual exposure to increasing levels of competition. In comparison, those fighters that enter the UFC after the acquisition of their organization to which they were contracted are usually higher paid and face high-level talent immediately. These contracts are exclusive in nature, meaning that once signed the fighter can only compete for the UFC and cannot compete for another MMA promotion without the permission of the UFC.

5.2.1. Rewarding successful fighters

UFC fighter contracts are performance-related and structured in such a way as to reward those fighters that stimulate ticket and pay-per-view purchases. New UFC fighters are typically signed to four fight contracts. Fighters are paid a basic appearance fee, with an additional bonus paid for winning their fight. For lower-level fighters, this bonus is usually equal to that of the appearance fee but is more variable for higher-profile fighters who are paid more (in excess of US$50,000). Those higher-profile fighters that are able to stimulate ticket and pay-per-view purchases are termed 'draws' for their ability to 'draw in' this paying audience.

For example, Table 10.2 lists the salaries (including win bonuses) for three selected UFC fighters from their first appearance in the UFC. This table shows the progression up the pay scale that fighters make as they win more fights. Our three examples demonstrate the pay scale for (1) a low-level fighter brought in from a regional promotion, (2) a fighter from 'The Ultimate Fighter' reality TV show and (3) an established high-level fighter.

The first of these, welterweight fighter Jon Fitch, entered the UFC after accumulating a 9–2 win-loss record in a variety of US regional MMA promotions. While initially only paid the entry-level rate of US$4000 base pay and a US$4000 win bonus, his eight successive wins illustrates how his base pay and bonus increased incrementally with each fight.

Table 10.2 Salaries of three selected UFC fighters

Fighter	UFC record (won–lost)	Fights								
		1	2	3	4	5	6	7	8	9
Jon Fitch	8-0	8	8	16	20	28	36	44	60	
Forrest Griffin	7-2	24	24	24	16*	32	16*	32	44	250
Anderson Silva	8-0	36	50	71	90	120	140	200	N/A	

Note: Salaries in US$1000, losses are asterisked.

Our second fighter, Forrest Griffin, was the light heavyweight winner of the first season of 'The Ultimate Fighter' and had a contract in which he initially received US$12,000 as his basic salary, with an additional US$12,000 for winning. This rose to US$16,000 plus US$16,000 until he became a main event fighter, at which point he was signed to an upgraded contract. For Griffin this was his ninth fight, a championship fight at UFC 86 that he won against Quentin Jackson, in which he gained a substantial purse of US$250,000.

Our final fighter is the Brazilian middleweight Anderson Silva. He entered the UFC after having already competed in the Japanese-based promotion Pride FC, which at the time was a significant rival to the UFC. His salary in his first bout was considerably higher than that of regular UFC debutants. In his second fight, he challenged and successfully won the UFC Middleweight title. His successful title defences have seen his pay rise significantly.

5.2.2. Rewarding exciting fighters

As the central product of the UFC, its events must satisfy the demands of its consumers so the UFC introduced additional event bonuses to encourage exciting fights. These additional bonuses are awarded at each UFC event for 'Fight of the Night', 'Knockout of the Night' and 'Submission of the Night'. These bonuses have risen from US$30,000 in early 2007 to US$60,000 at the end of 2008, and had been as high as US$80,000 at some events in between. These bonuses are several times greater than the pay received by the lower-tier fighters, who are often on contracts worth less than US$10,000 per fight. Thus these bonuses provide an incentive for the fighters to provide an entertaining fight that will be enjoyed by the audience live in the arena and watching on TV, reinforcing the excitement associated with the UFC brand.

5.2.3. Eliminating unsuccessful fighters

Although new UFC fighters are usually signed to four bout contracts, very few of these see out all of these fights because these contracts contain clauses that allow the UFC to terminate them should the fighter lose. There are two main reasons for this decision. The first is that the UFC, despite significantly expanding the number of events that it holds, has only so many events at which fighters can compete. For example, in 2007 the UFC held 19 events. These events comprised 171 individual bouts and featured 194 individual fighters. During this time, the majority of these fighters only competed in a single bout and only 20 per cent competed in three or more bouts (Table 10.3).

The second reason is that the UFC is looking to maintain its reputation as the promotion in which the most talented fighters compete. Analysis shows that in 2007, 59 fighters left the UFC and have not since returned to the organization (Table 10.4). Of these, only five left the UFC after having won their final bout. The other 54 were released by the UFC after losing one or more of their previous bouts. These figures indicate that a significant proportion of the fighters that enter the UFC are unsuccessful and soon leave, while the UFC remains in a dominant position to retain the more talented, successful fighters. An exception to this pattern is that exciting fighters with losing records may be retained by the UFC as their performances add to the entertainment value of the overall product.

5.2.4. The evolutionary trajectory of a business ecosystem

In his explanation of the growth of a business ecosystem, Moore (1996) described how an innovation trajectory is a central component of its development. By innovation, he meant an improvement in performance; for the UFC this means an improvement to its central product,

Table 10.3 Number of bouts competed in by UFC fighters in 2007

Number of bouts	Number of fighters	Percentage of fighters
1	90	46.4
2	65	33.5
3	35	18.0
4	3	1.5
5	1	0.5

Table 10.4 UFC record of fighters leaving the organization in 2007

		Lost				
		0	1	2	3	>3
Won	0	0	17	18	4	0
	1	1	4	5	1	1
	2	0	0	1	2	0
	3	0	0	0	1	1
	>3	0	0	1	1	1

the events it holds. As each event comprises a number of bouts between fighters, it is the quality of the fights and of the fighters themselves that ultimately determine the performance of the UFC product.

In the early days of the UFC, fighters were versed in only a single martial art. However, as competition intensified, fighters began to cross-train, to develop additional disciplines that they could incorporate into their combat style. By 2009, top-level fighters require both striking (including but not exclusively boxing, kickboxing, karate and tae kwon do) and grappling acumen (wrestling, Brazilian jiu-jitsu and judo) if they are to successfully compete. This multi-discipline ability is still emerging and it is anticipated that fighters will continue to become better skilled competitors. Accordingly, we observe that the recruitment, retention and elimination of fighters from the UFC create an evolutionary trajectory in which the quality of the core UFC product is steadily improving.

5.3. Benefits of operating in the UFC's business ecosystem

As the most prominent MMA organization in North America, the UFC has developed a significant profile through its events and TV programming. This has benefited its fighters, a number of whom have translated the success and exposure they have achieved in the UFC into financial opportunities elsewhere. For example, former UFC heavyweight and light heavyweight champion Randy Couture has opened his own gym, Xtreme Couture, and launched his own Xtreme Couture clothing range in partnership with Affliction Clothing. He has also starred in several Hollywood movies, including 'The Scorpion King', and featured on a number of other US TV shows. Elsewhere, former UFC middleweight champion Rich Franklin is a partner in the American Fighter range of leisure clothing and gyms, while both Franklin and lightweight contender Roger Huerta have begun acting careers. These examples, along with those in the next sections, illustrate how being part of the UFC business ecosystem provides significant benefits to actors that they would not realize elsewhere.

Connected to the development of the fighters themselves are the training camps and gyms to which they belong and in which improve their fighting skills. In the very early years of the UFC such entities did not exist. Over time 'camps' emerged where, in the absence of dedicated MMA training facilities, groups of fighters would train together to improve their MMA skills. The Lions Den, formed by MMA pioneer Ken Shamrock, was one of the first of these, along with Pat Militich's Militich Fighting Systems (MFS) and Team Quest. These early gyms were primarily formed by the fighters themselves because they needed training facilities in which to practice and improve.

Since the UFC began to explode in popularity in 2005, a number of training camps and gyms have risen to prominence in the USA. Jackson's MMA, Xtreme Couture, American Top Team (ATT), the American Kickboxing Academy (AKA) and Team Sityodtong are just five of the leading training camps to which UFC fighters belong. For example, six past or present UFC fighters train at Jackson's MMA, eight at Xtreme Couture, eighteen at ATT, eight at AKA and six at Team Sityodtong.

These training camps have risen to prominence through their fighters appearing in the UFC. As the UFC has positioned itself as the pinnacle of MMA, these training camps have by association acquired the reputation as the best in their field. They have benefited financially through the percentage of the salaries they receive from the fighters and through the revenues generated by providing classes to those novices and intermediate martial artists at their gyms. The popularity of MMA has led to an expansion in the number of gyms offering MMA training and some of these organizations have been quick to realize the commercial opportunities associated with the brand reputation they have acquired. For example, the Las Vegas-based Xtreme Couture gym has a franchise scheme whereby other gyms can license the Xtreme Couture name for US$50,000. Through a similar approach, the Florida-based American Top Team has expanded to 23 gyms across the US east coast. In each case the expansion of these networks of gyms seeks to satisfy a growing need from the UFC's audience to also practice the sport they have consumed. This participation aspect represents a reinforcing feedback into the practicing martial artist's interest and consumption of MMA and the UFC, further supporting the development of the UFC's business ecosystem.

Since its acquisition by Zuffa, the UFC has sought to profit from sponsorship revenues. As the UFC audience has grown, these revenues have started to be realized as the audience size and demographic have given other companies good reason to sponsor the UFC and its fighters. At each of its events, whether free or on pay-per-view, the UFC sells a number of sponsorship spaces. Physical sponsorship spaces include decals on the floor and frame of the Octagon and the preparation point that fights pass through immediately prior to entering the Octagon. The main event fights themselves are sponsored and read out by the ring announcer. A number of further sponsorship spaces occur during the broadcast, including the 'Fight Cards' that precede each bout and the 'Turning Point of the Night' at the end of the telecast. Similarly, the fighters have the logos of their sponsors on their shorts, t-shirts and caps, along with a banner that the fighter's entourage holds against the Octagon during the fight introductions.

These sponsors are particularly drawn to the 18–34 male demographic that watch the UFC events more than any others and can be divided into three categories. The first category is MMA-specific apparel companies such as TapouT, Sprawl, Cage Fighter and Warrior Wear, who sponsor fighters to wear their products. The second category includes companies that produce sports-related goods, including energy drinks such as Xyience and Rockstar, and athletic performance supplements such as BSN and Progenex. These first two categories of sponsors are much more closely connected to the UFC as their products directly relate to consumers that want to associate with an MMA lifestyle. In the final category are the 'blue chip' sponsors, international brands that have started to sponsor the UFC so as to reach the UFC's demographic. This category includes Budweiser, Burger King and Harley Davidson.

6. Conclusions

In this chapter we have started to describe how the development of a business ecosystem around the UFC, which includes its roster of fighters, television networks, sponsors, training camps and sporting goods manufacturers, has created a co-evolutionary dynamic in which these actors share in the success of the UFC. These elements are also investigated in the two chapters that follow on the growth of soccer leagues in the USA and Japan. But whereas soccer is already a global sport facing particular national challenges as it continues to expand internationally,

MMA is still a nascent sport and has yet to gain widespread recognition. As a growing firm, the UFC faces the challenge of acquiring mainstream acceptance and support, as evidenced by it still being illegal to hold MMA events in a number of US states. The UFC has, however, successfully positioned itself as the organization in which the most talented MMA compete. As the pinnacle of the MMA world, other fighters are drawn towards it with the hope of competing in the organization and testing their skills. This is also what the US public now believes, that the UFC has the most talented fighters on its fight cards, and this belief has grown to the extent that the UFC brand is bigger than that of any individual fighter. The increased exposure that the UFC has gained, along with the male 18-34 demographic to which it has most appeal, has brought in higher-profile sponsors, such as Budweiser, Harley Davidson and Burger King. The halo effects of being associated with these 'blue chip' firms has in turn lent credibility to the UFC and provided it with increased mainstream exposure. As the UFC is still on an upward growth path, this allows it to continue to return a greater proportion of its revenues to its employees, the fighters. This in turn provides greater incentives for potential and actual MMA fighters to want to enter the UFC because the livelihood that can be achieved through fighting in the UFC becomes more attractive.

MMA is a sport in which fans demand drama, with fights being competitive and where 'anything can happen' (Andrew et al., 2009). Going forward, the UFC faces the continuing tension of maintaining credibility as a professional sport and providing its customers with the entertainment they expect. Its retention of the most successful fighters ensures that its shows feature the most skilled competitors. However, fights between skilled practitioners do not always translate into entertaining bouts. The UFC continues to build up 'draws', fighters who can sell tickets based on their personality and skills, and to create compelling storylines between competitors in a similar manner to professional wrestling organizations such as World Wrestling Entertainment (WWE). The UFC has so far proven itself adept at entrepreneurial opportunism, expanding its business ecosystem in North America. Further challenges will come as it attempts to expand into international markets and establish its brand identity globally.

Notes

1. 'Mixed Martial Arts Unified Rules of Conduct: Additional Mixed Martial Arts Rules', http://www.state.nj.us/lps/sacb/docs/martial.html, retrieved 05.09.2002.

2. http://www.sherdog.com/news/news/26-million-tuned-in-to-see-dramatic-conclusion-2659, retrieved 12.04.2005.

References

Andrew, D.P.S., Kim, S., O'Neal, N., Greenwell, T.C. and James, J.D. (2009) 'The Relationship Between Spectator Motivations and Media and Merchandise Consumption at a Professional Mixed Martial Arts Event', *Sports Marketing Quarterly*, 18(4): 199–209.

Arthur, W.B. (1989) 'Competing Technologies, Increasing Returns and Lock-in by Historical Events', *Economic Journal*, 99(394): 116–131.

Arthur, W.B. (1990) 'Positive Feedbacks in the Economy', *Scientific American*, 262(February): 92–99.

Bhidé, A. (2000) *The Origin and Evolution of New Businesses* (New York, NY: Oxford University Press).

David, P.A. (1985) 'Clio and the Economics of QWERTY', *American Economic Review*, 75: 332–337.

Downey, G. (2007) 'Producing Pain: Techniques and Technologies in No-Holds-Barred Fighting', *Social Studies of Science*, 37(2): 201–226.

Ford, S.J. and Garnsey, E.W. (2007) 'Failing to Disrupt: The Case of the Network Computer', *International Journal of Technology Intelligence and Planning*, 3(1): 6–23.

Garnsey, E.W., Heffernan, P.B. and Ford, S.J. (2007) 'Diversity and Uniformity in the Evolution of Early Information and Communication Technologies', in E.W. Garnsey and J. McGlade (eds), *Complexity and Co-evolution: Continuity and Change in Socio-economic Systems* (Cheltenham: Edward Elgar Publishing): 177–203.

Gentry, F. (2004) *No Holds Barred: Ultimate Fighting and the Mixed Martial Arts Revolution* (Lytham: Milo Books).

Gomes-Casseres, B. (1996) *The Alliance Revolution: The New Shape of Business Rivalry* (Cambridge, MA: Harvard University Press).

Goodwin, B. (1994) *How the Leopard Changed Its Spots: The Evolution of Complexity* (London: Weidenfeld & Nicolson).

Iansiti, M. and Levein, R. (2004) *The Keystone Advantage: What the New Dynamics of Business Ecosystems Mean for Strategy, Innovation, and Sustainability* (Boston, MA: Harvard Business School Press).

Langlois, R. (1992) 'External Economies and Economic Progress: The Case of the Microcomputer Industry', *Business History Review*, 66(1): 1–50.

Meltzer, D. (2008a) 'UFC's Greatest Hits: The Early Days', http://sports.yahoo.com/mma/news?slug=dm-ufcearly111708&prov=yhoo&type=lgns, retrieved 17.11.2008.

Meltzer, D. (2008b) 'UFC's Greatest Hits: The Middle Years', http://sports.yahoo.com/mma/news?slug=dm-ufcmiddle112408&prov=yhoo&type=lgns, retrieved 24.11.2008.

Metcalfe, S. (1998) *Evolutionary Economics and Creative Destruction* (London: Routledge).

Moore, J. (1993) 'Predators and Prey: A New Ecology of Competition', *Harvard Business Review*, 71(3): 75–86.

Moore, J. (1996) *The Death of Competition: Leadership and Strategy in the Age of Business Ecosystems* (Chichester: John Wiley).

Nelson, R.R. (1995) 'Recent Evolutionary Theorizing About Economic Change', *Journal of Economic Literature*, 33(1): 48–90.

Nelson, R.R. and Winter, S.G. (1982) *An Evolutionary Theory of Economic Change* (London: Belknap Press).

Plotz, D. (1999) 'Fight Clubbed: Ultimate Fighting Ought to Be a Great American Sport. Instead, Cable Companies, Sen. John McCain, and a Squeamish Public Are Killing It', http://www.slate.com/id/46344, retrieved 17.11.1999.

Rogers, E.M. (1995) *Diffusion of Innovations*, 3rd edn (New York: Free Press).

Shapiro, C. and Varian, H. (1999) *Information Rules: A Strategic Guide to the Network Economy* (Boston, MA: Harvard Business School Press).

11
Learning from Failure: Is Major League Soccer Repeating the Mistakes of the North American Soccer League?

John D. Francis

1. Introduction

There is no question that the most popular sport in the world in terms of participation, viewership and business is football (known in the USA as soccer). Even though there is widespread participation among Americans under the age of 18, interest in soccer lags behind several other sports and is virtually ignored by the US media (Brennan, 2007). This apparent lack of interest has not, however, stopped investors and others from attempting to develop professional soccer in the USA in order to tap into the sport's enormous global market. In fact, the Los Angeles Galaxy of the Major League Soccer (MLS) created a stir in January 2007, when the club signed David Beckham, who agreed to leave Real Madrid, the professional Spanish football club, for a five-year, US$250 million contract in Los Angeles.

Paying a large salary to an international superstar in an attempt to draw attention to an American soccer league is a formula that has been used before. In 1975, the Brazilian soccer star, Pelé, signed a three-year, US$7 million deal with the New York Cosmos of the North American Soccer League (NASL). Although NASL saw tremendous growth during Pelé's playing years, the league folded in 1984, just six years after his departure. In similar fashion, MLS, looking to capitalize on revenue and growth potential, added Beckham. Many critics argue that MLS is following in the same footsteps as the now defunct NASL and is destined to meet a similar end, and that the USA will never have a successful soccer league which can rival or develop stars like other nations' leagues

(Bloom, 2007). MLS, on the other hand, argues that it is not making the same mistakes and that professional soccer has unlimited potential in the USA.

Of the many issues surrounding MLS' ultimate success, the importance of using NASL's failure as a critical source for learning seems relevant. While experiential learning is important for all firms, it is most important when organizations are relative newcomers to markets and when the advantages of learning are the strongest (Thomas et al., 2007). The importance of failure as a learning experience has received increased attention from organizational scholars as a determinant of how firms grow and evolve in the face of uncertainty (Miner et al., 1999; Sitkin, 1992). Failure experience has been viewed as a form of 'survival-enhancing learning' (Baum and Ingram, 1998), which can be both a valuable resource and a contributor to an organization's success if proper lessons are learned (Kam, 2004). On the surface this type of learning seems likely, however, research suggests that executives can be inclined to attribute unfavorable outcomes (such as prior failures) to uncontrollable external forces making learning difficult (Schwenk, 1986). In these cases, constructive evaluation of a prior failure does not occur causing organizations to repeat mistakes. In the case of MLS, critics argue that exceeding its salary cap by paying Beckham an enormous salary is similar to NASL's past strategies and that MLS is repeating the same mistakes.

To explore this criticism, this chapter examines the extent to which MLS is following similar or dissimilar strategies from the defunct NASL. Using a case methodology, learning theory is applied as to whether MLS executives learned from NASL's previous failure or whether they are ignoring earlier lessons. The chapter examines key success factors for successful sports leagues and their applications to the structure of NASL and the primary determinants of its failure. The chapter also explores the case of MLS, its ongoing evolution and its considerations concerning David Beckham.

Using organizational learning theory, this research contributes to the literature in several ways. First, it provides a test of whether executives learn through failure. Although there has been much written on the significance and nature of learning capabilities, there exist very few studies addressing the problems of learning from failure and more specifically the issues involved in learning vicariously from the failure of others. Lastly, it adds to the growing body of literature on the globalization of sports business by providing insight into how organizations attempt to grow professional sports leagues in challenging environments that lack extensive historical connections to them.

2. Learning from failure

Scholars have long asserted that the actions of organizations are based partly on the learning that comes from experience (Cyert and March, 1963; Levinthal and March, 1993; March, 1991; Simon, 1991) and that learning from failure is a primary type of experiential learning. For example, Cyert and March (1963) argue that firms learn mainly through encountering problems rather than by experiencing success. They maintain that dealing with problems, as opposed to success, is more likely to cause cognitive change and exploration behavior. Researchers have suggested that two types of learning occur – exploitative and exploratory. *Exploitative learning* results in what O'Driscoll, Carson and Gilmore(2001: 73) refer to as competence leveraging, where a firm applies existing competencies to new market opportunities "in ways that do not require qualitative changes in the firm's assets or capabilities". *Exploratory learning* involves changes in company routines and experimentation with new alternatives (see, for example, Dodgson, 1993; March, 1991), which, if successful, change the nature of company competencies and increase their innovative performance. While this second type of learning is more useful for developing unique advantages, researchers believe that firms typically concentrate more on exploitative learning because they are often unsure of which new capabilities to learn. Also, "by the time knowledge is needed it is too late to gain it; before knowledge is needed it is hard to specify precisely what knowledge might be required or useful" (Levinthal and March, 1993: 103).

Researchers increasingly maintain that vicarious learning from other organizations' experiences is also an important way to acquire knowledge (Ingram and Baum, 1997; Kim and Miner, 2007; Miner et al., 1999). However, to date the literature is somewhat incomplete in its elaboration on how this type of learning occurs. To this end, this study further examines questions of whether and how organizations learn vicariously from others by examining the cases of NASL's failure and MLS' start in the USA.

3. North American Soccer League and Major League Soccer

The study uses a historical case, contemporary case comparison methodology for a number of reasons. First, the research question applies to learning from an organization that is no longer in existence, and therefore accessing data through personal interviews or questionnaires is extremely difficult. Furthermore, any data collected in this way would likely be skewed as a consequence of NASL's eventual fate. A team of four researchers carried out extensive secondary research of sports media coverage, specialized trade publications and books to obtain case material on both NASL and MLS. In the sections below, we evaluate both leagues in terms of the actions taken during their development in relation to our research questions. The researchers looked for events, incidents, strategies and interactions indicative of key concepts. While it is possible to begin with a prior set of codes, given the nature of this study, we used an inductive approach to analysing the data (Glaser and Strauss, 1967). The questions posed were: (1) How did NASL structure itself at its start and how did this change during its lifespan? (2) What factors were stated as leading to its success/failure? (3) How did MLS originally structure itself? and (4) What has MLS done differently and what are the stated reasons for this? After independent analyses were undertaken, the team met and assembled interconnected themes found in their data gathering. The following section describes some of the key highlights during the historical development of both leagues.

Professional soccer is historically, and remains, a 'second tier' sport in America, in terms of popularity and audience demand. NASL and MLS employed various actions to grow their sport, increase its impact and raise profits for their leagues. For a professional sports league to be successful, there are several critical success factors that it must possess. These factors are identified as a basis for the motivation and comparison of NASL and MLS. First, the competition must have audience appeal. The fans have to feel connected to the athletes on the field, understand the rules of the game and be entertained by the action. Thus, leagues generally pay high salary and signing fees to attract star players to add to their audience appeal. Second, professional leagues must have favorable television contracts. Games must be broadcast on TV to increase exposure, legitimize the brand and provide large revenue streams. Third, to be successful in the long run, leagues must be able to achieve profitability. Startup leagues are not immediately profitable due to large infrastructure costs (such as stadiums, player salaries, training facilities and such) with very little revenues being accrued. Even teams with existing leagues may experience losses in a given year due to various factors. Therefore, in order to develop a sustainable business model in the long run, owners must have deep pockets to be able to absorb losses in the interim. Fourth, leagues have to obtain a certain level of control to ensure the consistent quality of games. Franchise locations must be strategically placed throughout a mix of large and small markets so that a variety of fans have opportunities to experience games first-hand. Leagues must also ensure that there is consistency regarding the number of teams in order to build intriguing story lines and rivalries to increase fan interest.

3.1. The North American Soccer League

The North American Soccer League was the first US professional soccer league, which started in 1968 on the heels of England's World Cup victory and the attention that brought to soccer in English speaking countries. In 1967, two professional soccer leagues, the United Soccer Association and the National Professional Soccer League, began in the USA. The timing of these two leagues was undoubtedly related to the World Cup victory of the previous year. The National Professional Soccer League was unsanctioned by the Fédération Internationale de Football Association (FIFA), soccer's organizing body, but had a national television contract with CBS. However, the ratings for matches were so poor that the contract was cancelled the following year. In order to better leverage soccer, the two leagues merged in 1968 to form the North American Soccer League or NASL (Jose, 2003).

As with any startup, NASL's main tasks were to grow interest in its product and generate revenue in its new markets. One growth strategy involved changing soccer rules to make the game more appealing to American fans. Such changes included a clock that counted time down to zero, similar to other timed American sports. Also, as many Americans dislike ties, shootouts were introduced to decide a winner in matches that ended in a draw. In addition, to improve the quality of its product NASL began bringing high-profile foreign players to the USA. A side effect of this move was that most American players did not end up playing (Newsham, 2005). For example, NASL's highest profile club, the New York Cosmos, signed the captain of West Germany's World Cup winning squad, Franz Beckenbauer, the Italian goal scorer Giorgio Chinaglia and, most famously, Pelé, widely considered to be the greatest soccer player of all time (Weiland, 2006).

The Cosmos played at Giants Stadium and drew over 73,000 fans in their 1978 championship win. Overall, the Cosmos averaged 40,000 fans per game during the late 1970s. To attract Pelé to the new league, his Cosmos contract made him the highest paid athlete in the world, making twice the amount of the highest earning baseball player (the most popular professional sport at the time in the USA). A result of this was that NASL hugely over-relied on these foreign players, who grossed a large percentage of the payroll and left American players with lower salaries (Avila, 1997).

Even though Pelé had been retired from the sport for nearly two years when NASL's Cosmos decided to bring him on he was still a global icon and gave the USA a formal introduction to the sport of world class soccer. This was seen as a strategic move that would not only benefit the Cosmos and NASL, but would also increase the overall popularity of soccer in the USA (Newsham, 2005). Pelé was the first international player to make the move to an American team, and he showed other players around the world that this could be done successfully (Anderson, 1977). At the time, he was the most transcendent athlete in all of sports and probably the only soccer player who had the clout to help legitimize the game in the USA. Pelé's three years with the Cosmos were hugely successful for the league and the game of soccer in the USA. During Pelé's first year with the club, the Cosmos' gate revenue increased by $3 million. Average home attendance increased to nearly 32,000 in Pelé's first year, up from an average of 3500 in 1974. Pelé and the Cosmos also drew large crowds when playing away from New York, with an average away attendance of nearly 20,000 during Pelé's three-year tenure with the team. Although Pelé came to the USA at the age of 34, he still had athletic ability as evidenced by his leading the Cosmos to the 1977 NASL title in his final year with the team.

When Pelé retired from NASL in 1977, soccer had become the fastest growing sport on the youth, college and pro levels in the USA (Jose, 2003). There were nearly 50,000 registered players in youth soccer leagues in 1967, and that number skyrocketed to close to a million by 1977 (Miller, 1977). Clearly, NASL did not view the growth associated with Pelé as temporary, but rather as something it could build on and sustain (Yannis, 1978). For example, NASL added six new teams to the league the year following Pelé's retirement in hopes of continuing to capitalize on the sport's recent success and momentum. A NASL team's future projected average net income from ticket sales, concessions and television was around US$1–$2 million a year in 1977, which was comparable to an National Football League (NFL) franchise at the time (Miller, 1977). With projections this high, it did not seem farfetched to proclaim that soccer had secured a permanent position in mainstream America. Commenting on the expectations of the state of soccer after Pelé's retirement in 1977, the NASL's commissioner stated,

> Within ten years soccer will not only be the number one sport in the US, but also the major soccer center of the world. America will win the World Cup. More people will watch and play soccer here than

in any other country. It's a question of better marketing from here on in. (ibid.: 187)

Those were strong words from NASL's chief and were eventually too optimistic for a sport that had just lost a huge piece of its brand image. In hindsight, this opinion was far from being the reality, but it is also easy to forget how popular and close to the mainstream soccer was in the USA.

However, the overall average attendance of NASL was less than 15,000 per club, with some clubs averaging fewer than 5000 (Jose, 2003). League attendance continued to decline until NASL folded in 1984. While soccer remained the world's most popular sport, there was no professional soccer in the USA for 12 years. Even though NASL ultimately failed, some long-term good did result from the league's attempts. First, it introduced soccer to the North American sports scene on a large scale and was the major catalyst in soccer becoming one of the most popular sports at the grassroots level. To this day, American college and high school soccer leagues still use certain NASL rules (ibid.). Second, NASL provided a case from which MLS could learn and hopefully avoid making similar mistakes (Wahl, 2005).

3.2. Major League Soccer

In 1993, the US Soccer Federation promised FIFA it would establish a professional league in the States. In exchange, FIFA would allow the USA to host the 1994 World Cup tournament (Markovitz and Hellerman, 2001). This decision surprised many due to the perceived lack of soccer interest and NASL's failure a decade earlier. However, the 1994 US World Cup tournament boosted the highest to date attendance.[1] Two years later, MLS officially started playing in ten cities. Now in its 14th season of existence, as it stands, MLS has recorded losses of US$350 million as a league, and only two teams, the LA Galaxy and FC Dallas, have been able to turn a profit (Holmes, 2004).

When MLS began, executives looked to take a more conservative approach than had NASL. And while many of their strategies have been perceived as cautious, in 2005 MLS signed international soccer superstar David Beckham to play for the LA Galaxy franchise. As Christine Brennan, a columnist for the *USA Today* wrote, "David Beckham coming to the United States is like Tiger Woods meeting Brad Pitt on the red carpet. This transcends sports."[2] Many similarities between the signing of Beckham and the signing of Pelé have been noted, including that both were the highest paid sports figures of their time, and both were brought to the USA in attempts to generate appeal to uninterested consumers.

To date the Beckham experiment has been perceived as not as successful as it was poised to be in July 2007. Even though the LA Galaxy enjoyed spikes in season ticket sales, huge draws in seats and the associated financial success, the team suffered from two disappointing seasons in 2007 and 2008. In October 2008, LA Galaxy signed contracts with AC Milan for Beckham to play in Italy, effectively limiting his commitment to MLS. Even though Beckham is a significant draw for Galaxy games (Galaxy averaged 28,132 fans per game on the road, nearly 10,000 more than any other MLS team), the league itself only benefited slightly, with its average attendance raising 6.9 percent to 16,459 in 2008. As for the main measure of impact for sports leagues, TV ratings, Beckham did not help improve MLS' ESPN rating, drawing 0.2 ratings for his Galaxy games – the same rating that non-Beckham MLS broadcasts earned (compared to Women National Basketball Association's rating of 0.4 and National Basketball Association's rating of 1.4) (Mickle, 2008).

3.3. League comparisons

While the MLS' move to bring David Beckham to the USA can be seen as similar to NASL's strategy, many other strategies have been distinctly different and provide examples of 'learning from failure' by MLS. The following section, summarized in Table 11.1, outlines several areas in which research reveals how MLS has differentiated itself from NASL on key dimensions.

First, the MLS was set up as a single-entity league. This means the league controls all teams, among which the revenues are allocated, and

Table 11.1 Key similarities and differences between NASL and MLS

	NASL	MLS
Ownership	Individual owners	Single entity moving toward individual
Locations	Owners determined, erratic	Strategic locations, stable growth
Stadiums	Mixed use facilities	Moving towards soccer specific
Players	Large numbers of internationals	Designated player rule
Rules	NASL specific	International rules
Media	Limited televised matches	Mixed media; internet and television, every game broadcast
Community relations	Owner dependent	League-sponsored youth development leagues in every city

the league, rather than individual teams, negotiates all player contracts.[3] This gives the MLS a strong, centralized leadership, which has already been mentioned as a key success factor. By having the league control all these aspects, the design attempts to limit the destructive behavior that was displayed by individual owners during NASL's over-expansion period and subsequent decline. For example, NASL allowed many owners to start new teams only to see them fail within a year or two due to a lack of revenues. Overall, it appears the owners within NASL were myopic and greedy, and the league became a victim of its own sporadic and inconsistent success. The Cosmos' success lured executives into an overly optimistic view of growth and the ease of achieving it. NASL expanded too quickly for its talent base as it rushed to challenge the other major sports for the lucrative television market. In the end, there were neither enough quality players nor enough patience among league executives to grow NASL more solidly.

MLS franchises are not allowed to offer stars exorbitant contracts to outspend each other. To limit owner spending, MLS put a salary cap of US$2.4 million on every team.[4] Another change that the MLS made to its structure was having each team start a local development team or soccer academy for younger players. MLS hoped to encourage and develop homegrown US soccer talent, while creating an infrastructure that might bridge the gap between a successful youth soccer movement and professional soccer. MLS also limits the number of international players on a team to four and the number of international players in the entire league to eight, so that American fans can relate more to the domestic players on the field.

MLS has other factors in place that further differentiate the league from NASL, such as an emphasis on soccer-specific stadiums. The emphasis on these types of stadiums is to increase attendance by creating a soccer-friendly atmosphere. Also, because individual teams own the stadiums, they no longer have to lease facilities, as they did before, which were costly and usually unfavorable.[5] MLS has also secured television deals with four different networks so that all regular season matches are televised live. The shortest deal, with HD Net, is three years long, while the league's deal with Fox Soccer Channel runs for 11 years (Mickle, 2007).

4. Discussion

This chapter focuses on learning and how advantages can be created for firms learning vicariously from others' failures. The study describes the case of professional soccer in the USA comparing NASL and MLS in terms of their commonalities and differences in order to ascertain whether MLS is repeating the mistakes of NASL. The analysis indicates that vicarious learning from the failure of NASL appears to have had a major impact on MLS' startup, structure and strategies.

As stated previously, organizational learning can generally be classified as either exploratory, where major organizational changes are involved, or exploitative, where learning is applied incrementally. Analysis reveals that while MLS has recently imitated certain NASL strategies, it initially positioned itself very differently from NASL in almost all aspects providing evidence that MLS has applied both types of learning. Upon startup, MLS claimed itself to be the 'anti-NASL' and did not reach out to former NASL executives (Trekker, 2006). In its early actions, more exploratory forms of learning appear present as major changes and differences from NASL strategies were attempted. This is evidenced by the league's chosen form of governance, which emphasized centralized ownership, and its conservative growth strategies.

Over time, however, the cases suggest that exploitative learning occurred within MLS. For example, the league, while improving its revenues, does continue to lose money and operate below the periphery of mainstream sports fans in the USA. Therefore the Beckham move and the designated player rule can be viewed as attempts to address problems with one part of the league's model while not scrapping the whole. The financial and brand building potential of signing a foreign soccer star with the celebrity magnitude like David Beckham's mirrors NASL's signing of Pelé. While NASL ultimately folded, Pelé's short-term impact on ticket sales, sponsorships, merchandise sales and brand awareness is undeniable. MLS officials and Anschutz Entertainment Group (AEG) executives felt that Beckham would provide this same short-term spark for the MLS, which, in combination with improved league structures, would result in long-term growth. In addition to the signing of Beckham, MLS has relaxed its rules regarding the number of international players a team can acquire. Recently the league has brought in Mexican stars that are attractive to the growing Hispanic market in the USA.

Another example of incremental trial and error learning is the inaugural SuperLiga tournament, which began in 2007, pitting the best teams from the MLS and the Mexican League against each other. Again, this type of tournament is not unique, but is being imitated in an effort to exploit the current capabilities of MLS while addressing certain marketing weaknesses and demographic trends in the USA. All of these moves indicate that while MLS initially made moves opposite NASL, they have changed in certain ways and actually realize that good soccer means incorporating the best players wherever they can source them while at the same time remaining financially conservative. Sports biggest draw is the star power of its athletes. Fans emotionally identify with stars and pay to see them on the field. As Dolles and Söderman (2011) state in their chapter "Learning from Success", soccer is simultaneously global and local. Successful clubs emphasize and capitalize on both elements in developing their teams and promotional strategies (Dolles and Söderman, 2008).

Of the major theoretical arguments against learning from failure, the biases or myopia of executives are presented as major barriers to learning. For example, bounded rationality (Simon, 1955) and imperfect cognitive representations (Gavetti and Levinthal, 2000; Thagard, 1996) have been shown to simplify complex relationships and interactions between choices and actors, leading firms to emit inappropriate or standardized responses when dealing with unstable and changing stimuli (Tversky and Kahneman, 1986; Walsh, 1995). Research suggests that individuals are vulnerable to a range of cognitive biases (Lovallo and Kahneman, 2003; Westphal and Bednar, 2005), such as learning myopia (Levinthal and March, 1993). Levinthal and March (1993: 104) argue that "earning is likely to be misleading if the experiential record on which it draws is a biased representation of past reality, and thus of future likelihoods". However, it can be expected that these types of barriers to learning would be lessened if actors played no part in the previous failure, which is true in this case. NASL executives were not utilized in the development of MLS (Trekker, 2006), and MLS strongly differentiated itself from the outset. If cognitive bias was present, it lay in MLS' strong reaction against imitating NASL's earlier actions and in distancing itself from NASL's failures.

Another barrier to learning from failure is that executives can be overly optimistic and can mistakenly attribute performance to incorrect causes. Lovallo and Kahneman (2003) contend that managers tend to make decisions based on 'delusional optimism' rather than on rational assessment. Since learning may appear to eliminate failures, it fosters optimistic expectations, and because firms promote people who lead successful activities, leaders tend to be optimistic people. While past and current MLS leadership has been confident in its promotion and the future of the league, the optimism is more conservative than that of NASL executives when compared to public statements made about the growth and popularity of soccer in the USA. It is likely that there will always be optimism surrounding the future of organizations, however, MLS is doing so many things differently than the former league, it is difficult to suggest that its leaders' optimism is preventing them from learning from the previous failure.

Additionally, in examining both cases, there have not been any suggestions that exogenous causes led to the failure of NASL. Instead, most of the blame has been placed on NASL team owners' overly aggressive growth goals. Overall, it appears that when there is a large failure that is blamed on former executive mismanagement, learning conditions are enhanced. For the current case, these conditions appear to have resulted in cautiousness. In particular, it may have led to an emphasis by MLS executives on pursuing different actions than the previous league, including a patient and slower growth approach and more of a focus on the long-term impacts of league growth decisions.

Interestingly, a by-product of this approach has been the seeming elimination of some of the flamboyance and marketing buzz that was part of NASL's popularity and overall branding. Soccer's popularity in the USA surged during the mid-1970s when Pelé played for the Cosmos, creating interest in several key market segments, including soccer and non-soccer fans alike. Satterlee (2001) suggests that one of these segments was comprised of mainstream periodical writers, who presented the sport to a largely ignorant and apathetic audience. His analysis of several print sources published during Pelé's three seasons with the New York Cosmos reveals that the media were chiefly concerned with both entertaining and educating their audiences. In addition, the rhetorical strategies these writers employed were effective in undercutting stereotypes and presenting soccer in a way that was more appealing to the 'average American' (ibid.). To date, MLS has not achieved this type of media appeal. Creating a more interesting appealing product to fans and the media is essentially the largest task for the future development of the league. As Don Garber, upon taking over as commissioner of MLS in 2000, admitted, "the biggest challenge facing MLS is turning what is enormous interest in the sport into television viewers and game attendees" (Cassidy and Bronson, 2000: 31). His primary focus has been on improving the sport by offering a better product and focusing on developing a local fanbase.

Overall, these case studies indicate that vicarious learning from the failures of previous organizations can contribute to the success of future organizations. The managerial hubris and misperceptions that can create learning failures seem to be diminished when current executives are not part of the original failure, and when the failure is not attributed to external causes. In these situations, both exploratory and exploitative learning are utilized as part of developing the new organization. No study is free of limitations, and our effort to understand and conceptualize the learning that took place from NASL's initial soccer league start versus the MLS in the USA is no exception.

Studying the demise of organizations is always difficult due to changing perceptions of the failure's causes and the actions that were going on concurrently. Also, there are always limitations to generalizing when using cases to explain organizational phenomenon. We do believe that both the specific conclusions are applicable to many organizations and decision-makers when attempting to build learning capabilities in their organizations. The basic premise of this chapter has been that, although the barriers to learning from failure in organizations are deep rooted and numerous, by understanding the mechanisms at work when examining learning from others, organizations can improve their track records of learning vicariously.

Notes

1. 'Coming to America, The "Greatest Show on Earth" came to the U.S., with Brazil Beating Italy in the Final', http://www.cbc.ca/sports/soccer/fifaworld cup/features/story/2009/11/21/spf-1994-world-cup.html, retrieved 15.11.2009.
2. 'Beckham Looking Forward to US Challenge' (January 2007), http://abcnews.go.com/GMA/story?id=2786923, retrieved 20.10.2007.
3. http://web.mlsnet.com/about/, retrieved 13.05.2008.
4. 'MLS OKs "Beckham Rule" to Attract Superstar Players' (2007), http://soccernet.espn.go.com/news/story?id=391320&&cc=5901, retrieved 13.05.2008.
5. http://web.mlsnet.com/about/, retrieved 13.05.2008.

References

Anderson, D. (1977) 'Pelé's Legacy: The Game and the Man', *New York Times* (28.08.1977): 166.
Avila, A. (1997) 'Soccer League Kicks Off Season', *Hispanic Magazine*, 10(3): 14.
Baum, J. and Ingram, P. (1998) 'Survival-enhancing Learning in the Manhattan Hotel Industry, 1989–1980', *Management Science*, 44(7): 996–1016.
Bloom, H. (2007) 'Trumpets Please – The Arrival of David Beckham', *Sports Business News*, http://sportsbiznews.blogspot.com/2007/07/trumpets-please-arrival-of-david.html, retrieved 20.10.2007.
Brennan, C. (2007) 'Beckham or Not, U.S. Soccer Interest Near Nil', *USA Today* (22.08.2007), http://www.usatoday.com/sports/columnist/brennan/2007-08-22-soccer-column_N.htm, retrieved 06.09.2010.
Cassidy, H. and Bronson, C. (2000) 'Don Garber', *Sporting Goods Business*, 33(7): 30–33.

Cyert, R.M. and March, J.G. (1963) *A Behavioral Theory of the Firm* (Englewood Cliffs, NJ: Prentice-Hall).
Dodgson, M. (1993) 'Organizational Learning: A Review of Some Literatures', *Organization Studies*, 14(3): 375–394.
Dolles, H. and Söderman, S. (2008) 'The Network of Value Captures: Creating Competitive Advantage in Football Management', *Austrian Economic Papers*, 55(1): 39–58.
Dolles, H. and Söderman, S. (2011) 'Learning from Success: Implementing a Professional Football League in Japan', in H. Dolles and S. Söderman (eds), *Sport as Business: International, Professional and Commercial Aspects* (Houndmills, Basingstoke: Palgrave Macmillan): 228–250.
Gavetti, G. and Levinthal, D. (2000) 'Looking Forward and Looking Backward: Cognitive and Experiential Search', *Administrative Science Quarterly*, 45(2): 113–137.
Glaser, B. and Strauss, A. (1967) *Discovery of Grounded Theory: Strategies for Qualitative Research* (Chicago, IL: Aldine).
Holmes, S. (2004) 'Soccer: Time to Kick It Up a Notch', *Business Week* (22.11.2004), http://www.businessweek.com/magazine/content/04_47/b3909099.htm, retrieved 11.05.2008.
Ingram, P. and Baum, J.A.C. (1997) 'Opportunity and Constraint: Organizations' Learning from the Operating and Competitive Experience of Industries', *Strategic Management Journal*, 18: 75–98.
Jose, C. (2003) *North American Soccer League Encyclopedia* (Haworth, NJ: St Johann Press).
Kam, J. (2004) 'Developing Strategy by Learning to Learn from Failure', *Journal of General Management*, 29(4): 58–73.
Kim, J. and Miner, A. (2007) 'Vicarious Learning from the Failures and Near-failures of Others: Evidence from the U.S. Commercial Banking Industry', *Academy of Management Journal*, 50(2): 687–714.
Levinthal, D.A. and March, J.G. (1993) 'The Myopia of Learning', *Strategic Management Journal*, 14: 95–112.
Lovallo, D. and Kahneman, D. (2003) 'Delusions of Success: How Optimism Undermines Executives' Decisions', *Harvard Business Review*, 81(7): 56–63.
March, J. (1991) 'Exploration and Exploitation in Organizational Learning', *Organization Science*, 2(1): 71–87.
Markovitz, A. and Hellerman, S. (2001) *Offside: Soccer and American Exceptionalism* (Princeton, NJ: Princeton University Press).
Mickle, T. (2007) 'A Year of Firsts in TV Deals', *Sports Business Journal*, http://www.sportsbusinessjournal.com/index.cfm?fuseaction=search.show_article&articleId=54892&keyword=mls, retrieved 02.10.2007.
Mickle, T. (2008) 'ESPN Kicks Up Efforts to Bolster MLS Ratings', *Sports Business Journal*, http://www.sportsbusinessjournal.com/article/58480, retrieved 03.05.2008.
Miller, L. (1977) 'The Selling of Soccermania', *New York Times* (28.08.1977): 187.
Miner, A., Kim, J.-Y., Holzinger, I. and Haunschild, P.R. (1999) 'Fruits of Failure: Organizational Failure and Population Level Learning', in A.S. Minder and P. Anderson (eds), *Advances in Strategic Management: Population Level Learning and Industry Change* (Greenwich, CT: JAI Press): 187–220.

Newsham, G. (2005) 'When Pele and Cosmos Were Kings', *Guardian* (10.06.2005), http://www.guardian.co.uk/football/2005/jun/10/sport.comment, retrieved 20.04.2007.

O'Driscoll, A., Carson, D. and Gilmore, A. (2001) 'The Competence Trap: Exploring Issues in Winning and Sustaining Core Competence', *Irish Journal of Management*, 22(1): 73–90.

Satterlee, T. (2001) 'Making Soccer a "Kick in the Grass"', *International Review for the Sociology of Sport*, 36(3): 305–317.

Schwenk, C.R. (1986) 'Information, Cognitive Biases and Commitment to a Course of Action', *Academy of Management Review*, 11(2): 298–310.

Simon, H. (1955) 'A Behavioral Model of Rational Choice', *Quarterly Journal of Economics*, 69(1): 99–118.

Simon, H. (1991) 'Bounded Rationality and Organization Learning', *Organization Science*, 2(1): 125–134.

Sitkin, S. (1992) 'Learning Through Failure: The Strategy of Small Losses', in B.M. Staw and L.L. Cummings (eds), *Research in Organizational Behavior* (Greenwich, CT: JAI Press): 231–266.

Thagard, P. (1996) *Mind: Introduction to Cognitive Thought* (Cambridge, MA: MIT Press).

Thomas, D.E., Eden, L., Hitt, M. and Miller, S. (2007) 'Experience of Emerging Market Firms: The Role of Cognitive Bias in Developed Market Entry and Survival', *Management International Review*, 47(6): 845–867.

Trekker, J. (2006) 'Chelsea MLS and the NASL', *Fox Sports* (04.08.2006), http://community.foxsports.com/blogs/JamieTrecker/2006/08/04/Chelsea_MLS_and_the_NASL, retrieved 20.05.2009.

Tversky, A. and Kahneman, D. (1986) 'Rational Choice and the Framing of Decisions', *Journal of Business*, 59(4): 251–278.

Wahl, G. (2005) 'Franz Beckenbauer', *Sports Illustrated*, 103(2) (11.07.2005): 148.

Walsh, J.P. (1995) 'Managerial and Organization Cognition: Notes from a Trip Down Memory Lane', *Organization Science*, 6(3): 280–321.

Weiland, M. (2006) 'Kick Off', *New Republic*, 234(23) (19.06.2006): 42.

Westphal, J.D. and Bednar, W. (2005) 'Pluralistic Ignorance in Corporate Boards and Firms' Strategic Persistence in Response to Low Firm Performance', *Administrative Science Quarterly*, 50(2): 262–298.

Yannis, A. (1978) 'Soccer Stepping into the Big Time', *New York Times* (20.02.1978): C1.

12
Learning from Success: Implementing a Professional Football League in Japan

Harald Dolles and Sten Söderman

1. Going international – the global spread of football

The transformation of football (or 'soccer' in the American context) into a global sport has several dimensions. These include: the migration of elite football talent, such as players and coaches, and the subsequent support of their fans, between nations, as well as within and between continents; the design and manufacturing of clothing, footwear and equipment for football professionals, amateurs and fans which forms a worldwide industry built on the branding of sports and merchandizing goods; the integration of new media technologies and the use of multiple new media platforms regarding the global transfer of images, information and messages produced and distributed by newspapers, magazines, radio, film, television, video, satellite, cable and the internet; and finally, the ideological dimension of the transfer of values centrally associated with football and its governing institutions. The declaration of the Japanese Football Association (JFA) exemplifies these multiple dimensions: "Through football, we realise the full benefits that sports can bring to our lives – the soundness of our bodies, the expansion of our minds, and the enrichment of our societies."[1]

Key features that have contributed to the global spread of football include:

- The worldwide acceptance of rules governing football and the internationalization strategies of football's governing institution, Fédération Internationale de Football Association (FIFA) and its six continental confederations.
- The fostered co-operation between national and international governing institutions, like the FIFA 'Goal – a project for the future of

the Game' initiative, which aims to support poorer national football associations.[2]
- An increase in the number of established professional leagues, the increasing importance of regional and global competitions and the growth of competition between national teams.

The 1993 establishment of the J-League, Japan's professional football league, to be run as an independent business according to Morris (1995), can certainly be considered as part of football's international development and, as to Hirose (2004a: 38), it is "an exceptional case of creating a whole new market out of the blue – totalling a cumulative flow of JPY 472 billion [€3,600 million] over the first ten years". *The Economist* (1994: 109) has described J-League's instant success as a puzzle. Light and Yasaki (2003: 40) highlight the J-League as an outstanding success, "attracting crowds that could not previously have been dreamt of for football in Japan".

This chapter takes the implementation as well as the immediate and sustainable success of the J-League during their first decade as a neglected research example, and is structured as follows: after providing a brief introduction into the development of football in Japan and identifying the research gap, we apply a conceptual network of value captures for the football business for analysis. This framework will be used to highlight distinctive features of the J-League's establishment and practice, as such taking a deductive research approach. In the last section, we will conclude how the changes associated with the establishment of the J-League have changed the international attractiveness of Japanese football.

2. Development of football in Japan

In the late 1980s, when the idea of the J-League began to materialize, according to Manzenreiter (2004), the prospect of a professional football league in Japan received a merely lukewarm welcome. Football had been played in Japan for more than a century without either establishing a self-sustaining basis or attracting substantial audiences (Horne and Bleakley, 2002). It is claimed that football entered Japan first in 1873 through a British naval commander who was teaching at Tokyo's naval academy and who started kicking a ball around with students between drills. Football then spread slowly via academic institutions. The first national championship was held in 1921 shortly after the set-up of the Japanese Football Association (JFA) on 19 September of the same year.

Compared to baseball (the Japanese professional baseball league was established in 1935), football held a position of minor importance in Japanese sports, and the all-Japanese championship in football, the Emperor's Cup, was contested almost exclusively by college and college old-boy teams. Nonetheless, Waseda University's victory in the 1963 Emperor's Cup was the last of its kind for a college because Japanese firms of the 1950s began to form sports teams to improve morale and to help employees identify with their employer. By moving towards mass consumption, company sport was broadcasted more extensively on TV. Surpassing the goal of uniting employees, the purpose of sports teams was now to advertise on TV and in newspapers (Horne and Bleakley, 2002; Manzenreiter, 2004). To increase their competitiveness, players were scouted especially for these teams, finally out-competing college football, and the first non-university win of the Emperor's Cup went to the Furukawa Electric company team in 1964. During the following decade, football in Japan only survived because of the supporting framework of corporate sports, however, it never acquired a competitive edge to enable it to challenge the dominant positions of professional baseball, golf and sumo.

The incorporation of the J-League in 1991 and the opening match on 15 May 1993 were intended to change sporting culture in Japan. Foreign ideas about the various ways in which football should be governed, structured, played and consumed were gradually institutionalized within Japanese sports during this process and over the course of the first decade of the J-League's existence. McDonald, Mihara and Hong (2001: 43) state "it is noteworthy that both the Japanese Baseball League and the J-League adapted these sports based on unique Japanese cultural and social patterns". The development of professional football in Japan therefore provides a promising area for research which, to date, has not been extensively covered. Some of the existing literature on the J-League has been provided by journalists (for example, Moffett, 2002; Ōsumi, 1998). While there are a few case surveys available (Harada and Ogasawara, 2008; Light and Yasaki, 2004; Manzenreiter, 2002; Probert and Schütte, 1997; Schütte and Ciarlante, 1998), most of the academic research in the field takes a sociological approach. For example, previous studies by Light and Yasaki (2002, 2003) and Sugimoto (2004) analyse the promotion of the J-League as a community-based sport for the future development of all sports in Japan, focusing on community and school sport. The studies also promote the idea that sport might simply be an opportunity to interact socially and to identify oneself as belonging to a specific group of fans.

The impact of both the Japanese sports lottery (toto) in 2001 and the 2002 FIFA Football World Cup on the development of the J-League is examined by Funk et al. (2006). Shimizu (2000, 2002) contrasts the behaviour of the supporters of the Urawa Red Diamonds team – the largest fan group in the J-League – with other football supporting cultures in Europe. Among the supporters in Japan, women are much more present in the football arena than is the case in Europe. As such, Manzenreiter (2006, 2008a) addresses the conjunctions of football, masculinity and gender relations in Japanese society in his research. By conducting two surveys on J-League games, Sumino and Harada (2004) analysed the relationship between affective experience at the arena in Japan, team loyalty and intention to attend further games. In a similar attempt, Nakazawa et al. (1999) categorized Japanese fans into three segments according to J-League attendance. The relationship between new team entry in the J-League and the options of team identification or brand switching by fans is examined by Harada and Matsuoka (1999).

The research on the globalization of football by Close and Askew (2004), Horne (1996, 2000, 2002), Horne and Bleakley (2002), Horne and Manzenreiter (2002), Manzenreiter (2002, 2004), Manzenreiter and Horne (2004, 2007) and Nogawa and Maeda (1999) might be placed within ethnosociologies – as MacAloon (1992) refers to it – when examining the cultural meanings attached to social changes involving the rise of football in North-East Asia and its development in Japan. The use of public sport facilities in Japan and the planning, construction and operation of the football World Cup arenas in Japan are analysed by Manzenreiter (2008b) and Nogawa and Toshio (2002). A socio-linguistic approach is taken by Ophüls-Kashima (2003) explaining the history of names, team emblems, team songs and mascots of Japanese football clubs. In addition, an insider's view of the development of professional football in Japan from the JFA is provided by Hirose (2004a, 2004b).

The existing body of work on the J-League's business system and impact can be categorized as descriptive and explorative. As an example, Hirose (2004a, 2004b) reflects on the design process and the costs of establishing a professional league. To him, the initial success of the J-League owed a great deal to high mass media exposure deriving from media reporting, not simply from advertising. Manzenreiter (2002), however, suggests causal links between the success of J-League's clubs and sponsoring engagements by firms as well as the support by local communities. "Community pride" also constituted one of seven contributing factors quoted by Mahony et al. (2002), where the overall focus was on spectator motives and an attempt to measure influence on the behaviour of the J-league audience. Matsouka, Chelladurai and Harada (2003) reported on J-League team identification and satisfaction and the reasoning behind future game attendance. The Japanese results appear to be in line with studies conducted elsewhere. Manzenreiter and Horne (2007) also identified the fan's capability and willingness to spend on football and those consumer products advertised through the game as the economic base for professional football in Japan. However, they conclude that "reducing the role of spectators to pure consumers would do injustice to the complexity of motives and objectives that draw people into football support" (ibid.: 574).

From the literature review, three main limitations in the current state of management research regarding Japanese football were identified. Firstly, the findings of those research streams have neither been systematically consolidated into a framework nor validated by means of a broader empirical survey. Secondly, given its economic impact, the business perspective in the development of football in Japan still needs to be addressed in further research, thus challenging existing 'Westernized' assumptions based on management theory about how the football business should be organized and managed. Thirdly, Japanese football is increasingly becoming part of the global network of interdependency chains in the football business, therefore adding further dimensions to the research on sport as a global business.

3. Research framework and methodology

In order to capture this global development of football in research, three factors must be highlighted. Firstly, international studies of the sports business must emphasize the interconnected political, economic, cultural and social patterns that contour and shape modern sport (Smith and Westerbeek, 2004). Attention must also be given to how these patterns contain enabling and constraining elements on people's actions. Secondly, in order to describe and analyse the international spread of sports and its related industries, it is useful to adopt a long-term perspective. A historical and comparative approach helps to explain how the present pattern of global sport has emerged out of the past (Brändle and Koller, 2002; Dolles and Söderman, 2005a, 2005b; Lanfranchi et al., 2004). The third point concerns the concept of internationalization itself. This concept refers to the growing interconnectedness in a political, economic, cultural and social sense. A multitude of transnational or global economic and technological exchanges, communication networks and migratory patterns characterize this interconnected global pattern in professional sports (for example, as described in Dolles and Söderman, 2008a; Harada and Ogasawara, 2008).

The complexity, specificity and changing nature of the football business and its environment places strain on conventional approaches to theory building in management sciences and hypothesis testing (Söderman, Dolles and Dum, 2010). Early sports management research offered no theory for examining the professional football club and its business environment. To enable advances in both knowledge and practice, we have favoured a framework approach to theory building rather than developing a model of the football business. A model abstracts the complexity of the football business to isolate a few key variables whose interactions are examined in depth. The normative significance of the model then depends on the fit between its assumptions and reality. Porter (1991: 97) concludes: "No one model embodies or even approaches embodying all the variables of interest, and hence the applicability of any model's findings is almost inevitably restricted to a small subgroup of firms or industries whose characteristics fit the model's assumptions."

Instead of developing a model, our approach was to build a framework based on 'value captures'. Our understanding of value captures is based on Barney's (1991) conceptualization of sustained competitive advantage. A football club's resources can only be a source of competitive advantage when they are valuable. Resources are considered to be value captures when they enable a football club to conceive of or implement strategies that improve its efficiency and effectiveness. Valuable football club resources possessed by a large number of competing clubs cannot be sources of sustained competitive advantage. A football club enjoys a competitive advantage when it implements a value-creating strategy combining bundles of valuable club resources. These strategies require a club-specific particular mix between the different products a club might offer and the customer groups. Thus, the framework concept is applied and is particularly valuable because it encompasses many variables and seeks to capture much of the complexity. "Frameworks identify the relevant variables and the questions which the user must answer in order to develop conclusions tailored to a particular industry and company. In this sense they can be seen as almost expert systems" Porter (1991: 98).

The approach to theory embodied in the framework method is contained in our choice of included variables, the way we organized the value captures, the proposed interrelations among the value captures, and the manner in which alternative patterns of value captures and club management's choices might affect outcomes. A way of dealing with this holistic complexity is offered by network theory. According to Gummesson (2006: 176) network theory is also "intuitive, reflecting how we think and act in practice". By reviewing all the variables in the football business, we aim to cover the complexity and context of the whole network, thus concurring with Gummesson (2007) that this network, although structurally consistent of its parts, is something other than the linear sum of its parts.

The chosen methodology reflects the exploratory nature of this research. We searched the websites of top European football clubs and the football governing institutions, FIFA and UEFA (Union des Associations Européennes de Football), for management issues and stories of success or failure of professional football clubs. These searches yielded a number of documents, articles and reports that were placed in the literature pool. We then applied a qualitative content analysis in order to identify possible value captures in professional football management based on the method suggested by Mayring (1994, 2000a, 2000b). This structural approach consisted of the following steps: (1) formulating structural categories for interpretations extracted from the data; (2) extracting definitions, examples and rules for codification of the structural categories; (3) compiling the data by attaching sequences identified in the documents collected in the literature pool; and (4) performing qualitative analyses of the assembled data.

An academic literature review followed, in order to provide scientifically based evidence to support the preliminary composition of value captures. These articles were added to the literature pool. In cases where strong scientifically based research did not exist, we decided to produce syntheses of research summarizing the evidence taken from practice. Finally, to evaluate our observations and findings we conducted about 20 narrative interviews with the J-League management, the JFA and football clubs in Japan, Germany and Sweden. The research framework was also presented and discussed during two research workshops. Some comments received during this stage of the development of the framework were very general in nature, or related to fundamental concerns about the cases and theories we used or the assumptions we made. Other comments were more specific and detailed in nature. We responded to the more general, broad-based comments, concerns and issues in order to develop a general framework designed to be applied by the management of a professional football club. As a result of this progressive development of the framework, we provide a more thorough, comprehensive and precise analysis that might also serve as a basis for future research on the subject.

4. The network of value captures in professional football

The research framework of value captures in professional football as developed by Dolles and Söderman (2008b) has three key dimensions (Figure 12.1): (1) the product and its features, (2) the customers and (3) the business process and strategic vision. The following explanations – 1.A to 1.F as well as 2.A to 2.E – constitute individual factors in the network of value captures and, when combined, they illustrate multiple interlinked relationships in football management. Having combined the six 'offerings' with the five groups of 'customers', 30 relations appear. Each of these constitutes a value capture and an equivalent value creation. Factor 1.F meets 2.A when the *merchandise product* is co-produced or sold to the *fans*. Then, the *players* (1.E) are of interest to the *sponsors* (2.D) or the *media* (2.C). Thus, a mixture of such relations constitutes the bulk of the football industry, acknowledging that not all lines are equally important.

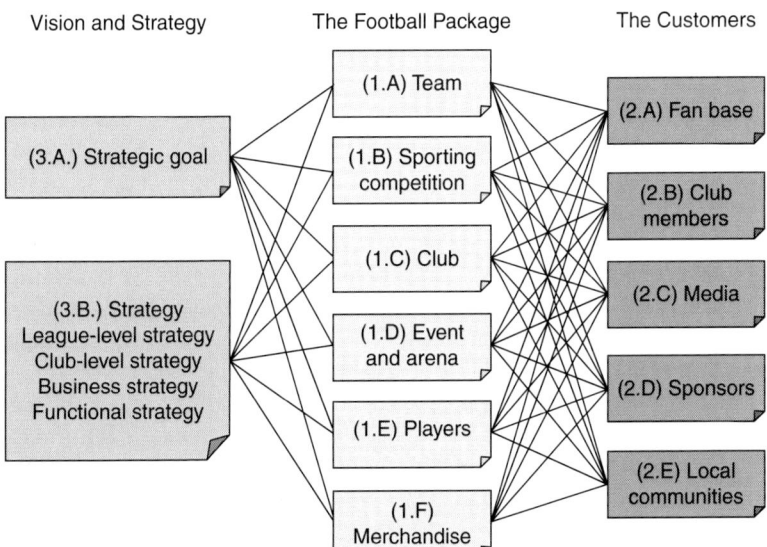

Figure 12.1 Network of Value Captures in professional football
Source: Dolles and Söderman (2008b).

By adding the strategy dimension to the framework of value captures we introduce the vision and imagination of the future of the club, which influences the club-specific composition of the football package. The multiple dimensions of the football package are central to the level of strategy aggregation. The network *level of strategy* (3.B) is closely connected with the *league's procedures* of promotion and relegation (1.B), the costs of scheduling *matches* for the club (1.C), requirements to develop their *arenas* (1.D) and/or a regulated labour market for *player movements* (1.E).

The problem of defining the product in the football business is partly the result of every individual having their own experience and expectation of the game, or events around the match – a 'certain something else' associated with the football experience. It is not one single product, service or entertainment that a football club offers. We can consider the following possible 'offerings': (1.A) *team*; (1.B) *sporting competition*; (1.C) *club*; (1.D) *event and arena*; (1.E) *players*; and (1.F) *merchandise*.

1.A: ***Team; i.e., top performance team***. Football is a team sport. Nonetheless, 11 skilled players do not necessarily comprise a winning team. A team with superior physical ability alone cannot beat an opponent that has good technique and a carefully planned strategy.

1.B: ***Sporting competitions; i.e., league structures***. Football as a team sport also requires co-ordination among the competing teams, because the game involves at least two distinct teams which must agree on the rules of the game. Leagues need to be organized by the club's national governing body, depending on the division in which their teams play. In order to manage competition efficiently, rules also need to be developed for determining a champion.

1.C: ***Club; i.e., administration***. Hosting a winning team has a dual meaning for professional sports organizations. Not only must the players on the sporting team be able to give their utmost to the cause of winning, but the financial and administrative structure (marketing, public relations and so on) behind them must also work in an exact manner to ensure that business goals will be achieved.

1.D: ***Event and arena; i.e., the football match and arena***. A sporting event (a football match) is intangible, short-lived, unpredictable and subjective in nature. It is produced and consumed simultaneously by the spectators in the arena, in the most part with a strong emotional commitment from the fans. In recent years, football games have been transformed into media events for the benefit of millions of spectators, few of whom were in attendance at the live event. Such mediatized events go so far as to affect the stadium or arena they are attached to. Arenas of most of the top clubs represent the state of the art in sports leisure multiplex architecture.

1.E: *Players; i.e., stars, top players as assets*. Players and their development are of prime concern to football managers. Football clubs send out their scouts to discover young players in the immediate region, or worldwide, and to sign contracts with them, since some of them might later find their way into a professional team.

1.F: *Merchandise*. Football merchandise means goods held for resale but not manufactured by the football club, such as flags and banners, scarves and caps, training gear, jerseys and fleeces, footballs, videos and DVDs, blankets and pillows, watches, lamps, tables, clocks and signs.

Why do supporters choose one team over another? Cost is certainly not the only nor prevalent argument for fans in the football business. Rather, fun, excitement, skilled players and regional 'embeddedness' might all be good reasons for supporting a team. Consequently, the variety of offerings creates a broader customer approach in football, addressing (2.A) the *spectators and supporters*, (2.B) *the club members*, (2.C) *the media*, (2.D) *the sponsors* and (2.E) *local communities*.

2.A: *Fan base; i.e., spectators and supporters*. When it comes to sales in the football business, the main attention is created by the supporters, in relation to ticket sales and merchandising. Fan motivation and behaviour vary depending upon the type of fan. By introducing the international dimension, we distinguish two different types of fans. 'Local fans' exhibit their behaviour because of identification with a geographic area; that is, they are either born, living or staying in the home region of the club. 'International fans' live abroad and do not get many opportunities to see the team play live. Their attendance is mainly virtual, via the radio, television or internet.

2.B: *Club members; i.e., membership*. Football by its very nature is fun; it involves exercise and is competitive. For this reason, football clubs facilitate opportunities for their active members to engage in exercise and to play football in a team. Others may join the football club as passive members to support their favourite team.

2.C: *Media*. The media is the main sales channel. Football's importance for the media business can be seen in the increasing amounts of money paid for broadcast rights, as well as the growth in the number of sports-oriented radio talk shows and TV networks.

2.D: *Sponsors; i.e., sponsorships*. Football is a natural area for sponsorship as it carries very strong images, has a mass international audience and appeals to all classes. Depending on the level of sponsorship, the benefits for the sponsors might include, but are not limited to: product category exclusivity, naming rights, the sponsor's logo on jerseys, uniforms, websites, perimeter advertising (boards and/or banners) in the arena, VIP tickets, advertisements in the club's official magazine and cross-promotional arrangements. Sponsorship deals are promoted either by the club or an intermediary agency specializing in sponsorship activities.

2.E: *Local communities; for example, public authorities, local sport governing bodies*. Football is firmly rooted in the local setting and plays a vital part of the cultural and social make-up of local communities. As a result, community funds or pooled resources are sometimes used as a last resort to keep clubs in business. In this sense, football clubs remain largely untouchable by economic forces that determine the fate of other companies. Clubs which mismanage their finances, however, are relegated to lower divisions or are liquidated.

The highest and broadest level business objective is the ***vision of the club*** (3.A). This is a statement of broad aspiration, as it deals with where the club hopes to be in the future. This is not about winning the next game, it is the attempt by the club management to define where it expects the club to be at a later point in time: to win the championship; to stay in the league; to make profit; or to go international. With the exception of merchandising, the football business lacks the option of producing and storing inventory for future sale, as the main characteristic of football is its ambiguity and the uncertainty of the outcome of a game.

In order to reach the goals attached to the vision of where the club should be in the future, what kind of ***strategies*** (3.B) should be applied? Strategies can be articulated for different activities within the club, where the lowest level of aggregation is one specific task, while the highest level of aggregation encompasses all activities within the club. A logical extension of this distinction is the league-level strategy.

5. The analysis of the J-League's development

Now that the network of value captures in professional football has been articulated, attention moves to the analysis of the development of professional football in Japan. We begin by introducing the *strategic vision* and *objectives statements* (3.A) of the J-League:[3]

- To raise the level of Japanese football and promote the diffusion of the game through the medium of professional football.
- To foster the development of Japan's sporting culture, to assist in the healthy mental and physical growth of Japanese people.
- To contribute to international friendship and exchange.

Other than these ideas of strategic direction and objectives taken from the J-League mission statement, it was said that the founders of the J-League in the late 1980s had no interest in catching up with Chinese and South Korean football. "They did not want to compete only with other Asians, or become moderately good at anything" (Moffett, 2002: 19). Hirose (2004a: 52) adds,

> what became evident through my interviews with key players in the process was that business success was not the ultimate goal for the whole group of founders but the primary goal was to start the business in order to improve the level of football playing and be able to beat the Korean national team one day.

A new professional league should drive the national team to a level where it could compete beyond the confines of Asia and turn Japan into a regular FIFA World Cup qualifier – as well as being the competition's first Asian co-host of this tournament (Sugden and Tomlinson, 2002). Certainly, by successfully hosting half of the FIFA World Cup in 2002, and, for the first time in Japanese footballing history, advancing to the final 16 teams, the JFA successfully accomplished their targets. Shortly after the FIFA World Cup in October 2002 the JFA announced the next 'JFA President's Mission', which aimed to further promote and develop Japanese football, thus linking the JFA's *vision* (3.A) with *strategy* (3.B), the *national team* (1.A) and the *fan base* (2.A). The 'JFA Declaration, 2005' proclaims:

> By 2015, we will become one of the top 10 football associations of the world, and realise the following two objectives: 1. The football Family of Japan, the fans with a true love for football, will number 5 million strong. 2. The Japan National Team will be ranked among the top 10 teams in the world.[4]

By interlinking the strategic *vision* (3.A) with the *team* (1.A) and all five *consumer groups* (2.A to 2.E), one major difference compared to football in Europe became obvious in this declaration. Popular enthusiasm for football in Japan is tied to the success of the national squad. "The national team will be good if the local teams are good, the local teams will be good if they are well supported locally, and local support will be strong if the national team does well" (Probert and Schütte, 1997: 15; also Horne and Bleakley, 2002).

Another particularity of Japanese football becomes apparent by connecting different *levels of strategy* (3.B), *sporting competition* (1.B), as well as *media* (2.C) and *sponsors* (2.D). The main objective for the J-League during the first decade since its establishment was to survive due to the extreme simplicity of its contracts, organizational structures and substantial investments in marketing (Harada and Ogasawara, 2008). The J-League markets itself as an autonomous, non-profit organization, like the Championnats of France and the German Bundesliga. The English Premiership League was founded in 1992 as a limited company and La Liga Espanola is a private organization, independent from the Spanish Football Association (RFEF) of which it is a part. The striking difference is that most of the decisions concerning sponsorship and licences are dealt with centrally by the management of the J-League, whereas in Europe, the clubs are responsible for their own deals. This is partly due to the fact that football was, and still is, not yet rooted in Japan's sporting culture. We might assume, therefore, that the clubs and JFA must work together off the pitch to create sufficient support so that football may become self-sufficient in its essence in order to attract spectators, fans and supporters.

In its first few seasons, the J-League and its members had to co-operate to survive in a country where football was overshadowed by baseball, sumo and golf. If the football clubs were to settle their own sponsorship deals, player and TV contracts from the start, many teams would have left the J-League with financial problems. By having contracts, sponsorship deals and TV rights all decided centrally, the J-League hoped to accumulate larger sums of money, which it would then distribute equally among its member teams. This synchronized effort at equitable financial support and public exposure/marketing aimed to increase support for football as a whole, as opposed to just one or two teams. Following in the footsteps of the US model, this was believed to achieve higher competitiveness by giving equal growth opportunities for each individual team. Currently, over 35 companies sponsor the J-League, including multinational enterprises such as Canon, Coca Cola, Fuji Xerox, Johnson and Johnson, Adidas, Nike, Mizuno and Puma.[5] Divided into 13 sponsorship levels, these sponsors cover the same goods and services, competing against each other to become each team's supplier. The US influence on the J-League is also visible in the franchise system of all football merchandise, such as kits, balls, refereeing equipment, nutrition (soda) drinks and all other imaginable *merchandise* (1.F).

The J-League started with a clear belief that the only way to gain the all-important support of the general public in the beginning was to create a true 'home-town' system with a close mutual commitment between the football club and the local people (interlinking strategic *vision* (3.A), *club* (1.C), *fans* (2.A) and the *local community* (2.E)). Basing themselves on the German experience, the J-League founders wanted to create the sort of atmosphere where local people are passionately involved in the fortunes of the home club. Equally, they tried to avoid the franchise type of sports league organization that is common in the USA, where a team's home depends on the preference of the legal owner. This home-town base is still a condition of J-League membership: "Each club must designate a particular locality as its hometown. It must cooperate in sports activities conducted in the area to grow as a club that takes part in activities in the community and promotes sports in the region."[6]

A further condition for J-League membership refers to the *arena* (1.D) in terms of pitch conditions, spectator capacity and floodlight conditions. The *players* (1.E) are also mentioned in the membership conditions since each J-League team must have a minimum number of players who have concluded the standard professional contract approved by the JFA, and coaches employed at all levels should hold the appropriate licence. Furthermore, it is a requirement for each club to operate a reserve team and youth teams (refer to *team* (1.A) and to have active *club members* (2.B)).[7]

In connecting strategic *vision* (3.A) with the network *level of strategy* (3.B) and *sporting competition* (1.B), it is obvious that the prospect of expanding the influence of the football game to East Asia moved FIFA towards complying with some particularities introduced by the J-League, giving local influence to football in the early years. In order to make the league both "easy to understand and exciting for the greatest possible number of people" (Manzenreiter,

2004: 295), the J-League adapted European practices, with a two-stage season system and a final play-off between the winners of the two stages. From 2005, once the general understanding of football had risen in Japan following the league's first decade, J-League 1 was played as a single season-long league without separate stages.[8] A one-point system for games ending in a tie was introduced only in 1999 and finally adopted for all J-League matches in 2003. Previously, tied games had been followed by a race for the 'V(ictory)-goal' within 30 minutes of overtime and, if still undecided, by a decisive penalty shoot-out (Horne, 1996; Sakkā Hyōron Henshūbu, 1999: 28–29).

The J-League started with ten *teams* (1.A) in 1991, expanded to 16 in 1996, rising to 20 in 1998, and implemented a *two division system* (1.B) in 1999 (J-League 1: 16 teams; J-League 2: 10 teams).[9] In the J-League's 17th season (2009), for the first time 36 football clubs participated; 18 clubs in J-League 1 and 18 clubs in J-League 2, with further clubs targeting J-League membership. By implementing the two division system and the single long season, promotion and relegation play-off have been introduced in Japan.[10] Nonetheless, in fulfilling the club's obligations to the J-League organization, Japanese professional football clubs will not drop down from the second J-League as is the case across Europe. Additionally, a J-League 2 club, even if it qualifies on the pitch, can only be promoted if it satisfies the formal requirements for entry to J-League 1.[11]

One major challenge during the establishment of the J-League was that *club membership* (2.B) had to be defined within Japanese society. In most European countries, football is organized through clubs, with active members taking part in competition, and non-active members, that is, people who do not or no longer actually pursue football actively. In Japan, however, this was not at all common. Influenced by the American system, Japan's football was provided by companies, on the one hand, and schools, colleges and universities, on the other.

Linking *club* (1.C), *merchandise* (1.F), *fans* (2.A) and *sponsorship* (2.D) during the planning phase of the J-League, the founders expected their main audience not to be active *members* (2.B), but merely football fans: "Spectators at the average baseball game were very different from the J-League's target market. Baseball was a very male-oriented game, and most people in the crowd were men over 40 years old who liked to go along and relax with beers and their business friends. Watching the game itself didn't always seem to be the main reason for going" (Probert and Schütte, 1997: 9). The J-League targeted people who played and enjoyed football and who are passionately involved in the action on the pitch. Match attendance included not only families – there was not so much as a hint of the hooligan tendency that keeps young women and children away from visiting the arena in Europe – but also teenage girls, who came to cheer on individual players. Creating a football supporting culture was one of the major tasks of the first decade of the J-League. The hard core of fans could make as much noise as any crowd in the world (see, for example, Shimizu, 2002), but "a few rows away, the other side of an invisible line, shouting and singing became as embarrassing as it would be in a shopping centre" (Moffett, 2002: 78). Those fans were, for the most part, purely occasional spectators and the challenge remains to convert them into regular spectators.

Football itself was marketed in Japan as a "new, improved product, now on sale", in the mould of a marketing principle well-known to Japanese marketing professionals (Horne and Bleakley, 2002; Watts, 1998). Different to European practices, associated *product marketing and merchandising* (1.F) is centralized in the J-League. "The unified marketing system allowed consistent pricing, design and quality, ensuring responsible trademark management and equal exposure for each club" (Probert and Schütte, 1997: 8). This strategy reflects the fundamental principle of the founders of the J-League that all teams should have an equal chance of exposure and an equal share of the merchandising revenue. In the same vein, the J-League practices a method of distributing *media revenues from broadcasting rights* (2.C) equally to all J-League teams irrespective of performance (Horne and Bleakley, 2002), challenging prevailing European practices in professional soccer (and even other sports, like baseball, in Japan).

To handle the *merchandising business* (1.F), in the early years the J-League engaged one sole supplier, Sony Creative Products, a subsidiary of Sony Music Entertainment, to create characters and logo marks for every team, constituting a completely new strategy in the football business. Sony Designers scanned team emblems and mascots used in the NFL, NBA and European football leagues and came up with animated cartoons: the Yokohama Marinos were given a seagull dressed up in a sailor's uniform, the Kashima Antlers a deer (Figure 12.2). Team strips for the football clubs were chosen by a J-League committee, and the colours were deliberately jazzy in order to appeal to supporters (Ophüls-Kashima, 2003): bright orange for S-Pulse, lime green and yellow for Bellmare.

Figure 12.2 J-League – sample team emblems and mascots

6. Conclusion: creating a new market for football in Japan

The network of value captures constitutes a number of paths for a club to enter when succeeding in this growing industry. Without a local *fan base* (2.A) and *local revenues* (2.E) a football *team* (1.A) cannot expect to survive and prosper beyond its market of origin. Attracted by the huge potential market and the growing popularity of football in Japan, Europe's top football clubs, like Manchester United, Real Madrid, FC Barcelona and FC Bayern Munich, pay increasingly regular visits to Japan. Besides Bayern Munich, the German Bundesliga Clubs VfL Wolfsburg, Schalke04 and Borussia Dortmund are becoming popular in Japan because Makoto Hasebe, Atsuto Hasebe and Shinji Kagawa, just to name three of the top stars of Japanese football, are playing successfully there. In an effort to attract Japanese fans, European teams have built on the fact that they have a Japanese *player in the squad* (1.E), for example, in 2008 VfL Bochum played a friendly against Yokohama Marinos for this objective (when Shinji Ono was in the squad). This activity was further supported by the German Bundesliga Organisation in order to pursue its strategic overseas marketing policy (*league-level strategy* 3.B).

Among the European top football clubs, FC Barcelona went so far as to open a temporary fan shop in Yokohama during its stay in Japan in 2006, which was considered a great success:

> Over the last few days, more than 30 people have signed up as members, but the most important thing is that there has been a big flow of visitors and we have given out a lot of information.... Even more than the players, the Japanese fans stress the value of teamwork, the philosophy of the Club and our one hundred year history.... They are highly knowledgeable about the Club and very loyal.[12]

By means of follow up and service to their international fans, FC Barcelona have placed their club news at the disposition of their Japanese fans via the Japanese language version of the club's website, which also allows them to purchase official club products online (linking the *event* (1.D) with the *fans* (2.A) and the *merchandize* (1.F)). However, the problem still remains how to convert this attention to foreign clubs into revenue streams for Japanese football (Dolles and Söderman, 2005c).

Of the Japanese football clubs themselves, Urawa Reds' activities also target the international market. Their collaborative agreement with Germany's FC Bayern Munich plays a core role in them becoming the best-known Japanese team in Europe. This partnership was signed in January 2006 with the aim of: (1) playing team friendlies against each other in both countries (1.D); (2) sharing scouting information (1.A, 1.E); (3) accepting each other's players for training and the development of exchange systems for youth players (1.E.); (4) mutual merchandising support (1.F); (5) friendly matches and training camp co-operation (1.A., 1.D., 1.E); and (6) co-operation for promotional activities (2.A., 2.C., 2.D).[13] Bayern Munich and Urawa Reds played friendlies in 2006 and 2008 and the Reds U-15 team visited Germany. Red Voltage, the official Urawa Reds shop, now has a corner dedicated to Bayern goods and the official Urawa Reds website is linked to Bayern's Japanese language page. Bayern Munich celebrated Urawa Reds' J-League championship victory in 2006 with a large-screen congratulatory message at their own home match at the Allianz Arena. The invitation for Urawa Reds to play in Austria was also mediated by Bayern Munich. It is indicated that the further strengthening of exchange and meetings between club officials is set to make the partnership even closer.[14]

One of the key ingredients of the business of football is its simultaneously global and local character. An immense amount has been written about the football phenomenon in the popular press, but little systematic research has been conducted in proportion to the size of the sport's general acknowledgement (Dolles and Söderman, 2005a, 2005c). In addition, the existing case studies in the field need to be complemented by a conceptual framework that builds on theories. In this chapter, we have identified, defined and described those business parameters in professional football that vary from the parameters of any other business. The ambition in this chapter has been to apply a framework that enables a more profound analysis of this phenomenon. By identifying six value offerings and five customer categories we can construct up to 30 value captures. In the real world, these captures are preceded by the management strategy intent and require strategies on different levels of aggregation. The captures constitute a number of paths on which a club can enter to succeed in this ever-growing industry.

Knowing how those value captures are interlinked is, therefore, of significant practical relevance and importance. As suggested in sports management research (FGRC, 2004; Schewe and Littkemann, 2002) and by football executives (Mayer-Vorfelder, 2005), the sporting success of a football club might increase its revenue potential; however, the extent to which this potential is fulfilled depends on the club's strategy, on sound club and product management and on good working relations with all customer groups. Furthermore, the framework relies on the condition that professional football is embedded in the socio-cultural environment in which football has evolved, is performed, sold and consumed. In this sense, our network of value captures aims to link context, practices and institutions of a specific industry and responds to the calls for building theoretical models that capture the international dimension of sports (Maguire, 2005; Smith and Westerbeek, 2004).

Notes

1. http://www.jfa.or.jp/eng/declaration2005/index.html, retrieved 26.01.2009.
2. http://www.fifa.com/aboutfifa/developing/news/newsid=71368.html, retrieved 03.01.2009.
3. http://www.j-league.or.jp/eng/mission/, retrieved 25.01.2009.
4. http://www.jfa.or.jp/eng/declaration2005/index.html, retrieved 26.01.2009. In December 2010 Japan is placed no. 43 in the FIFA world ranking, http://de.fifa.com/worldfootball/ranking/lastranking/gender=m/fullranking.html#confederation=0&rank=188, retrieved 13.01.2010.
5. http://www.j-league.or.jp/eng/sponsors/, retrieved 26.01.2009.
6. http://www.j-league.or.jp/eng/d1and2/, retrieved 15.10.2005.
7. http://www.j-league.or.jp/eng/jclubs/, retrieved 20.01.2009.
8. http://www.j-league.or.jp/eng/d1and2/, retrieved 15.10.2005.
9. For a full description on all Japanese professional teams refer to the J-League Databook (Tsuboi and Yaki, 2002) and the J-League's club guide, http://www.j-league.or.jp/eng/clubguide/, retrieved 27.01.2009.
10. See http://en.wikipedia.org/wiki/J._League_Promotion/Relegation_Series for full details, retrieved 27.01.2009.
11. http://www.j-league.or.jp/eng/jclubs/, retrieved 15.01.2009.
12. http://www.fcbarcelona.com/eng/noticias/noticias/n05061401.shtml, retrieved 20.10.2005.
13. http://www.urawa-reds.co.jp/english/club-in_the_world.html, retrieved 25.01.2009.
14. http://www.urawa-reds.co.jp/english/club-in_the_world.html, retrieved 25.01.2009.

References

Barney, J. (1991) 'Firm Resources and Sustained Competitive Advantage', *Journal of Management*, 17(1): 99–120.

Brändle, F. and Koller, C. (2002) *Goal! Kultur- und Sozialgeschichte des modernen Fussballs* (Zürich: Orell Füssli).

Close, P. and Askew, D. (2004) 'Globalisation and Football in East Asia', in W. Manzenreiter and J. Horne (eds), *Football Goes East: Business, Culture and the People's Game in China, Japan and South Korea* (London: Routledge): 243–256.

Dolles, H. and Söderman, S. (2005a) 'Transfer of Institutional Practices in Sports – From European Football to the Development of Professional Football in Japan (J-League)', in W. Dorow (ed.), *The Transfer of Organisational Practices: Enhancing Competitiveness in Asia/Pacific – European Business Relationships* (Frankfurt/Oder: European University Viadrina): 81–105.

Dolles, H. and Söderman, S. (2005b) 'Globalization of Sports – The Case of Professional Football and Its International Management Challenges', *DIJ Working Paper*, No. 05/1, Tokyo: German Institute for Japanese Studies.

Dolles, H. and Söderman, S. (2005c) 'Implementing a Professional Football League in Japan – Challenges to Research in International Business', *DIJ Working Paper*, No. 05/6, Tokyo: German Institute for Japanese Studies.

Dolles, H. and Söderman, S. (2008a) 'Mega-sporting Events in Asia. Impacts on Society, Business and Management: An Introduction', *Asian Business and Management*, 7(2): 147–162.

Dolles, H. and Söderman, S. (2008b) 'The Network of Value Captures: Creating Competitive Advantage in Football Management', *Austrian Economic Papers*, 55(1): 39–58.

Economist (US) (1994) 'Goal! Says Japan: Soccer is challenging baseball's grip of the Japanese imagination' (22.10.1994): 109.

FGRC (eds) (2004) 'The State of the Game: The Corporate Governance of Professional Football 2004', *Football Governance Research Centre Research Paper*, No. 3, London: Birkbeck, University of London.

Funk, D.C., Nakazawa, M., Mahony, D.F. and Thrasher, R. (2006) 'The Impact of the National Sports Lottery and the FIFA World Cup on Attendance, Spectator Motives and J. League Marketing Strategies', *International Journal of Sports Marketing and Sponsorship*, 7(3): 267–285.

Gummesson, E. (2006) 'Qualitative Research in Management: Addressing Complexity, Context and Persona', *Management Decision*, 44(2): 167–179.

Gummesson, E. (2007) 'Case Study Research and Network Theory: Birds of a Feather', *Qualitative Research in Organizations and Management: An International Journal*, 2(3): 226–248.

Harada, M. and Matsuoka, M. (1999) 'The Influence of New Team Entry Upon Brand Switching in the J-League', *Sport Marketing Quarterly*, 8(3): 21–30.

Harada, M. and Ogasawara, E. (2008) *Supōtsu manejimento* (*Sport Management*) (Tokyo: Taishukan).

Hirose, I. (2004a) 'The Making of a Professional Football League', in W. Manzenreiter and J. Horne (eds), *Football Goes East: Business, Culture and the People's Game in China, Japan and South Korea* (London: Routledge): 38–53.

Hirose, I. (2004b) *J-Riigu no manejimento. hyakunen kōsō no seido sekkei wa ikanishite sōzōsareta ka (The J-League Management: How the Organzational Plan of the One Hundred Year Vision Was Created)* (Tokyo: Tōyō Keizai Shinpōsha).

Horne, J. (1996) ' "Sakka" in Japan', *Media, Culture and Society*, 18(4): 527–547.

Horne, J. (2000) 'Football in Japan: Is "wa" all you need?', in G. Finn and R. Giulianotti (eds), *Football Culture: Local Contests and Global Visions* (London: Frank Cass): 212–229.

Horne, J. (2002) 'Professional Football in Japan', in M. Raveri and J. Hendry (eds), *Japan at Play: The Ludic and the Logic of Power* (London: Routledge): 199–213.

Horne, J. and Bleakley, D. (2002) 'The Development of Football in Japan', in J. Horne and W. Manzenreiter (eds), *Japan, Korea and the 2002 World Cup* (London: Routledge): 89–105.

Horne, J. and Manzenreiter, W. (eds) (2002) *Japan, Korea and the 2002 World Cup* (London: Routledge).

Lanfranchi, P., Mason, T., Wahl, A. and Eisenberg, C. (eds) (2004) *100 Years of Football. FIFA 1904–2004* (London: Weidenfeld and Nicolson).

Light, R. and Yasaki, W. (2002) 'J-League Football and the Rekindling of Regional Identity in Japan', *Sporting Traditions*, 18(2): 31–45.

Light, R. and Yasaki, W. (2003) 'Breaking the Mould: Community, Education and the Development of Professional Football in Japan', *Football Studies*, 6(1): 37–50.

Light, R. and Yasaki, W. (2004) 'Winds of Change for Youth and Children's Sport in Japan? A Case Study of the Kashima Antler's Football Development Program', *Asian Journal of Exercise and Sport Science*, 1(1): 63–74.

MacAloon, J. (1992) 'The Ethnographic Imperative in Comparative Olympic Research', *Sociology of Sport Journal*, 9(2): 104–130.

Maguire, J. (2005) *Power and Global Sport: Zones of Prestige, Emulation and Resistance* (London: Routledge).

Mahony, D.F., Nakazawa, M., Funk, D., James, J.D. and Gladden, J.M. (2002) 'Motivational Factors Influencing the Behaviour of J-League Spectators', *Sport Management Review*, 5(1): 1–24.

Manzenreiter, W. (2002) 'Japan und der Fußball im Zeitalter der technischen Reproduzier-barkeit: Die J.League zwischen Lokalpolitik und Globalkultur', in M. Fanizadeh, G. Hödl and W. Manzenreiter (eds), *Global Players: Kultur, Ökonomie und Politik des Fußballs* (Frankfurt/Wien: Brandes & Apsel/Südwind): 133–158.

Manzenreiter, W. (2004) 'Japanese Football and World Sports: Raising the Global Game in a Local Setting', *Japan Forum*, 16(2): 289–313.

Manzenreiter, W. (2006) 'Fußball und die Krise der Männlichkeit in Japan', in E. Kreisky and G. Spitaler (eds), *Fußball: Die männliche Weltordnung* (Frankfurt/Main: Campus): 296–313.

Manzenreiter, W. (2008a) 'Football in the Reconstruction of the Gender Order in Japan', *Football & Society*, 9(2): 244–258.

Manzenreiter, W. (2008b) 'The "Benefits" of Hosting: Japanese Experiences from the 2002 Football World Cup', *Asian Business and Management*, 7(2): 201–224.

Manzenreiter, W. and Horne, J. (eds) (2004) *Football Goes East. Business, Culture and the People's Game in China, Japan and South Korea* (London: Routledge).

Manzenreiter, W. and Horne, J. (2007) 'Playing the Post-Fordist Game in/to the Far East: The Footballisation of China, Japan and South Korea', *Football & Society*, 8(4): 561–577.
Matsouka, H., Chelladurai, P. and Harada, M. (2003) 'Direct and Indirect Interaction Effects of Team Identification and Satisfaction on Intention to Attend Games', *Sport Marketing Quarterly*, 12(4): 244–253.
Mayer-Vorfelder, G. (2005) ' "König Fußball" in Deutschland – Wirtschafts- und Kulturgut', in K. Zieschang and C. Klimmer (eds), *Unternehmensführung im Profifussball: Symbiose von Sport, Wirtschaft und Recht* (Berlin: Erich Schmidt): 1–16.
Mayring, P. (1994) 'Qualitative Inhaltsanalyse', in A. Böhm, A. Mengel and T. Muhr (eds), *Texte verstehen: Konzepte, Methoden, Werkzeuge* (Konstanz: Universitätsverlag): 159–176.
Mayring, P. (2000a) 'Qualitative Inhaltsanalyse', *Forum Qualitative Sozialforschung (Forum: Qualitative Social Research)*, 1(2): Article 20, http://nbn-resolving.de/urn:nbn:de:0114-fqs0002204, retrieved 04.02.2009.
Mayring, P. (2000b) *Qualitative Inhaltsanalyse. Grundfragen und Techniken*, 7th edn (Weinheim: Deutscher Studienverlag).
McDonald, M., Mihara, T. and Hong, J.B. (2001) 'Japanese Spectator Sport Industry: Cultural Changes Creating New Opportunities', *European Sport Management Quarterly*, 1(1): 39–60.
Moffett, S. (2002) *Japanese Rules. Why the Japanese Needed Football and How They Got It* (London: Yellow Jersey Press).
Morris, K. (1995) 'How Japan Scored', *Financial World Magazine* (14.02.1995): 82–86.
Nakazawa, M., Mahony, D.F., Funk, D.C. and Hirakawa, S. (1999) 'Segmenting J. League Spectators Based on Length of Time as a Fan', *Sport Marketing Quarterly*, 8(4): 55–65.
Nogawa, H. and Maeda, H. (1999) 'The Japanese Dream: Football Culture Towards the New Millennium', in G. Amstrong and R. Giulianotti (eds), *Football Cultures and Identities* (London: Macmillan): 223–233.
Nogawa, H. and Toshio, M. (2002) 'Building Mega-events. Critical Reflections on the 2002 World Cup Infrastructure', in J. Horne and W. Manzenreiter (eds), *Japan, Korea and the 2002 World Cup* (London: Routledge): 177–194.
Ophüls-Kashima, R. (2003) 'Schiffe, Kirschblüten, Eichhörnchen und Hirschgeweihe. Die Struktur japanischer Vereinsnamen und die Konstruktion von Identität im japanischen Fußball', in R. Adelmann, R. Parr and T. Schwarz (eds), *Querpässe. Beiträge zur Literatur-, Kultur- und Mediengeschichte des Fußballs* (Heidelberg: Synchron Wissenschaftsverlag der Autoren): 79–90.
Ōsumi, Y. (1998) *Urawa Rezzu no kōfuku (The Happiness of Urawa Reds)* (Tokyo: Asupekto).
Porter, M.E. (1991) 'Towards a Dynamic Theory of Strategy', *Strategic Management Journal*, 12(Special Issue): 95–117.
Probert, J. and Schütte, H. (1997) 'Goal! Japan Scores in Soccer', *INSEAD Teaching Cases* (Fontainebleau: Insead).
Sakkā Hyōron Henshūbu (1999) 'J-riigu no hikari to kage: J-riigu cheaman Kawabuchi Saburō intabyū' ('Rise and Fall of the J-League: Interview with Chairman Kawabuchi Saburō'), *Sakkā Hyōron*, (4): 18–34.

Schewe, G. and Littkemann, J. (eds) (2002) *Sportmanagement. Der Profifussball aus sportökonomischer Perspektive* (Schorndorf: Hofman).
Schütte, H. and Ciarlante, D. (1998) *Consumer Behaviour in Asia* (New York, NY: New York University Press).
Shimizu, S. (2000) 'Sapōtā. Sono hyōshō to kioku soshite ima tsukurarete iku mono toshite' ('Supporters. Their Symbols and Memories in Regards to the Club they Support'), *Gendai Supōtsu Hyōron*, (3): 75–90.
Shimizu, S. (2002) 'Japanese Soccer Fans. Following the Local and the National Team', in J. Horne and W. Manzenreiter (eds), *Japan, Korea and the 2002 World Cup* (London: Routledge): 133–146.
Smith, A. and Westerbeek, H. (2004) *The Sport Business Future* (Houndmills, Basingstoke: Palgrave Macmillan).
Söderman, S., Dolles, H. and Dum, T. (2010) 'Managing Football: International and Global Developments', in S. Chadwick and S. Hamil (eds), *Managing Football: An International Perspective* (Amsterdam: Elsevier): 85–101.
Sugden, J. and Tomlinson, A. (2002) 'International Power Struggles in the Governance of World Football: The 2002 and 2006 World Cup Bidding Wars', in J. Horne and W. Manzenreiter (eds), *Japan, Korea and the 2002 World Cup* (London: Routledge): 56–70.
Sugimoto, A. (2004) 'School Sport, Physical Education and the Development of Football Culture in Japan', in W. Manzenreiter and J. Horne (eds), *Football Goes East: Business, Culture and the People's Game in China, Japan and South Korea* (London: Routledge): 102–116.
Sumino, M. and Harada, M. (2004) 'Affective Experience of J. League Fans: The Relationship between Affective Experience, Team Loyalty and Intention to Attend', *Managing Leisure*, 9(4): 181–192.
Tsuboi, Y. and Yaki, T. (2002) *J. League Kanzen Databook 2002* (Tokyo: Kanzen).
Watts, J. (1998) 'Soccer *shinhatsubai*. What are the Japanese Consumers Making of the J. League?', in D.P. Martinez (ed.), *The Worlds of Japanese Popular Culture: Gender, Shifting Boundaries and Global Cultures* (Cambridge: Cambridge University Press): 181–201.

Index

ABN-AMRO, 27
Achrol, R. S., 172
Ackerman, F., 123
Adams, T., 101
Adidas-Salomon-Reebok-Group, 3, 27
Aegon, 27
Affliction Clothing, 207
Agarwal, S., 147
agenda-setting theory, 100, 112
Agndal, H., 171
Ahuja, G., 184–5
Ajax Cape Town (South African franchise), 18
Ajax FC satellite supporters, 15–16, 28–30
  consumption behavior of, 25–8
  identification with, 21–5
  limitations/prospects of, 28
  loyalty of, 25
  research methodology, 19–21;
    materials and procedures, 20;
    respondents to, 19
  team identification and, 16–18
Alreck, P. L., 19
American Fighter, 207–8
Amis, J., 142–4, 149, 155–8
Amstel, 27
Amstrong, G., 36
Anderson, A., 15–31
Anderson, D., 218
Anderson, D. F., 16–17
Anderson, J. C., 172
Andersson, T., 80, 91
Andreff, M., 3
Andreff, W., 3
Angelini, J. R., 102–3
Anschutz Entertainment Group (AEG), 222
Antoncic, B., 171
Argyris, C., 125
Arthur, W. B., 196
Asian County Board, 165
Asian Gaelic Games, 165

Askew, D., 231
Auckland Institute of Technology (AUT), 185
Audet, M., 125
Augé, B., 115–33
Auld, C. J., 75–95, 137–9, 145–9, 174
Aurier, P., 8, 116, 118–21, 124
Australian Football League (AFL), 18
Austrian, Z., 75, 78
Avila, A., 217
Axelrod, R., 123

Baade, R., 75–6
Backoff, R. H., 158
Bae, S., 35–50
Baer, R., 22
Bailey, K. D., 19
Bairner, A., 158, 161–2
Baker, J., 46
ban (GAA), 161
Barcelona FC, 15, 244
Barney, J., 157, 233
Barrett, J. J., 163
Baslé, G., 116, 121
Baum, J. A. C., 180, 214–15
Beckenbauer, F., 217
Becker, G. S., 54
Beckham, D., 213, 214, 219–20, 222
Bednar, W., 223
Beijing Organizing Committee, 3
Bell, S. J., 36, 46
Bennett, D., 75
Ben-Porat, A., 15
Benson-Rea, M., 170–89
Berger, P. W., 47
Bergkamp, D., 18
Bernard, R. H., 39
Berrett, T., 142–5, 149
Berry, L. L., 46
Bessant, J., 171, 180
Bessy, O., 115, 119–22
Best, D. L., 47
Bhidé, A., 196

251

Billings, A. C., 99–103
Birkinshaw, J., 171, 180
Birrell, S., 102
Black, J. A., 157
Blankenburg-Holm, D., 172–3, 180
Bleakley, D., 229–31, 240, 243
Bloody Sunday, 162
Bloom, H., 214
Blumenthal, D., 46
Blundel, R., 171
Boal, K. B., 157
Bob, U., 75, 77, 93
Bohner, G., 46
Bond, E., 22
Bonnar, S., 200
Borgatti, S. P., 173
Bourke, A., 8, 138, 153–67
Brändle, F., 232
brands
  favorite, 44
  global, 4
  team, 5, 28
Branscombe, N. R., 16–17, 23
Brass, D. J., 170–3, 184–5
Breheny, M., 163
Brennan, C., 213, 219
Breuer, C., 6, 53–70
Brief, A., 146, 197–202
broadcasting, 197–8, 216, 240
Bronson, C., 224
Brookfield, J., 188
Brown, S. L., 178
Browne, K., 18
Bruce, T., 101
Bull, C., 75, 80, 91–3
Burke, V., 137, 149
Burt, R. S., 184–5
business ecosystem
  co-evolutionary dynamics of, 195–6
  MMA, 202–9
  UFC, 195–6, 202–9
Buss, D., 47
Butzen, P., 55

Calbreses, T., 180
Callède, J. P., 122
Campbell, A. J., 172–4
Campbell-Hunt, C., 174
Capranica, L., 102

Carlson, B. D., 21
Carson, D., 175, 215
Cashman, R., 78
Casper, J. M., 16–18
Cassidy, H., 224
Cawley, J., 54
central brokers
  bridging structural holes with, 184–5
  communication and, 185–8
  coordination, resource and mechanism, 181–4
  networks and, 171–4
  strategic focus and, 180–1
Chae, J. S., 37–8, 45
Chalip, L., 77–8
Championnats of France, 240
Champion (sportswear), 44
Chapman, J., 157
Chelladurai, P., 154, 158, 232
Chetty, S. K., 171–4, 180, 188
Chinaglia, G., 217
Chung, Y. C., 37–8, 45
Cialdini, R. B., 23
Ciarlante, D., 230
Cleveland Browns, 17–18
Close, P., 231
Coalter, F., 55
cognitive mapping
  construction of, 123–5, 126, 127
  definition of, 125
  as sports facilities analysis tool, 123–32
  sports management actors and, 127–32
cognitive states, conflict and, 139
Cohen, J., 105
Coleman, R., 75, 78–9, 91
Collins, D., 137, 149
commercial sport events, *see* sport events
communication conflicts, 141
  see also conflicts
competitive advantage, sports bodies/organizations and, 156–7
conflicts
  affecting individual's role, 146–8
  definition of, 139–40
  management of, 137–8

negative consequences of, 140
in sports organizations, 140–8
Connor, K. R., 157
consumer characteristics approach, 37
consumer decision-making styles, 36–50
Consumer Style Inventory (CSI), 37, 39
consumer typology, 37
consumption value, 119, 120
Cooke, A., 57
Cooper, R. G., 173
coordination mechanism, 183–4
Corfman, K. P., 117
Cossette, P., 125
Cousens, L., 170
Couture, R., 200, 207
Coviello, N. E., 170–1, 175, 180
Cowan, R., 181
Croke Park, 162–3
Crompton, J., 75, 77–9, 91, 93
Cronin, M., 159
Cruijff, J., 18
CTIME (time people spend to reach the sport facility), 56, 57–64
Cunningham, G., 101
Cuskelly, G., 137–9, 146, 155
Cuthill, M., 80, 93
Cyert, R. M., 215

Darcy, S., 78
David, P. A., 196
Davie, A., 197, 198
Davis, M., 77
Dawson, A., 77
Deaton, A., 65
De Burca, M., 159
decision-making styles
American college-aged consumers, 41–7
approaches to, 37
characteristics of, 37, 39, 40
research topics in, 37–8
South Korean college-aged consumers, 41–7
De Dreu, C., 139
Dejonghe, T., 77
Delaney, K., 79
Delbridge, R., 171, 180

Denzin, N. K., 178
Desbordes, M., 122–3
Devine, A., 159–60
Devine, F., 159–60
Dietz, B., 16
Dimmock, J. A., 16, 21
Dodgson, M., 215
Doherty, A., 148–9
Dolles, H., 1–11, 15, 18, 23, 75, 100, 223, 228–46
Dominick, J. R., 105
Donavan, D. T., 16–17, 21
Dong, L. C., 174
Douglas, P. H., 55
Dowling, M., 171
Downey, G., 197
Downward, P. M., 54, 77–8, 81
Droege, S. B., 174
Dum, T., 23, 233
Dunne, A., 164–5
Dunning, E., 159
Durvasula, S., 37–8
Dwyer, L., 77
Dyer, J. H., 171–2, 183, 188

Eagleman, A. N., 99–112
Eastman, S. T., 99–103
Eckstein, R., 79
Eden, C., 123
Eisenhardt, K. M., 178, 180
Eklund, R. C., 21
Emirbayer, M., 173
Emperor's Cup, 230
End, C. M., 19, 23
English Premier League (EPL), 1, 2, 17, 240
Erickson, G. S., 170
Eriksson, K., 173
European football leagues, 1
Everett, M. G., 173
Evrard, Y., 8, 116, 118–21, 124
exploitative learning, 215
exploratory learning, 215

facebook, 29
failure, learning from, 213–15
Falconer, H., 140
Falt, E., 1

fans
  die-hard, 17, 25
  fair-weather, 17, 25
  family and teenage girls, 243; *see also* team identification
  international, 15, 18, 237, 244
  local, 237, 242–3
  purchasing behavior, 16, 109, 216, 221, 223
Fan, X. J., 37–8, 45–6
Faulkner, B., 78, 80, 91–2
Faust, K., 173
Fédération Internationale de Football Association (FIFA), 1, 2, 155, 217, 228
Fertitta, F., 199
Fertitta, L., 199
Finance, 3, 78, 160, 238
Fink, J. S., 16–17, 108
Fisch, R., 158
Fitch, J., 204, 205
Fletcher, K., 47
football (soccer)
  commercial representation of, 1
  development of, in Japan, 229–32, 238–43
  global spread of, 213–14, 228–9
  leagues, *see* English Premier League; German Bundesliga; J-League; Major League Soccer; North American Soccer League
  management, 235–8
  media coverage and, 2, 213
  other sport comparisons to, 2
  popularity of, 1–2, 213–14, 224, 229–30, 244–6
  value captures in, 235–8
Football World Cup, 2, 3, 23, 78, 93, 217, 218, 219, 231, 239
Ford, D., 171
Ford, J., 158
Ford, S. J., 194–211
Forester, J., 156
Formula One, 2, 3–4
Forsyth, P., 77
Fort, R. D., 78–9
Foxman, E. R., 47
Fox Soccer Channel, 221
Francis, J. D., 10, 213–25

Frank, R. H., 55
Franklin, R., 207–8
Fredline, E., 78, 80, 82, 91–2
Freeman, L. C., 173
Friedman, R., 141
Fulton, G., 161–2
Fulton, W., 77
functional model of value, public sports facility, 124
Funk, D. C., 16, 231

GAA, *see* Gaelic Athletic Association (GAA)
Gaelic Athletic Association (GAA)
  ban, 161
  Croke Park and, 162–3
  international activities of, 164–5
  managing/organizing change, 161–5
  profile of, 158–61
  Strategic Vision and Action Plan (2009–2015), 162
Galaskiewicz, J., 172
Garber, D., 224
Gardial, S. F., 117
Garnham, N., 158
Garnsey, E. W., 195–6
Gavetti, G., 223
Gentry, F., 194
geographic proximity, socialization agent, 17, 23
German Bundesliga, 240
Geser, H., 173
Gibson, H. J., 174
Gill, R., 158
Gilmore, A., 215
Gladden, J. M., 20, 22
Glaser, B., 216
globalization of football (soccer)
  features contributing to, 228–9
  J-League and, 229–32, 238–43
  management and, 231–2
  research framework/methodology, 232–5
  value captures network in, 235–8, 244–6
global value of sports facilities, 115–16
  cognitive mapping, 123–32
  and consumption value, 116–20
  dimensions of, 120–3

Godbey, G., 146
Goldberg, J., 123–5, 127, 131
Golembiewski, R. T., 158, 166
Golfing Union of Ireland, 155
Gomes-Casseres, B., 171, 180, 183, 196
Goodwin, B., 195
Goodwin, J., 173
Gorman, W. M., 54
Gracie, R., 194, 197
Granovetter, M. S., 184
Grant, R. M., 157
Gratton, C., 75, 78–9, 91
Greenwood, P. B., 16–18
Grewal, D., 46
Grieco, M. S., 173
Griffin, F., 200, 205
Gross, B., 118
Grove, J. R., 16, 21
Gucciardi, D. F., 21
Gulati, R., 171, 183
Gummesson, E., 171, 234
Gwinner, K., 18, 21

Hafstrom, J. L., 37–8, 45
Hair, J. F., 68
Håkansson, H., 170–3, 183, 188
Halinen, A., 170, 175
Hanneman, R. A., 173, 175
Harada, M., 230–3, 240
Hardin, M., 101–2
Harris, M. J., 19
Harris, N., 78
Harvey, J., 139, 170
HD Net, 221
Healy, P., 164
Heffernan, P. B., 195
Heinonen, H., 19
Hellerman, S., 219
Hellgren, B., 171
Hesterly, W. S., 171
Hicks, J. R., 55
Higgs, C. T., 101
Higham, J. E. S., 174
Hilairet, D., 115, 119–22
Hill, C., 158
Hill, J., 78
Hiller, H. H., 79
Hinch, T. D., 174
Hinings, B., 138, 142

Hinnings, C. R., 157–8
Hirose, I., 229, 231
Hirschman, E. C., 121
Hite, J. M., 171
Hiu, S. Y., 37, 45, 47
Hoang, H., 171
Hodur, N., 78
Holbrook, M. B., 117, 121
Holmes, S., 219
Hong, J. B., 230
Horne, J., 91, 229–32, 240, 242–3
Hosking, D. M., 173
Houlihan, A., 1, 16
Houlihan, B., 153
Houston Rockets, 15
Howard, D. R., 23
Hoye, R., 137–9, 146, 154–5, 174
Hoyle, R. H., 19
Huberman, M. A., 178, 180
Huerta, R., 208
Huff, A. S., 175
Hui, S., 79
Humphreys, B. R., 54
Hums, M., 155, 157, 162

Iansiti, M., 196
Indian Premier League (IPL), 2
Ingram, P., 214–15
instrumental values, sports facility dimensions
   functional/knowledge, 120–1
   hedonistic, 121
   self-expression function, 121–2
   social link function, 121–2
   symbolic, 122–3
intentionally created networks, 172
inter-coder reliability, 105
international activities, 153–4, 163, 164–5
international franchises, 4
International Olympic Committee (IOC), 2, 155
Internet as survey method, 19
Irish Ladies Union, 155

Jackson, Q., 205
Jackson, S., 147
Jacobson, B. P., 16–18, 21
James, J. D., 16–18, 22

256 *Index*

Janda, S., 16–17, 21
Japanese Football Association (JFA), 225, 228
Jarillo, C. J., 172
Jehn, K., 141
Jenkins, M. C., 37–8, 123
Jeong, G., 91
J-League
  development of, 229–32; analysis, 238–44; emblems and mascots, 243–4
  global spread of football, 228–9
  growth of, 242
  main objective for, 240–1
  marketing of, 242–3
  network of value in, 244–6
  strategic direction and objectives of, 239–40
Johannisson, B., 173
Johanson, J., 172–3, 183
Johnson, N. B., 174
Jonard, N., 181
Jones, C., 75, 79–80
Jones, D., 1, 16
Jones, G., 158
Jones, I., 16, 18, 21
Jose, C., 217–19
Judd, C. M., 19
Jurkowitsch, A., 46

Kahneman, D., 223
Kahn, R., 140, 146–7
Kam, J., 214
Kane, M. J., 100
Kanters, M. A., 16–18
Katz, M., 120
Kelly, S., 163
Kendall, E. L., 36–9, 46–8
Kensicki, L. J., 108
Kerr, A. K., 15–31
Kerr, C., 194–211
Késenne, S., 55
Kikulis, L., 138
Kim, D., 46
Kim, J., 215
Kim, K., 79
Kim, M. S., 46
King, B., 91
King, C. W., 37–8

King, D., 140
King, L., 140
Kirkman, B., 142
Kluivert, P., 18
Kolbe, R. H., 16–18, 22
Koller, C., 232
Kotler, P., 36, 172
Kramer, R., 140
Krane, V., 101
Krejcie, R. V., 39
Kunkel, J. H., 46
Kushner, R. J., 170

Lai, A. W., 118
La Liga Espanola, 240
Lancaster, C., 54
Lanfranchi, P., 232
Langfield-Smith, K., 123, 127
Langlois, R., 195
Larmer, B., 15
Larson, J. F., 103
Laukkanen, M., 123
Lavoie, M., 55
Lavy, M., 46
learning from failure, 213–15
Lechner, C., 171
Leeds, M., 94
Leistritz, F. L., 78
leisure service providers, 140
Lenskyj, H. J., 100
Lera-López, F., 55
Levein, R., 196
Levinthal, D. A., 215, 223
Lewis, M., 19, 100
Liddell, C., 200
Light, R., 229–30
Lincoln, Y. S., 179
Liu, R.-J., 188
Liverpool FC, 17, 30
Lloyd, K. M., 75–95
London County Committee, 165
Long, S. J., 65
Los Angeles Galaxy, 213, 219
Lovallo, D., 223
Lovell, J., 75, 80, 91, 93
Low, B. S., 47
Lynn, S., 101
Lysonski, S., 37–8

Index 257

MacAloon, J., 231
MacIntosh, D., 138
MacLean, J., 155, 157, 162
Madrigal, R., 16, 23
Maeda, H., 231
Maguire, J., 246
Mahony, D. F., 17, 23
Major League Baseball (MLB), 2, 15
Major League Soccer (MLS), 219–20, 221–5
  learning from failure and, 215
  NASL and, 213–14, 215–17, 220–1
Mallin, C., 155
management of professional sports, 16, 155, 214, 216, 233, 236
Manchester United, 15
Manzenreiter, W., 91, 229–32, 241
March, J. G., 159, 163, 215, 223
marketing and merchandizing, 228
Markoczy, L. A., 123, 125, 127, 131
Markovitz, A., 219
Martin, S. G., 170–89
Martineau, P., 46
mass media, Olympic Games coverage by, 99–100
  gender/race portrayals, 101–3
  nationality portrayals, 103
  research: discussion, 108–9; findings, 105–8; limitations, 109–10; methodology, 104–5; prospects, 110–11; purpose, 103–4; questions, 104
Matsouka, H., 232
Mattsson, L.-G., 172–3
Mayer, J., 149
Mayer-Vorfelder, G., 246
Mayring, P., 234
McCain, J., 198
McCombs, M. E., 100
McDonald, M., 230
McDonald, M. A., 16
McGough, J., 19
McLeod, P., 82, 92
McNamee Review, GAA, 161
McNary, E. L., 99–112
media, 17, 138, 216, 220, 224, 228, 235, 237
  see also mass media, Olympic Games coverage by

Medina, F., 141
Medlin, C. J., 175
Meenaghan, T., 170
Melnick, M. J., 16–17
Meltzer, D., 198, 200
Metcalfe, S., 195
Mexican League, 222
Meyer, M., 79
Meyrowitz, B., 197, 198
Mickle, T., 220–1
Mihara, T., 230
Miles, M. B., 178, 180
Militich, P., 208
Miller, L., 218
Mills, H., 145
Milman, A., 91
Milne, G. R., 16, 22
Miner, A., 214–15
Ming, Y., 15
Misener, K., 148–9
Mistry, K., 142, 145, 149
Mitchell, J. C., 173
Mitrano, J. R., 19
mixed martial arts (MMA), 194
  business ecosystem and, 202–9
  unified rules, 198–9
  see also Ultimate Fighting Championships (UFC)
Mixed Martial Arts Unified Rules of Conduct, 198, 199
MLS, *see* Major League Soccer (MLS)
MMA, *see* mixed martial arts (MMA)
Model of Participation in Physical Activity, 54–5
Moffett, S., 230, 239, 243
Möller, K., 170, 172–3, 188
Moore, J., 195–6, 206
Moran, A., 159
Morgan, D. W., 39
Mouzas, S., 172–3
MTIME (maximum willingness to spend travel time), factors influencing, 64–8
Muehling, D. D., 47
Muellbauer, J., 65
Muniz, A. M., 30
Munro, H. J., 171
Murrell, A. J., 16

Nakazawa, M., 231
Nash, R., 19
NASL, see North American Soccer League (NASL)
National Basketball Association (NBA), 2, 15
National Football League (NFL), 2, 17–18, 218
national governing bodies (NGBs), 153–4, 166–7
  GAA: Croke Park and, 162–3; international activities, 164–5; management practice, 161–2; profile, 158–61
  sports organizations: characteristics, 154–6; competitive advantage/strategic change, 156–8
National Hockey League (NHL), 2
National Professional Soccer League, 217
National Sports Organizations (NSOs), 139, 142, 174–5, 183, 187–8
Neale, M., 141
Nelson, J. K., 39, 41
Nelson, R. R., 196
networks, sports professionalization, 170–1
  actors in, 173–4
  concepts: constructs, 173–4; context, 174; effectiveness, 172–3; organic/intentionally created, 171–2
  NZAS, stages of development, 174–9
  see also central brokers
network theory, 234
Nevada State Athletic Commission, 199, 201
New Balance (sportswear), 44
New Jersey State Athletic Commission, 198
Newman, B., 118
Newsham, G., 217–18
New York Cosmos, 213, 217, 218
New Zealand Academy of Sport (NZAS) system, 174–88
New Zealand Olympic Committee (NZOC), 174–5
Nichols, G., 138–9, 145–6

Nike, 3
Nisbett, R. E., 47
Nobeoka, K., 172, 188
Nogawa, H., 231
Nolan, L., 141
Nordhaus, W. D., 54–5, 57
North American Soccer League (NASL), 213–14, 217–19, 221–5
  MLS and, 215–17, 219–21
Northcraft, G., 141

O'Driscoll, A., 215
O'Dwyer, E., 18
O'Guinn, T. C., 30
Ohl, F., 122–3
Olympic Games, 2–3
  NBC and, 2
  revenues generated by, 2–3
  see also mass media, Olympic Games coverage by
O'Neal, N., 141
Ono, S., 244
Ophüls-Kashima, R., 231, 243
organic networks, 171–2
organizational conflicts, 140–8
  see also conflicts
organizational learning theory, 214
Ortiz, T., 200
O'Sullivan, P., 170
Osumi, Y., 230
Owen, J. G., 78

Palakshappa, N., 170–89
Park, Y., 35
Parkes, R., 1, 16
Parkhe, A., 170–1, 173
Parvinen, P. M. T., 170, 172
Patterson, A., 171–2
Patton, M. Q., 178
Pawlowski, T., 53–70
Pease, D., 79
Pedenon, A., 115–33
Pedersen, P. M., 108
Pelé, 213, 217, 218
personal conflicts, 141
  see also conflicts
Peteraf, M., 157
Pettinger, R., 158, 166
Philips, L., 65

Pierce, S., 17, 26
Pihkala, T., 170–2, 181
Pizam, A., 91
planning process, sport events and, 79–80, 93–4
Plotz, D., 198
Pociello, C., 116, 121
Porter, M. E., 156–7, 233
Powell, W. W., 172, 185
Preuss, H., 76–7, 79–80, 94
Pride Fighting Championships (Pride FC), 201
Probert, J., 230, 240, 242–3
professional staff, organizational conflicts and, 138–9
psychic income, 79, 93
psychographic/lifestyle approach, 37
public actors, 7
public private partnership (PPP), 53
Puma, 3

Quirk, J. P., 78

Rajagopalan, N., 157
Rajala, A., 170, 172–3, 188
Ralston, D. A., 170–1, 173
Ralston, R., 78, 81
Rapún-Gárate, M., 55
Real Madrid, 15, 213
Rea, M. B., 170–89
recruitment and retention policy, 10, 203–7
Reebok, 44
relational approach and consumer behavior, 117–18, 120
relationship conflicts, 141
  see also conflicts
Richards, G., 79
Richards, L., 178
Richardson, B., 18
Rieck, J., 75–95
Rijkaard, F., 18
Ring, L. J., 38
Riordan, J., 54
Ritchie, J., 79
Rivenburgh, N. K., 103
Robbins, S., 141, 143
Robinson, N., 77
Roche, M., 79

Rogers, E. M., 203
role conflicts and ambiguity
  definition of, 146–7
  studies on, 147–8
role of sport, 1
Rosentraub, M., 75, 78–9, 82, 92
Rumult, R., 157
Ruseski, J. E., 54
Rustad, A., 80, 91

Sabo, D., 103
Sadler, A., 171, 180
Sakires, J., 148–9
Salwen, M. B., 108
Samuelson, P. A., 54–5, 57
Sartore, M., 101
satellite supporters
  of Ajax FC, 19, 24, 25–8
  definition of, 15
  team brands and, 5, 28, 29
Satterlee, T., 224
Schewe, G., 246
Schön, D., 125
Schrader, M. P., 16–18, 23
Schuler, R., 146–7
Schulz, J., 137–49
Schütte, H., 230, 240, 243
Schwenk, C. R., 214
second tier sport, professional soccer as, 216
Seidman, I. E., 175
Semaphore Entertainment Group (SEG), 197, 198
servuction, definition of, 116
Settle, R. B., 19
Shamrock, K., 197, 200, 208
Shapiro, C., 120, 195–6
Shapiro, D., 142
Shaw, D. L., 100
Sheth, J., 118
Shibli, S., 75, 78–9, 91
Shimizu, S., 231, 243
shopping style, 5, 38, 39, 45, 48, 50
  see also sport product purchasing
Short, J., 140
Silva, A., 205
Silverman, B. S., 180
Simon, H., 215, 223
Singh, H., 171, 183

Sitkin, S., 214
Slack, T., 138, 142–5, 149, 154–5, 157–8
Smith, N. F., 5, 15–31
soccer, *see* football (soccer)
social identity theory, 21
socialization agents, team identification and
  family/friends/peers as, 16
  geographic proximity as, 17
  media as, 17
Socioeconomic Demand Theory, 55
socio-linguistic approach, 231
Soda, G., 170
Söderman, S., 1–11, 15, 18, 23, 75, 100, 223, 228–46
Solberg, H. A., 76–7, 79–80, 91
Sony Creative Products, 243
Sony Music Entertainment, 243
Sorrentino, R., 140
Soutar, G., 80, 82, 92
Spanish Football Association (RFEF), 240
Spike TV, 200, 202
Sport and Recreation New Zealand (SPARC), 174
sport clubs
  conflicts in, 137, 144
  non-profit, 57–8, 68, 138
  strategic alliances, 4, 245
sport culture, *see* sport product purchasing
sport events, 2–3, 75–6, 91–5
  economic and social benefits/costs of, 2–3, 78–9
  funding of, 77–8
  hosting: community perceptions of, 79–81; economic and social benefits/costs of, 84–91
  involvement, demographic characteristics and, 82–3
  research methodology, 81–2
sportivization of society, 115
sport product purchasing, 35–6, 45–50
  athletic apparel information sources, 43
  brand preference, 44
  companion preferences, 43–4
  decision-making styles, 36–8

demographic description, 41
frequency, 41–3
hours per visit, 41
patterns, American/South Korean college consumer, 44–5
research methodology, 38–41
store preference, 43
trade, 3
sports demand, 54, 59–64
sports economics, 54–5
sports facilities, global value, 115–16, 132–3
  cognitive mapping; construction of, 123–7; management actors and, 127–32
  consumption value of, 116–20
  dimensions of, 120–3
sports facilities management, 53–4, 68–70
  CTIME (time people spend to reach the sport facility), 56, 57–64
  demand and travel time elasticities, 59–64
  descriptive statistics data, 57–9
  MTIME (maximum willingness to spend travel time), factors influencing, 64–8
  research methodology, 56–7
  theoretical background, 54–5
sports organizations
  characteristics: forms/activities, 155–6; grouping of, by sector, 154–5
  competitive advantage/strategic change in, 156–8
  conflicts in, 140–8
  definition of, 154
  and governing bodies, 155–6, 238
  see also national governing bodies (NGBs); sport events
sports policy, 127–9
Sproles, E. L., 38
Sproles, G. B., 36–9, 46, 48
Spurr, R., 77
Stewart, B., 77
Stigler, G. J., 54
Stjernberg, T., 171
Stoffel, J., 36

strategic change, sport organization, 156–8
Strategic Review Committee (SRC), 161–2
Strauss, A., 216
structural conflicts, 141, 143
  see also conflicts
structural holes, bridging, 184–5
structured network, 188
success, learning from, *see* J-League
Sueur, R., 80, 94
Sugden, J., 239
Sugimoto, A., 230
Suh, J., 16–17, 21
Sumino, M., 231
survival-enhancing learning, failure as, 214
Sutton, W. A., 16–18, 22
Suzuki, A., 15, 47
Swanson, S. R., 18, 21
Swart, K., 75, 77, 93
Swindell, D., 78–9, 82, 92

Tai, S. H., 37, 38
Tajfel, H., 20
tangible/intangible benefits, 78
task conflicts, 141
  see also conflicts
Taylor, P., 139
team identification
  Ajax FC, 18, 21–5
  consumption behavior, 25–8; loyalty, 25
  description of, 16
  factors/socialization agents of, 16–18
  fan communities and, 17–18
  Internet survey concerning, 19–21
  J-League, 243–4
  limitations/prospects, 28
  origins of, 18, 237
  sport marketers and, 18, 237–8
Thagard, P., 223
The Ultimate Fighter (TUF), 200–2, 204, 205
Thiabult, L., 138, 142
Thiel, A., 149
Thomas, D. E., 214

Thomas, J. R., 39, 41
Thorelli, H. B., 183
Thuathaigh, G. O., 160
Tikkanen, H., 170, 172
Tilke, H., 3
Tobin, J., 65
Tomlinson, A., 239
Toohey, K., 77–8
Törnroos, J.-Å., 170, 175
Toshio, M., 231
Trail, G. T., 16–17
Trait, A., 123
transactional approach and consumer behavior, 116–17, 118
travel time elasticities, recreational sports and, 53–4
  demand and, 59–64
  research methodology, 56–7
  theoretical background of study on, 54–5
  see also sports facilities management
Trekker, J., 222–3
Tribou, G., 122–3
Tsuboi, Y., 246
Tucker, K. B., 16–18, 23
Tuggle, C. A., 101
Tuominen, M., 172–3
Turco, D., 82, 91–2
Turner, J. C., 20
Tversky, A., 223
twitter, 29
2006 Winter Olympic Games, *see* mass media, Olympic Games coverage by

UEFA (Union des Associations Européennes de Football), 234
UFC, *see* Ultimate Fighting Championships (UFC)
Ultimate Fighting Championships (UFC)
  acquisition of, 199–200
  ban on, 198
  co-evolution, business ecosystem and, 195–6, 202–9
  launch of, 197–8
  media coverage of, 200–3
  recruitment/retention of fighters in, 203–7

Ultimate Fighting Championships
  (UFC) – *continued*
   research methodology, 197
   sponsorship of, 209, 210
   trialability of product, 202–3
   unified rules of, 198–9
Underwood, R., 22
United Nations (UN) Director of
  Communications, 1
United Soccer Association, 217
Usai, A., 170
US media coverage of Olympic Games,
  see mass media, Olympic Games
  coverage by
US Soccer Federation, 219
Uysal, M., 79
Uzzi, B., 172

value captures football management,
  network of, 235–8
van Basten, M., 18
Vancouver Organizing
  Committee, 3
Van Sell, M., 146
Varamäki, E., 170–2, 181
Variance Inflation Factor (VIF), 68
Varian, H., 68, 195–6
Veal, A. J., 77
Verdin, P. J., 157
Verhoeven, M., 143–4
Vernhet, A., 7, 115–33
Verstraete, T., 125
Vesalainen, J., 170–2, 181
vicarious learning, 215, 222, 224
Vincent, W., 38
volunteer management,
  organizational conflicts and, 138–9
Von Allmen, P., 94

Wahl, G., 219
Walker, G., 158
Wall, V., 141
Walsdorf, K., 101
Walsh, G., 36, 38
Walsh, J. P., 223
Wanke, M., 46
Wann, D. L., 16–18, 21, 23, 25–6

Wasserman, S., 170–1, 173
Watts, J., 243
Watzlawick, P., 158
Weakland, J. H., 158
Weiland, M., 217
Weiller, K. H., 101
Welch, D., 172, 188
Welch, L., 172, 188
Wensing, E. H., 101
Westerbeek, H., 232, 246
Westphal, J. D., 223
Wharton, R., 103
White, D., 199, 200
Whitford, M., 76
Whitson, D., 138
Wicker, P., 53–70
Williams, J. E., 47
Williamson, P. J., 157
Wilson, D., 154
Wilson, D. T., 172
Wilson, H., 170–1
Wilson, J., 79
Wimmer, R. D., 105
Winter, S. G., 196
Wirth, A., 123, 127
Witt, P., 180
Wolfe, R., 170
Women National Basketball
  Association, 220
Wood, A., 77
Wood, N., 108
workplace violence, 140
  see also organizational conflicts
World Alliance of Mixed Martial Arts
  (WAMMA), 203–4
World Extreme Cagefighting (WEC), 201
World Fighting Alliance (WFA), 201
WOW Promotions, 197, 198

Xiao, J. J., 37–8, 45–6
Xtreme Couture, 207

Yaki, T., 246
Yannis, A., 218
Yasaki, W., 229–30
Yin, R. K., 174
Yoshioka, C., 147

Zaharopoulos, T., 99
Zaheer, A., 170
Zeitham, L., 117
Zellner, A., 70
Zhang, J., 79
Zhang, Y., 157
Zimmerman, J. -B., 181
Zimmerman, M., 21
Zotos, Y., 37–8
Zuffa LLC, 199, 202, 209